ENGLAND'S CHILD

Cyril F. Johnston with the 20-ton bourdon for Riverside Church on display at the Gillett & Johnston Bellfoundry, Croydon, England, 1930

ENGLAND's CHILD

The Carillon and the Casting of Big Bells

JILL JOHNSTON

CADMUS EDITIONS

SAN FRANCISCO

First published in the United States in 2008 by
Cadmus Editions
Post Office Box 126
Belvedere Tiburon
California 94920
www.cadmuseditions.com

Distributed by National Book Network, NBN
www.nbnbooks.com

Catalog-in-Publication Data is available from the Library of Congress

Design and typeset Print Means Inc. • New York • NY
www.printmeans.com
Cover design by Ingrid Nyeboe
Printed by Sheridan Books Inc. • Ann Arbor • Michigan

First Edition
ISBN 0-932274-71-4
ISBN 13: 9780932274717

This book is dedicated to
INGRID NYEBOE

and to the memory of my half-sister
LADY ROSEMARY PRICE

My luck was to belong to a dead man
—Jean-Paul Sartre

*Cyril Frederick Johnston was without question
the greatest bellfounder of the 20th century*
—James R. Lawson

CONTENTS

ACKNOWLEDGMENTS

I have had extraordinary support in my long run to research and write this book.

Without my partner Ingrid Nyeboe, whose enthusiasm for the subject dates from 1981 when our searches and travels first began, I cannot imagine how the book would ever have come into being. Ingrid's determined, never-give-up style of investigation, her computer expertise, constant encouragement and readings and editing of the manuscript in progress, and inventive suggestions in problem-solving, have been way beyond any call.

I credit my agents John Brockman and Katinka Matson (president of John Brockman Inc.) with a certain imaginative vision in taking on bells, and in reliably offering support for the writing as it unfolded. To my publisher, Jeffrey Miller of Cadmus Editions, a gift of professionalism, kindness, reassurance, patience, and attention to detail, I am deeply obliged.

Without my English relatives—half-brother Arthur F. E. Johnston, half-sister Lady Rosemary E. Price and her husband Sir David Price—this book would be missing much family lore and a spirited interest in the legacy of Cyril F. Johnston. Especially to my half-sister and her husband, I owe thanks for their gracious hospitality in the final years of my effort.

For vetting my manuscript, and their enthusiasm for the subject, I offer special thanks to Professor Joseph Clair Davis and to David Cawley, Vicar of Leicester Church, England.

John Lampl of British Airways liberally facilitated many of my trips to the UK. And Stephen Rabson of the Peninsular & Oriental Steamship Navigation Company (the P&O) made the contact for a memorable crossing on the *Oriana* from New York to Southampton.

Special thanks must be extended to members of the GCNA, the Guild of Carillonneurs of North America, among them, Lyle John Anderson, R. Robin Austin, Beverly Buchanan, Laurel Buckwalter, Marilyn Clark, Tom Collins, Joe Connors, John Courter, Wylie Crawford, Bill De Turk, Jim Fackenthal, Todd Fair, John Gouwens, George Gregory, Frank K. Griesinger, Margo Halsted, J. Samuel Hammond, John W. Harvey, the late James Lawson, Dionisio Lind, George Matthew Jr., Gordon Slater, James B. Slater, James Smith, Richard Strauss, Brian Swager, Janet Tebbel, Sally Slade Warner, Richard Watson, Phyllis Webb.

Carl Scott Zimmerman, webmaster of the GCNA, has over the years repeatedly answered my email requests for data on bells worldwide.

From the beginning of researching this book, I have had the devoted interest of many of my American friends and my sincerest gratitude goes to Katherine Allard, Elizabeth Baker, Marcus Baram, Charlotte Bellamy, Miles Bellamy, Jill Boltin, Candace Chaite, Steven Corsano, Tom Davey, the late Teeny Duchamp, Lynn Fowler, Suzi Gablik, Paul Gruber and Keith Champagne, Geoff Hendricks, Jon Hendricks, Roberta Jellineck and Helge Mansson, Julie Martin, Ken Johnson, Jackie Monnier Matisse, Catherine Kehoe, Kenneth King, my daughter Winifred Lanham, my son Richard Lanham, Danny Moses, the late Sven Jesper Nyeboe, Vaughan Rachel, Phillip Rivlin, Jan Roby, Judith Smith, Michael Standard, Marianne Sturman, George Walsh, Randy Weinstein, and Dr. Stanley Weinstock.

Numerous people, both here and abroad, have been of immeasurable assistance, among them Eric Andersen, Nana Araujo, Roy Beatty, John Beyer, Ray Binwanger, Anton Brees Jr., Mike Bussey, Dr. Susan Deakins, Bern E. Deichmann, Dagmar Getz, Martin A. Gilman, Reverend Douglas Grandgeorge, James R. Houghton, the late Mrs. Don Hunter, Peter Hurd, Victor Jordan, Michael D. Lampen, David E. Magee, Deborah McKeon-Pogue, Maureen Nevins, Neno Pessoa, Herbie Schwagerl, David and Rebecca

Sinkler, Brother Stavros, Jane Thomas, Stephen Trombley, Harry van Bergen, Renee Ziemer.

To Darwin Stapleton, archivist of the Rockefeller Center Archive, I owe a special debt of gratitude for his interest and friendship over my book, and the ease with which he made it possible to obtain copies of the vast correspondence between John D. Rockefeller, Jr., his advisor Frederick Mayer, my father Cyril F. Johnston, and others.

In particular, many thanks to my friends, associates and archivists in the United Kingdom: Tony Delamothe and Friedericke Eban, Olga Edridge, the late Ronald D. Laing, Berna Moody, the late Nikos Stangos. Also to Alan Berry, Alan Buswell, Eric Bradley, Ariel Bruce, Ann Higgins, Ursula Carlyle, Arthur Casey, Stephen Coombes, Robert Fisk, Keith Fleming, the late Michael Howard, Allen Hughes, Douglas Hughes, Baroness Helena Kennedy, John Knox, John Mortimer, Frederick H.G. Percy, Mark Stephens, Nigel Taylor, Trevor Workman.

John Eisel, librarian of England's bell library, has consistently been a generous and reliable source of information.

I had kind assistance from Madeleine Lavine of the YMCA in Jerusalem, Israel.

In Holland and Belgium I was helped obligingly by the late Koen Cosaert, Dr. Josef Denyn, Geert d'Hollander, Joost Eijsbouts, Gret Huilbrecht, the late Kamiel Lefevére, the late André Lehr, Jacques Maassen, Eddy Marien, Luc Rombouts, Joost van Balkom and Joep van Brussel.

Mr. David Rockefeller extended significant patronage for which I am deeply grateful.

I am indebted to the Pauline Oliveros Foundation under whose auspices a number of friends and associates made contributions in support of my time in researching and writing the book: Christo and Jeanne-Claude, Merce Cunningham, Ann D'Harnoncourt, Mark di Suvero, Suzi Gablik, Geoffrey Hendricks, Kenneth King, Les Levine, the late Agnes Martin, Jackie Monnier Matisse (in memory of her mother Teeny Duchamp), Harry Mathews, Yoko Ono, Benedicte Pesle, Edwin Schlossberg, Gloria Steinem and Marianne Sturman.

In my two and one-half decades of working on the book, I may have overlooked several people who offered help along the way—be assured that I am grateful to each of you.

INTRODUCTION

My father, Cyril F. Johnston, was a great bellfounder, some say the greatest of the 20th century. He is pictured on the back cover of this book standing between King George V and Queen Mary. The date is May 12, 1925, the place the Gillett & Johnston bellfoundry in Croydon, Surrey, the occasion a viewing of the huge 10-ton bell made to anchor a 53-bell carillon destined for the Park Avenue Baptist Church in New York. Until this moment, the massive tower concert instrument called the carillon—indigenous to Belgium and the Netherlands since the 1500s—had never exceeded forty-six bells. In another four years, this number would be surpassed again, now to the unimagined size of seventy-two, with a weight of over 100 tons, as the Park Avenue bells were moved to and augmented at the newly erected Riverside Church. Backed financially by John D. Rockefeller Jr., Cyril Johnston built the three pioneering carillon instruments in the United States, those at Park Avenue and Riverside, and one to follow at the University of Chicago.

Historically, the carillon instrument is the "Child" of Belgium and Holland. But it became "England's Child" at the turn of the 20th century when two British bellfounders, Cyril Johnston and John Taylor, having rediscovered the lost secrets of accurately tuning carillon bells, began exporting the instrument to North America.

While all this was going on, Cyril Johnston, still unmarried in his mid-forties, was having a transatlantic affair with my American mother. At the very peak of his career, my mother gave birth in London—without benefit of marriage. The story of my English father's adventures and exploits in the brand-new American market for the carillon has long seemed inseparable in my mind from my birth.

I have been writing this book since I was born. I speak mystically of course. I did not begin writing qua writing until I was twenty-something, when my subject was far from bellfounding or from having anything to do with my father. After a certain number of years writing, I realized that I had become a writer to write this book. Then another number of years went by, a good many in fact, before the project at last became real. Conception was followed by a "pregnancy" of interminable length. There were abortions and miscarriages in the form of bombed contracts, outright opposition, failures of nerve, misguided readiness, and intriguing diversions. My birth was not a simple matter. And while we may think that we begin there, we have naturally origins of much greater complexity. Still, I begin with a humble fixation: a father unknown, *non noto,* a fact of high over-determination. In our society you must have a father as well as a mother. This we know has been true throughout the world for quite a few thousand years. It is of course only the father who, by claiming his children through the institution of marriage, makes them legal, or legitimate. In his name, his children perpetuate the system. You can get along sans father, very well in fact, but if such an absence is gilded by secrecy, and you are raised under false pretenses, you may end up like me on a quest to find out what happened and why and who exactly your progenitor was.

Without this direction and purpose in life, I might have been just a writer. In pursuit of my father, I have perforce undertaken a daunting study of his profession. A study in any department of world literature, or art, history, politics, psychology, would have been a lot easier for me. Luckily, at the same time, my father made something very interesting. The shape of a bell is for me a sacred icon. I am a bell. I am England's Child. I would not be here had the musical instrument called the carillon—that collection of chromatically tuned bells ranging in number from 23 to 77—not been under importation to America during the decade of the 1920s. It is the process by which bells are made, the art of bellfounding, which has often stupefied me. A craft older than your greatest grandmother, it involves a feat of scientific engineering encompassing innumerable technical details and trade secrets.

Secrets are an aspect of the trade that I can particularly understand. Anyone born without a legal father in my mother's time was raised secretly, i.e. with a cover story. It was a donnée of the condition, absolutely essential for social survival. My mother's cover was elemental enough, easily suggested by cultural interdiction. Following my birth in London, once she crossed the pond with me to live forever in America, and keeping in mind that three thousand miles at that time was a much bigger distance than it is now, she lied and told everyone including me (when I was old enough to grasp language) that she was a widow, her "husband" and father of her child having died of pneumonia in my infancy. She also told me his name, nationality and profession, but these were all true. As a "widow," my mother assumed the surname Johnston. Whether she assumed it legally or not, I never found out. Secrets denote both the personal sequestration that defined my birth, and the professionally classified information under which my father labored to make bells. Neither state has anything especially to do with the other, except by loose association. My father entered his father's bellfounding firm in 1902, at a very sensitive moment in the history of the craft, just when a revolution in the tuning of bells was underway. Guarding the secrets of tuning was an occupational desideratum, not exactly equivalent to my mother's all-consuming need to protect her past, but roughly similar in the fear it implies for any sort of future. My father was bent on outlasting his competition. My mother on surviving society.

Wherever I highlight my mother's secret, I mean to show or imply that this book would never have been written without it. As the determining circumstance of my birth, it shaped the future of a book devoted to my father and his profession. The carillon is itself something of a secret subject since, by my figuring, less than one half of one percent of the population ever heard of it. People are well aware of bells in towers, and the sounds they can make. They toll the time, they can toll for extraordinary events, they can disperse familiar melodies or hymns provided the tower is equipped with enough bells and a drum roll, now largely computerized, for automatic playing. These sounds are generally registered unconsciously. Like muzak, they form an audio environment, absorbed in a campus or village surround, or a cityscape noise and hum. To distinguish the harmonic sounds of a carillon, performed at a tower console by a carillonneur, from the common diatonic melodies of an automatic player, the listener must know that there is indeed an instrument called a carillon and to have had some exposure to its music. And since there are (at this writing) no more than one hundred and eighty such instruments in North America, it seems realistic to say that the carillon remains largely a secret, at least on this side of the Atlantic.

Equally obscure is the key role of John D. Rockefeller, Jr. in defining the new future of the carillon in America. He is of course famous as the conservator of the wealth his father made in Standard Oil, and in furthering his father's philanthropic interests. In bells and the carillon, JDR Jr. became a frontier man. His money was initially the rock behind Cyril Johnston's surging reputation as a bellfounder, as he met every experimental challenge set by Rockefeller and his advisors to create unheard-of monster bells, tuned for integration in newly colossal carillon instruments. Rockefeller, though a thrifty tycoon and pious churchgoer, turned out not to be immune to the frenzy for size and grandeur that captured America's imagination after the Great War and during the roaring 1920s. But bells are not purely secular or materialistic like the skyscrapers, ships and bridges that were then under fiercely competitive construction. Bells have crowned the towers of churches and universities—those two esteemed institutions singled out by the Rockefellers to endow. And bells have sacred functions and artistic purposes. So JDR Jr. could have rationalized. They are also hidden from view, an ideal site for a millionaire who craved anonymity.

Obscurity was hardly a goal of Cyril Johnston's. He sought publicity for his wares on a grand scale. His foundry in Croydon was the site not only of forging and furnaces and tuning, but of many social events celebrating important castings or the emergence of some new great bronze bell from its earthen-buried mould. He drew royalty, prime ministers, ambassadors, archbishops, famous entertainers, rich American donors, and world-renowned carillonneurs to his premises. The press was very obliging in writing up these events, also in covering bell installations around the world. Cyril Johnston himself cut a broad swath in advance of his contracts, in promoting his unusual goods and in marking his successes. He seemed to embody the idea of bellfounding as a profession célèbre. How, he might have wondered, would he fare in history?

Not surprisingly, whatever world once knew him outside or beyond his profession, has by now consigned him to anonymity. Bell people however know him well as an awesome historic figure. When I go to their meetings or Congresses, I am treated like the daughter of a famous dead man, a feeling I treasure, even while there may be unasked questions about my precise status as this daughter. They all know or could sense, I suppose, that I have been writing this book since I was born. I have never mentioned the suspicion I developed that my father deposited me in America along with his bells with a fathomless unconscious ambition. An American child, especially one he never introduced himself to, could grow up to tell the glorious story of his outrageously big bells and carillons, and his role in forging the carillon's new home in England's lost colony.

Such a long shot for history would obviously involve a trade-off. I have never imagined telling this story without an account of how I became the one to do it.

Chapter I

ARTHUR

We had never met as father and daughter. We had never looked into
each other's eyes, knowing, and now we never would
—Diana Petre, half-sister of J.R. Ackerley

September 8, 1978, London, England, a life-altering moment I
had gone to some trouble to arrange was due to happen at the
Ebury Street Steak House—a 1 P.M. lunch appointment to meet
Arthur, Cyril Johnston's only son. Arriving at 12:55, the maître d'
asked me if I wanted to wait at the bar, and while I pondered the
option, my lunch engagement walked in. Having never met him,
nor seen any pictures of him, it might have been difficult to pick
him out had there been more than a few clients in the restaurant
at that hour. But I doubt it. I knew from photos what his father
had looked like. The height, broad shoulders, coloring and dress
code should have made him easy to identify. On the phone a few
days earlier when I had called him from Marlborough to make the
appointment, neither of us had asked the other how we might be

recognized. And while I knew about him, so far as I was aware he knew nothing whatever about me. In case our shared surname would tip him off, I had fictionalized it.

In August, identifying myself as "Joan Castile," I had called Arthur from America, requesting an interview with him for a book about his father. At that time I was under contract for the third time for such a book. Why publishers signed me up, beginning in 1969, without any evidence that I had researched my subject, remains a capital mystery to me. It may be because I was undaunted myself, seeing nothing wrong with writing mythically about a father I never knew or met. On my second try in fact, I barely introduced him by name, and I think not by profession at all, filling up 430 pages (written all in lowercase, in a single paragraph), with diversionary anecdotes and appropriated quotes from a vast mythological literature. The results of this labor may well have led to my determination to meet Arthur, whose realness might have the effect of steering me toward history and factuality. On the face of it, I believe I decided to find Arthur because my mother was dying. My mother had warned me, by way of continuing her past attempts to protect me, never to look up any of my relatives in England. Arthur's appearance and her dying, occurring within two months of each other, were the two big events of my life in the late 1970s. The death of a mother, and a reincarnation, can I say, of the father? She died November 15 unaware of the adventure I had had abroad meeting the son of her onetime paramour. By introducing myself to him pseudonymously, I seemed *half* covered in my serious liability. How far I intended to go in my pose was uncertain as I flew off to England. I had waited twenty-eight years, from the time in 1950 when first I learned of Arthur's existence, to make an approach. On March 30th of that year our mutual father had died.

Soon after, I paid a visit to the tower of the Riverside Church in Manhattan, site of Cyril Johnston's famously oversized assemblage of carillon bells—72 of them— dedicated in 1931. I had been to the tower once before. When I was eight, my mother had taken me up, giving me the experience of my childhood. By that age, I was aware that my father had made bells, but with no clear idea what that meant. And for all I knew, the only bells he ever cast were at Riverside. The word "carillon" raises another question in my mind—I may have heard the word, but can't imagine I knew what it was really, or how it differed from other kinds of bells or collections of them. I never gave the matter any thought. I was simply agog to be in the tower belfry. The great thing at Riverside is that all the bells are fully on display. In most towers you can't see them, or you have to climb impossible enclosed spiral staircases to get to trapdoors beyond which they are imprisoned. The Riverside belfry, 50 feet high, 40 by 40 feet wide, is entered after a 20-floor elevator ride and a walk up two flights of stairs. Then you are in this drafty cavern in the sky, over a hundred tons of bronze hanging in it, an enormous presence, unimaginably awaiting an unseen hand to rouse it all from a practically deafening silence. Entering the belfry, I stepped hesitantly along a horizontal iron catwalk, passing within inches of three bells in a row weighing in the aggregate 79,712 pounds, more than twice that amount with their steel frames figured in. The biggest of the three, the *bourdon*—name of the heaviest bell in every carillon—is at 20 tons a gargantuan hunk of bronze. Hanging in the middle of this triumvirate, it scared me when I was a child. I had been led to believe somehow that if it went off in your presence it could make you deaf for life. I can see myself hastening past it, pressing forearms into each other against chest and forefingers into ears.

Climbing a zigzag series of iron staircases up toward the octagonal observation deck, 392 feet above ground, I passed slowly by all the bells, a whole forest seen up close or in depth. Looking down from any height I could single out the five mothers—the bourdon and its companions, the latter weighing between seven and ten tons. Midway was the landing or platform supporting the carillonneur's enclosed playing cabin. Peering into the door window, I saw a console vaguely, very vaguely, resembling a piano, more equivalently an organ. But really unlike anything most anyone has ever seen. No musician was sitting there that day. The keys are oaken batons resembling the ends of broom handles. They're not played with the fingers as on organs and pianos, indeed that would be impossible, but rather struck by the bottom edge of the hand when curled in a loose fist. Hands may be splayed also to press down a number of keys at once. A pedal board of square flat-topped wooden protuberances, for striking the notes of the heavier bells by foot, completes the key-board. The disconnect between player and bells is dramatic; the player in fact cannot see his or her instrument. Once a key or baton is struck, a transmission system linking it by wires, levers and pulleys up through a hole in the roof of the playing cabin to the clapper of the bell with its corresponding note, is activated. The clapper is then pulled against the inner membrane of the fixed or stationary bell to sound its note. Riverside, way beyond the minimum of two octaves defining a carillon, has six and one-half octaves of tones and semitones.

As a child, what impressed me in the tower more than any-thing, more even than the bell that could deafen me, was the fact that my surname was all over the place. Every bell bore the name of my father's firm, Gillett & Johnston, inscribed around its uppermost band. The smallest ones at the top of the belfry, the least weighing ten pounds, also had the founder's monogram, CFJ, stamped into them. This tower with its bells could have been a kind of Taj Mahal—a mausoleum built by my father to his own everlasting memory. I may have imagined it in some way or other like this. But in fact, not unlike the Taj, the Riverside tower cum bells was built or I should say financed by a man as a memorial to a woman, here John D. Rockefeller, Jr. to his mother Laura Spelman Rockefeller. When I got much older, taking into account the Taj and its six other companion sites around the world, all deemed wondrous, I presumed to add another: Riverside the Eighth Wonder.

My second visit to the tower, on my own in 1950, was inspired by Cyril Johnston's death on March 30th. A junior in col-lege in Boston, I had heard about it by mail from my mother. There were two envelopes. An obituary notice from *The London Times* fell out of one. In the other was a letter my mother wrote to try to explain the date away. She had good reason. Until this moment I believed, as she had never wavered in telling me, that Cyril Johnston had died in my infancy. The cause, she had said, was pneumonia. Now I was to understand that the man I had always thought dead had been alive all that time and had just actually died. And that the reason for such a colossal lie was that my mother, as it appeared now from her letter, had not really been widowed by Cyril Johnston throughout those years but divorced from him. She placed great weight by implication on the shame of divorce. Anyone older, more experienced or informed than I was, or less cloistered after ten years of school institutional life (boarding school and college) and before that six years living as I had in domestic confinement with my maternal grandmother, might have seen through this. In short, I accepted unquestioningly her new cover for her past as an unwed mother. I doubt that I had ever heard of unwed motherhood. If that was true, my mother imagined correctly that the way to go was to keep covering it up, she not being the one to try to educate me on the subject. She would leave it up to me to find out. In my mother's day, children generally were left to discover the most important things on their own.

So why did she inform me of Cyril Johnston's death just then, and thus her lie, with a new one added, further complicating her story? I believe she was upset about his death, and who best to tell but his only blood relative in America? Also, ghastly as it may seem, she must have understood that with his death, I now had no chance of ever meeting him. Anyway, in her world she was a "widow." Who would believe her divorcée tale, except a child like me? It would be another five years before I knew she had never been married, and I found out through an unexpected agency. I was looking at *East of Eden,* the film after the Steinbeck novel, a Cain and Abel story starring James Dean as the "Cain" figure (called Cal) and impelled by a dark secret the father (Adam, played by Raymond Massey) has told his two boys—that their mother was dead. Actually she had left home when the two brothers were infants. The father never knew where she went. But Cal (Dean), about 18, has found her somehow, operating as a

Madam in a brothel fifteen miles away from where he and his brother and father live. He is stalking her as the film opens. The secret of her status, both as dead but actually alive, and of her disreputable career, guides and powers the story. As it unfolded when I saw the movie (I figure in 1954, its release date), somewhere along its narrative I had what pop psych purveyors by the 1990s were calling a "light bulb" or an "aha" moment, and walked out of the theater saying to myself incredulously, "My mother was never married." This of course was the missing counterpart of her lie that Cyril was dead. Soon I was confronting her with my divinely imparted information, and my mother didn't try to deny it, but was furious I had found out. Now our past and future were decidedly undone. And our worlds would begin separating inexorably. Hers was one where her secret was safe. Mine was where it was not. In 1950 sometime after March 30th, the date of Cyril's death, I went instinctively to the Riverside memorial tower. Here was the one place in America with which I associated this twice-dead father. I was not yet familiar with any other markers. I went there not by way of mourning or memorializing him; I had not, after all, sustained a loss. It had to be a means of deploying the shock of my mother's lie, a shock probably left unabsorbed until her own death more than a quarter century later.

I went directly to the Riverside tower office, an aerie about 300 feet above street level with French windows giving on spectacular views of the Hudson River looking west toward New Jersey and north to the George Washington Bridge. Peering down on Riverside Drive, you'll see the dome of Grant's Tomb in a park across the street and slightly to the north, close enough to seem like a satellite of the church. Offices like those in the sky at Riverside have wind blowing through them even when there is none. There I found the eminent Belgian carillonneur Kamiel Lefévere, who had been playing the Riverside carillon since its installation in 1931. Even better than a "grave" marker in the form of a tower, I had unearthed a man who had known Cyril Johnston personally. On Lefévere's office wall was a photograph of Cyril flanked by King George V and his consort Queen Mary taken at the Croydon bellfoundry in 1925, a copy of which I would eventually own, and that would evolve into a monumentalized idea I developed of the bellfounder's station in life. (See back cover). No bells can be identified in the picture, even though bells are what the group is looking at. Actually their focus, as they stood gazing into a fortification of tall steel frameworks upon which bells were hanging, was Lefévere himself playing on a carillon demonstration instrument. Isolating the photo from its context—a viewing by King and Queen of Cyril's new carillon of 53 bells for J.D. Rockefeller Jr.'s Park Avenue Baptist Church in New York, the instrument that would end up at JDR's Riverside Church in an expansion scheme—the bellfounder could be construed as the royal couple's son. I had never seen the picture before. In fact I knew only one image of him. In a news clipping owned by my mother dated April 7, 1927, he is standing next to a newly cast seven-ton bell destined for the Houses of Parliament in Ottawa, the High Commissioner for Canada Mr. P. C. Larkin close by and wearing formal dress including top hat, leaning back a little and looking up, regarding the bell with some apparent awe. Introducing myself to Mr. Lefévere as Cyril Johnston's daughter, he overlooked somehow my undiluted American accent, calling me "Rosemary" and asking me how my "brother Arthur" was. Thus I found out I had two half-siblings. Barely able to catch their names, then failing to disabuse the renowned musician, I took on a sudden surprising imposture— a role in keeping with my American mother's private designation of me as her "secret child."

It was my first such deception, and would be my last until the approach to Arthur in September 1978, when I pretended quite the contrary thing—having no relationship at all. I was unsuited to any kind of posing. Once I understood the full extent of my mother's cover-up of my birth circumstance, I became reactively her opposite, an ungovernable truth teller. As such, my ambush of Arthur seems now an improbable aberration. Before meeting him I could be observed in an Italian restaurant on Belgrave Street behaving apoplectically, choking over a prawn appetizer. Dressed in smart livery, a costly three-piece black pants suit bought at

Jorge's on Madison Avenue in New York to impress myself, I was laughing and crying convulsively over jokey questions that an American traveling companion had been saying I could ask Arthur. A half hour later I walked sedately, however with profound apprehension, into the Ebury Street Steak House.

At 46, Arthur Francis Evelyn Johnston was just one year older than the age of his father at my birth. As I approached him and we were ushered to a table, I had barely time to register his features and attire—6'3" height, dark hair, some of what was left of it graying around the ears, dark hazel eyes, navy chalkstripe suit—before he launched a monologue on the history of his father's business, none of which I really heard, or that I remember. He was on a lunch break from his own business in Fleet Street Estates Management, and was in a hurry. I let him go on for ten minutes. I already knew I was not going to pose as "Joan Castile" for very long. I may have gone to the lunch imagining I had a choice, to keep up the surrogate pretense or to put Arthur straight. In relating the story afterwards, I liked describing it the former way, I suppose because it sounded more dramatic. However, only the day before, I had received compelling advice to tell Arthur who I was "as quickly as possible."

I had gone to see Diana Petre (pron. Peter), illegitimate half-sister of the distinguished English author and critic J.R. Ackerley. She was the author herself of *The Secret Orchard of Roger Ackerley,* Roger having been the mutual father of J.R. and Diana. J.R. had written about their father's "secret" (a whole family consisting of Diana, her twin sisters and their mother, Roger's mistress) in his wonderful memoir *My Father and Myself,* published posthumously in 1968. J.R. was himself born illegitimately, though he was unaware of it until his parents were married when he was 23. From my meeting with Diana, a lovely lady then 66, I salvaged mainly her counsel to waste no time in telling my half-brother the next day that I was his father's American daughter. Like me, as I knew from her book, she had been raised on the lie that her father was dead. When she was 17, "Uncle Bodger," as he was known to her and her twin sisters, actually did die, at which point Diana's mother notified the sisters that their "uncle" was really their father, turning Diana into a truth addict of the kind I could recognize. The timing of her mother's disclosure, occurring immediately following the death of the uncle/father, also echoed that overlap in my story. Another familiar feature to me was her mother's habitual silence following her stunning revelation. And the impact of the surprise, as I well knew, must have split her short history, creating a before and after of a powerful perplexity.

Of course exposures like what I contemplated at lunch with Arthur, challenging family history in a different way, are rife with the risk of rejection. In my case, I risked forfeiting information as well. Seizing a pause in Arthur's speech to pursue a brambly path toward disclosure, I kept myself in the dark over these potential consequences. I had not even asked myself if Arthur might have known somehow of my existence. I had supposed, correctly it would turn out, he did not. The surge to end my pose was very strong in any event. "Your father," I ventured, about to tell him something he knew quite well, "crossed the ocean many times between Britain and the United States transporting bells and seeking contracts . . . " Continuing, now telling him something he also knew but perhaps had never given much thought, "And he was well into his forties before he married . . . " Arthur was attentive, impassive. "Who *is* this woman?" he might have begun to ask himself. Now, hurtling toward revelation, opening up verboten territory, I posed the question, "Can't you imagine that before he married, your father had some girlfriends, or romances, on these trips . . . ?" If I hoped here for a helpful glimmer of understanding, none was forthcoming. So with this plunge into the personal, unexpectedly disregarding the presumed terms of our encounter, the public business of a great man, and reluctant to be misunderstood for another second, without more ado I announced, "My mother was one of these romances."

A hung moment transpired, as my words sank in. Then a teaspoon Arthur was holding fell out of his hand, clattering to a dish. The teaspoon served to say it all, with the expression on his face remaining appreciably the same. From that moment, he never betrayed a shadow of doubt that what I told him was true. Yet he showed signs of a future reserve and protectiveness, a plan to maintain me as a mystery figure, to keep the rest of his family in the ignorance he had shared with them until now, to possess me as an interest or curiosity of his own exclusively. Quickly he collected himself to switch our agenda, make himself interviewer instead of interviewee, and have me fill him in on this unknown, not exactly reputation-enhancing chapter in his father's past. Obligingly, I produced the story of how Cyril met Olive, my mother, aboard ship on an Atlantic crossing from Cherbourg via Southampton to Boston in 1927. When it came to her pregnancy, and her decision to go full term despite Cyril's protests, including his offer of the best most expensive abortion to be had on the Continent, Arthur glanced swiftly, covertly, at tables around us now occupied by other lunch clients, obviously hoping we had not been overheard. He could be pegged for a real English stiff, a Winchester/Cambridge button-down product—an impression belied somewhat by the mischievous glint in his hazel eyes. He seemed almost collusive with me until I presumed too much. He was looking, after all, at the results of the aforementioned failed relationship, a woman born (in London) against his father's wishes and without his involvement or legal sanction, now perhaps asserting herself as a kind of pretender to his family.

If this was not clear already, it loomed when the subject of my marriage came up, and I observed a common element between us, suspiciously interweaving our families: Arthur as older brother to his sister Rosemary; his father Cyril's identical role to his sister Nora; my son Richard the same to his sister Winifred. My newly met half-brother drew back visibly, gauging a distance he deemed proper, any playfulness gone from his eyes. Then when he asked if my children "were interested in all this" and I said, "No they don't care about it much one way or another," he nodded approvingly. When in August I had told my son, aged 20, about my upcoming meeting in London, he had said jauntily, "Maybe you could get a picture to see if we look alike . . . Arthur is a real blood relative, a half-uncle, he might give me an estate." My rejoinder: "You have a good sense of humor." An Englishman I know, a noted art critic and a man with a background similar to mine, told me, "they [the family] could easily be very interested," so long as I "didn't want anything—that terrible phrase." Of course I did want something. Call it "an estate" as my son had breezily specified. Not as commonly understood, but one I had long imagined, given my circumstances, as within the realm of possibility—the information upon which to base a book. The end of my mythic orientation to Arthur's father seemed at hand. In Arthur's person, I was faced with a tangible vibration. He was not what I imagined Cyril was exactly. But he was the son, he had a physical resemblance, he grew up with Cyril, he knew things, he could be an invaluable conduit.

Having come this far, Arthur may have looked inviting, but he presented a new unforeseen challenge. In revealing my true identity, I had risked shutting down a vital source. The proposed author "Joan Castile" had been put to rest during our luncheon, along with her book. And through my proper introduction of myself I had forfeited the opportunity of meeting Arthur's mother on the Monday following. He decided right then not to mention me to his mother, it being uncertain if she knew of me or not. He now planned to tell her that "Joan Castile" had already left by Monday when he had scheduled a meeting between the three of us. Given this and other signs of discouragement, I had no way of knowing then what a major role Arthur would play in the fulfillment, over the long haul, of my objective. He would never be able to tell me more than I knew or found out myself concerning his father's profession; and on family subjects he would be tight to cryptic. But just knowing Arthur, and experiencing his traditional resistance, was to become an educational bonus in my quest. Had I waited him out at our Ebury Street lunch, listening to all he had to say about his father's business, I would have heard only the official story—in essence how great Cyril Johnston was. His line would have been the same whether he was talking to Joan or to Jill, or to any interested party. I already knew his father was great. I wanted much more. "More" is well known from the investigatory biographical traditions. The origins of things, given the conjunction of my birth with my subject—i.e. Cyril Johnston's involvement with America and my American mother in the course of his carillon travels—were already a fixated interest.

Leaving the Ebury Street Steak House, with goodbyes and handshaking on the sidewalk outside, I tried to apologize to Arthur for my ruse in meeting him, saying, "I didn't think I could or should have introduced myself transatlantically." He agreed politely, possibly sincerely, "No, that would have been too unreal."

Many years later, and long after Arthur died, in 1993, aged sixty-one, a key to the origins of his father's bellfounding history—topmost in my list of real things to find once I had left mythology behind—came from another family source. My new and belated informant would alter my relationship to England and to this book.

In 1906, as the result of a botched order of five bells for a school in a northern suburb of London called Elstree, Cyril discovered the principle of tuning that was beginning to revolutionize bellfounding in the 20th century. It was his axial moment, soon catapulting his firm to the forefront of the craft, and at the new frontier of carillon building.

Chapter II

ELSTREE

All bells must harmonize perfectly in respect to one another
—François Hemony

*We have bells with us everywhere, and few people with musical ears have
not, at one time or another, puzzled themselves in attempting to
determine accurately the notes of their own church bells*
—Canon Arthur B. Simpson

*Canon Simpson of Fittleworth Sussex contended that no peal in England
was in tune, and that a good bell should be in tune with itself,
viz., have at least five tones in perfect accord*
—Cyril F. Johnston

England is a land of change-ringing, not of carillons at all.
During the 1600s the English were seized by a curious craze,
which grew and grew in popularity, and is pandemic to this day.
Some 40,000 Englishmen and women enjoy "The Exercise" as
they call it, climbing church towers every Sunday morning and at
sundry times to pull on ropes attached to bells that sound off
when they swing, making a godawful noise to the uninitiated, a

divine stentorian jumble to the participants. Americans can hear this sound, if they listen for it, in the popular film, *Four Weddings and a Funeral*. At least six thousand churches in England have these "rings" of from four to twelve bells, which are tuned to the diatonic scale. The ringers (as many as there are bells) stand in a circle in a room below the bell chamber each holding a rope which ascends through a hole in the ceiling and attaches to the spoke of a wheel fixed to an assigned bell. The bell starts in a mouth upwards position, and when set in motion by a pull on the rope in the room below, rotates clockwise 360 degrees, near the height of its arc the clapper meeting bell to sound its note. Stopping briefly back in the mouth upwards position, the next pull on the rope has the bell rotating in the opposite direction, anticlockwise; and so it goes, back and forth sometimes for hours on end. But there is a method, literally, in such seeming madness.

Sequence and timing are everything. Skills are involved. The Exercise is called change-ringing because each player's note is sounded in a serial, systematic order. The sequence of bells is altered according to set rules every time they are sounded. Such an order is a Method in the change-ringing taxonomy, and thousands of them have been devised since the 1600s. The Methods all have names, like *Single Oxford Bob Triples* or *Bristol Surprise Major*, which the ringers memorize, able to keep hundreds ready for use in their heads. Obviously the more bells there are in a ring, the greater the number of permutations that can be rung on them. On seven bells, 5,040 are the maximum number of changes possible, on eight bells 40,320. On twelve: 479,001,600. If a whole range is deployed, usually 5000 plus changes, it's called a peal, and it involves three to four hours continuous ringing: if you stop, you've lost it. At this level change-ringing is a competitive sport, and the players' official publication, *The Ringing World,* publishes weekly reports on peals around the nation successfully completed.

The carillon instrument, a particular invention of the Lowlands on the Continent dating from the 1500s, never caught on in England—a realm famously called the "Ringing Isle" by G. F. Händel after he arrived there in 1712 to be a court composer. The very presence of the carillon in Britain, numbering no more than fourteen instruments by now, is something of an insult to the pealing multitudes. Cyril Johnston, himself raised in change-ringing England, could seem to have been an unlikely prospect as a future builder of carillons. Like so many of his compatriots he was in fact an enthusiastic change-ringer. He joined the Ancient Society of College Youths (the earliest association of ringers with a continuous history, founded in 1637) in his twenties, and rang in 32 peals during his lifetime. The order that Gillett & Johnston had for five bells for the Elstree School in 1906 was simply for the clock to chime on. In numbers of bells, the carillon needs 23, comprising two octaves, to begin to qualify for carillon status. Cyril could not have been unconversant with this solo concert instrument, so notably ubiquitous across the Channel in Belgium, Holland and parts of northwestern France. But he was still far from making one. In 1906–07 as a result of the Elstree order, he found out what he would need to know to do it. In the meantime he would fill many orders for English rings, competing with other English founders in this demanding market.

In a short paper no more than 700 words that Cyril wrote in 1948, two years before his death, titled, "Why I Started an Intensive Study of the Tuning of Bells," he summed up this earliest turning point in his career. After his firm had installed five small clock bells, the largest weighing only 2 cwt. (hundredweight), in a "famous school at Elstree," the owners complained of the tone. They called in Dr. William Wooding Starmer, a famous organist and bell specialist, who recommended the bells be sent to a competitor firm to be re-cast.

"In my youthful enthusiasm," Cyril wrote, "this seemed to be a bit hard and I persuaded my father to allow me to experiment and at the same time to stop production of bells which were in progress at the Foundry." Untried and young though he may have been, his rivalrous instinct, which would later drive his competitors mad, was clearly auspicious. And his perfectionism was in evidence. Four years earlier in 1902 when he was just eighteen and barely out of school he had joined his father's firm as an apprentice. His father Arthur Anderson Johnston had been a bellfounder since 1877, when he joined a clock-making company as a third partner, introducing bells to its production line.

During that very time, a man with a most unusual mission was touring the country investigating England's bells. Canon Arthur Barwick Simpson, born 1828, a Rector at a small church in Fittleworth, Sussex, had undertaken to prove that all the bells in England were out of tune. His researches and writings on the subject, conducted over a 23-year period, would have a fantastic impact on the future of bellfounding. In 1895 and '96 the fruits of the Canon's study were published in the *Pall Mall Magazine*. Two essays—*Why Bells Sound out of Tune* and *How to Cure Them*—then appeared in 1897 as a book. Cyril Johnston discovered the work in 1906 after his Elstree bells were found wanting. He was not the first bellfounder to light upon Canon Simpson's findings. But he was only the second to take them seriously. The first, John William Taylor I of the John Taylor Co., based in the Midlands town of Loughborough, had been conducting his own experiments independently of Simpson, and had a good head start on Cyril. By 1895, when Cyril was just eleven, John William, who had been contacted by Canon Simpson, invited him to the foundry to discuss tuning issues. The two men met several times and corresponded. Within a year John William was casting bells tuned according to the Canon's prescription. Cyril's father Arthur A. Johnston, one of several other founders also approached by this bell visionary, never picked up the challenge. When Cyril did, in 1906, six years after Simpson's death, a small crisis developed in the Croydon foundry between father and son. The father continued resisting change or innovation. Cyril, to implement his new knowledge, needed a tuning machine and his father refused to get one for him. Once Cyril prevailed, buying the machine himself, and successfully recasting the Elstree bells, his father propitiously handed the bell side of the works over to him.

Canon Simpson's "prescription" for curing the dissonance he heard in all the bells of England, earthshaking as it would be for the 20th century world of bellfounding, was not a new one. During the 1600s, a glorious period on the Continent in art and music, the craft of tuning bells to a certain harmonic perfection had flourished unabated for at least forty years. Two brothers, François and Pieter Hemony, natives of Lorraine, are revered figures in the carillon lore. Between 1644 and 1684, as they moved on to Germany then the Netherlands, they tuned bells to a sound that had never been so beautiful before, and would not be again— once their secret died with them—until the early 20th century in England. Bells present very special tuning problems because of their rampant and unruly overtones. All musical instruments issue complex sounds, which conveniently arrange themselves subordinately with the fundamental note. If not tamed, the overtones in a bell tend to struggle for dominance. A bell made to hang alone is not such a problem, although a trained ear can be offended if a governing note is not discernible. When destined for integration with other bells in an instrument like a ring, a chime or a carillon, its intractable partials have to be brought under control for the sake of general harmony. In a (single) percussion instrument like a gong you can hear all sorts of overtones, which have no harmonic relation to each other, thus can't fuse to make an indivisible sound. The multi-vocality is intense. There's an impressive noise, not an identifiable note or pitch.

A single bell cast to be part of a ring or carillon is tuned so that its note in a diatonic or chromatic scale is clear, its sound unambiguous. Before the Hemony brothers, bellfounders cast and tuned a single bell roughly to its intended note. After a bell had been cast, the bronze was hewed out in a primitive fashion, the metal interior pared away with hammer and chisel to arrive at the proportions for emitting the right sound. Each bell was tuned without reference to its inner overtones or harmonics. In fact, no structural analysis had been made before of a bell's partials. The Hemonys, as bellfounders paralleled by their belated descendants John Taylor and Gillett & Johnston, had their own Canon Simpson in a blind man from Utrecht, Jacob Van Eyck. With Van Eyck as advisor, the Hemonys built their first carillon in 1644 for a tower in Zutphen, an eastern Dutch city. Van Eyck (c.1590–1657) was Utrecht's municipal carillonneur and a student of bell tones. He analyzed bell partials systematically, isolating the outstanding ones, five in number—the fundamental or strike note, the hum-tone an octave below, the nominal an octave above, a tierce and a quint in between the fundamental and the nominal—and measured the intervals between them. Intervals between overtones became important. Altering the bell model in the right places (the Hemonys, in advance of previous methods, put the bell on a lathe, turned not of course by electricity but by men, to file the inner surface at various levels), a consonant relationship between the partials or overtones was achieved, creating a harmonious chord. Apparently the Hemonys had wonderful ears, but to test for accuracy, auxiliary instruments were used, and have been since at least their time. Van Eyck had simply whistled at bells, the way you can whistle at a glass, to make them vibrate to his key. Now each overtone was tested through the sympathetic vibration of tone bars. The brothers employed a "metallophone" (a chromatic series of bronze or iron staves, a metal variant of the wooden xylophone), one forerunner of tuning forks, which were invented in 1752 and are used to this day even while sophisticated electronic computer-based methods have become prevalent.

For the first time in bellfounding, measurable information concerning bell notes was compared to measurable properties of the bell profile. Once a bell was in tune with itself so to speak, it was next requisitioned to be in tune with the other bells that altogether comprise an instrument like the carillon. "All bells," François Hemony wrote, "must harmonize perfectly in respect to one another." All the three principal notes in a bell—the fundamental or strike note, the hum note one octave below, or the nominal one octave above—must be tuned in precise accord with the same pitch in all the other bells. The complexities of bell-tuning were richly delineated by Canon Simpson in his 1895–96 essays. The bridge he made between the Hemonys and his own time included an exploratory knowledge of Hemony bells. To his travels throughout England, the Canon added the Continent, seeking out the bells of old master craftsmen to test, in particular surviving examples of the 50 carillons or parts of them that the Hemonys built altogether. In a nice historical coincidence, a tad more than 50 would be the number of Cyril Johnston's total output in carillons once he started casting them in 1922. I wonder if he registered that connection, or perhaps aimed at it subconsciously. His bells would be compared favorably to those of the Hemonys. He surely aspired to the Stradivarian reputation of François, the elder brother.

By the 1640s when the Hemonys built their first carillon, the instrument was not much more than a century old. The origins of a musical instrument like the carillon are not too hard to imagine. The numbers of bells in a tower first of all would have to increase beginning from one. A single bell, hit by hammer or swung by rope to sound the time or announce curfews or warn of fire or natural catastrophe or enemy attack, etc., gradually found itself with ever more companions. During the Middle Ages the numbers and size of bells in church towers increased throughout Christendom. With the invention of weight-driven clocks, both in England and on the Continent in the 14th century, bells were quickly connected to them. The adaptation of a greater number of bells to the clock gave rise to mechanically played tunes, historically called chimes. By the 15th century clocks were essential tower installations, with the large bell striking the hours, the clock mechanism lying immediately beneath. In that part of Europe sloping toward the North Sea west of the Rhine, i.e. the Low Countries, bells grew to have a prominence not found elsewhere. Towns competed architecturally in building beautiful towers to house their clocks and bells. By the late 1300s there were automatic players everywhere. Automation, most famously the jack or clock-jack, or jack-o'-the-clock as the English called it—one or two bronze-cast figures striking bells mechanically by cleverly devised connections to the clock—replaced the human bell ringer.

A split occurred—the clock chime as signal and the clock chime as "music." For the latter, a rotating drum, like a big music box or a player piano, was preset to play a combination of notes before the stroke of each hour. The commonest interval of signal was every quarter hour, and these usually formed an accretion of notes, the longest being on the hour or fourth quarter. These notes, sounded on four bells added to a heavier hour bell, are famously known as the *voorslag,* a Dutch word meaning fore-stroke (to announce the impending hour strikes)—a word enshrined in carillon history. The voorslag exists widely today in such as the Westminster or Cambridge, and Parsifal quarters; at Riverside Church the hourly tolling of the bourdon is preceded by the four Parsifal quarter-chiming bells. Combining both signal and "music," the voorslag led most directly to the carillon, a word derived from the French *quatrillon* (itself from the Latin *quadrillo*)—originally connoting bells hung on all four sides of a tower. An interest in tunes suggested by the voorslag inevitably grew with the addition of more bells. More and more bells were added until all the intervals of the chromatic scale were supplied. The next step was the keyboard, taking tunes or melodies beyond their mechanical sameness and allowing for variety and expression by a musician.

According to the late André Lehr, the preeminent Dutch carillon historian, a primitive baton keyboard appeared in Antwerp in 1480. But he considers 1510 as the year of the birth of the carillon. By preserved record, in that year a baton keyboard was built for a tower in Oudenaarde, Belgium. Now all the tones and semitones were played manually, alongside the automatic time-telling mechanisms.[1] Where clock and carillon co-exist, as they do today in many Western towers, the curious origin of the carillon in early clock mechanisms can be construed. And they remain united through the dependence of the clock (whether mechanism alone or mechanism with a face or dial) on several carillon bells, notably the bourdon, to strike the quarters and the hours. Of course many towers have only clock-bells, like the Palace of Westminster in London housing Big Ben, or One South Broad Street in Philadelphia, a 27-story "pedestal" for the 15-ton *Founder's Bell* [See Chapter X].

Gillett & Johnston, maker of the *Founder's Bell* in 1926, had roots dating from 1844 as a clock making firm exclusively. William Gillett (1823–1886) was an itinerant clockmaker and repairer from Hadlow, Kent. He moved to Clerkenwell in London, then to Croydon where he established permanent premises. Between 1844 and 1950, over 14,000 tower clocks were made at the foundry. When Cyril Johnston's father Arthur bought a partnership in Gillett's firm in 1877, and added the specialty of bells, he inadvertently altered the structure of bellfounding at that time, becoming the only founder to head into the 20th century with the capacity to sign for clock-bells, change-ringing sets, and carillons without having to order out for clock mechanisms.[2] Such an advantage would have made up to some extent for the handicap Cyril inherited as a latecomer to the bell field. His competitors John Warner (who folded in 1925), John Taylor and Whitechapel, both active to this day, collectively had centuries on him.

With his first step, in 1906, Cyril found his bible in Canon Simpson's passionate writings, urging the people of England to listen to their bells, to demand harmonious sounds; and exhorting the nation's church wardens to require this of bellfounders. It took Cyril just a few weeks, as he says in his 1948 paper, to hit upon the cause of trouble with his Elstree order, and correct the faults— "So that the bells might comply with the late Canon Simpson's theory that a good bell should have at least five tones in tune with itself." The longest paragraph in his short paper is a tribute to this teacher, who had died six years before Cyril discovered him. Recalling his Elstree episode as a "threatened catastrophe," Cyril said in effect that the Canon saved him. Thereafter he would invoke the great bell Utopian's name as a mantra in his business. Quoted in newspapers or identified in company brochures, Cyril had his bells tuned after the "five-tone Simpson principle"—a term that has survived with ubiquity, often simply as "Simpson tuning," in the bell literature. The John Taylor Co. on the other hand, destined to be Cyril's lifelong competitor and nemesis once he caught up with them in 1906, would claim the principle for their own, calling it the "Taylor True-Harmonic System." Taylor, it can be deduced from Cyril's retrospective paper, was the "competitor firm" that Dr. William Wooding Starmer recommended for recasting the faulty Elstree bells. Starmer had strong connections with Taylor, and became an influential consultant, a figure for Cyril to reckon with.

After 1906 and his Elstree breakthrough, Cyril, like Taylor, came up against powerful resistance in England to the new Simpson tuning. The countless old bells that Canon Simpson had condemned as out of tune, many dating from Medieval times, were to both ringers and church officials along with their congregations, historical treasures of inestimable value. Now they would become increasingly vulnerable to destruction and replacement by new and better bells, tuned on state-of-the-art principles. At that point, the new Simpsonite bellfounder tended to be viewed as simply a commercially avid man.

The Elstree School order was of course for brand-new bells. In Cyril's 1948 paper, he didn't say he recast the Elstree bells after the ones he had installed were condemned. He did say he was "very fortunate [in hitting] upon the cause of trouble within a matter of weeks."[3] The evidence of his recasting them is in Croydon foundry records listing "the first set of bells for Elstree School," cast in 1906, "replaced soon afterwards," in 1907. The notes, dimensions and weights of the bells, 10 in all, are itemized. So 1907 is the official date of G&J's first bells tuned on modern principles.

It would make him a major player in England's altered bellscape, and ultimately in America as well.

Chapter III

THE ROYAL EXCHANGE

Do Weel and Persevere
—Arthur Anderson (1792–1868)

In 1920 during a luncheon at the Croydon works, Cyril Johnston told his specially invited visitors that, "it was a well known fact . . . we English were too backward and modest about what we do, and bellfounders seemed to be the most backward of any." He went on in this bold vein, "Great things have been evolved and great problems mastered in the bell world during the last twenty years, and yet the public—and particularly the musical public—knows hardly anything of these things."[1] It had been fourteen years since Cyril mastered the art of tuning, and nine since his last manifest triumphs in bellfounding. In 1911 a grand total of thirteen orders had included the prize of restoring a venerable old ring of eight dating from 1629 for the Wimborne Minster in Dorset. At Cyril's 1920 luncheon, his visitors were there to see his new bells for London's Royal Exchange, a plum order he had chased for his English portfolio. His Wimborne and Royal Exchange undertakings bookended the Great War, when bellfounding took second place to munitions and other war work.[2] The Royal Exchange contract would be Cyril's first for the City of London. And the first bells in the City to be tuned on the Simpson principle. Mentioning the Hemonys in the same breath with Simpson, Cyril concluded his talk, "It has been left to England to perfect what was aimed at in Belgium three hundred years ago, so that to-day the finest bells in the world are being turned out by British hands."[3]

In a surviving photo from this luncheon, Cyril, aged 36, stands over the upturned tenor bell, a mallet held aloft in his right hand, a glint of pride and satisfaction in his face. His 34-year old sister and only sibling Nora, at that time involved in the London theatre as actress and producer, appears to his right holding a rope. Cyril was poised over a bell and also a very bright future. In a year's time he would be building his first carillon, and the first to be sent to North America, heralding a transatlantic movement as big in its way as the relocation of the world's art capital from Paris to New York after WWII.

The bellfounder's confidence hints at personal origins— beyond the disadvantage of inheriting a company that started up green just when its product was beginning to undergo transform- ations at large. A clue to Cyril's belief in himself lies where one might look first, to the mother. Née Amelie Charlotte Brouneau, born 1863, of French origin, Cyril's mother had him living at home with her until he married at the age of 46. She performed a social role extraordinaire in his business, entertaining guests for tea at the works or at their house, often having visitors overnight who were important to her son. I heard the relationship cap- sulized, if rather sourly, while I was visiting the Whitechapel bellfoundry in 1986, calling on Douglas Hughes, whose father Albert had been a fierce competitor of Cyril's in the UK market for peals. Hughes said, "Cyril's mother seemed to think he was sent from heaven and could do no wrong." Amelie had married a bellfounder (in 1881), and through her son, the more adored object, she stayed married in a sense, outliving her husband as she would by 25 years.

Another clue to Cyril's self-expansiveness can be found in his school records. At the Whitgift School in Croydon, with roots as a Grammar School dating from 1600, when Croydon was an industrious trading and market town of 2000 inhabitants, Cyril was a star. By 1902 the year he graduated he was Captain of the School, a Prefect or Headboy, and he held positions in the Cricket and Swimming Clubs, the School Magazine, the Literary and Debating Society, the Rifle Club, the Library, and the Natural History and Scientific Societies. As a cricket player he was said to be a fair batsman, generally making runs when most wanted—a talent called clutch hitting in American baseball. Cyril's widow, Mary Johnston, would tell an interviewer that her husband was "brainy and brilliant and not all that interested in joining his father's bellfoundry."[4] He would, she said, have preferred to go to university and enter the diplomatic service. If destined to be great at whatever he chose to do—an impression one can deduce from his school record—a high profile career would surely have appealed to him. And bellfounding was hardly that. In making the most of it, in fact developing a passion for it, he would have his moment in the sun, and challenge or astonish people who saw bellfounders as mere manufacturers, a plodding and anonymous breed. The way Douglas Hughes expressed it, "He tried to put himself in a class higher than he was."

I don't think he "tried." He was driven along an unusual path by convergent forces. His parents were an impressive couple. His father, a copious man with a walrus moustache and an evolved social consciousness, was a genial town father known in Croydon for his generosity and good works. Born in Yorkshire in 1851, the seventh and last child of a Scottish Baptist minister and an Englishwoman from Scarborough, he would be favored by an uncle-in-law after whom he was named, a benefaction with broad consequences. The class compass was skewed in this case. The uncle-in-law, Arthur Anderson, died very wealthy, but he was uncommonly poor to begin with. The object of his affections, the nephew named after him, had descended paternally from an orderly line of unexceptional middle class people in or around Greenock, a shipbuilding town on the Clyde in southwestern Scotland.[5] His father Robert Johnston, the Baptist minister, born in 1802, left Scotland in the 1820s to study for the ministry in the Yorkshire town of Bradford. Robert had tried to emulate his father William Johnston who was a printer, and an elder brother named William who had followed suit. Then he struck out on his own, pursuing a different profession and leaving home and country to do it, showing profile of a second son under primogeniture, even choosing the offbeat Baptist denomination, bearing the assigned epithet of "dissenting minister." In 1833 Robert established a small Baptist ministry in the beautiful Yorkshire town of Beverley. A year later he married Hannah Hill, the daughter of a Scarborough shipowner. Between 1835 and 1851 the couple had their seven children, with the seventh and propitiously named Arthur primed for success.

On the surface, Cyril Johnston's unremitting middle class paternal history yields little sign of his immoderate ambition to come. Unless by that very constancy, in exhausting itself at last a son with a mission is produced. But a model had emerged. Into an unremarkable family, an outsider can inject an idea of greatness that had not existed before. Arthur Anderson, his father's uncle-in-law, was a rare creation of Britain, with origins in a remote corner of the Isles. His story conforms to legendary tales of the obscure, impoverished, often abandoned child who makes good in a very big way. Born on February 19, 1792, in Lerwick, the Shetland Islands capital, by age 10 he was working as a "beach boy," curing fish for a general merchant. With little or no educational opportunities he seemed destined for the main fisherman class of the Shetlands. But three older men in his life, including his father and his employer, seeing that he had special qualities, with a superior intelligence and determination to learn, made sure he was exposed to some schooling and affairs of the world. Arthur's employer saved him from the press gangs, which periodically descended on the Islands to kidnap young boys for naval service.

And in 1808 when Arthur was sixteen, secured passage for him on a man-o'-war, seeing him off with the parting advice, "Do Weel and Persevere" which became his lifelong motto.

In 1808 Europe was in turmoil over the Napoleonic wars. It was three years after Lord Nelson's defeat of the Franco-Spanish fleet at Trafalgar, establishing the Royal Navy's supremacy. At first Anderson saw action as a Midshipman aboard *HMS Ardent*, a 64-gun ship of 1,422 tons built in 1796; then as Captain's Clerk on a 10-gun brig the *HMS Bermuda*. One mission of the *Bermuda,* in 1812, was to recapture a British brig aground near Boulogne. There could, I suppose, have been an engagement with an oversized enemy frigate such as Patrick O'Brien describes in his novel *Master and Commander,* with events in the same time frame. Anderson was discharged from service in 1815, a year after Napoleon's exile. Paid off in Portsmouth, tradition has him walking to London in a penniless state, and living in the city close to starvation until he found work. He was lucky in having one promising connection. Through his maternal uncle Peter Ridland, Anderson most auspiciously met Ridland's brother-in-law Christopher Hill, a shipowner from Scarborough. As impressed by the young Shetlander as the boy's elders at home had been, Hill would determine Anderson's fate to an extraordinary degree. And it was Hill's appearance that turned Anderson into a significant figure in and for the Johnston family. Hill introduced him not only to his future partner in business but to his wife-to-be, Hill's own daughter Mary Ann, older sister to Hannah who would marry Robert Johnston, Cyril's grandfather, in 1834.

Anderson's future partner, Brodie M. Willcox, a shipbroker with whom Christopher Hill had business dealings, hired him as a clerk. In 1822 when Willcox made Anderson partner, he married Hill's daughter—a happy conjunction of family and business concerns. Fifteen years later, in 1837, Willcox and Anderson founded what would become one of the world's mighty shipping lines, the P&O, or Peninsular & Oriental Steamship Navigation Company. By then Arthur Anderson had become linked through his wife Mary Ann to the Johnstons of Greenock and Beverley.

When Mary Ann remained childless in their marriage, the last child her younger sister Hannah had with Robert, in 1851, was named Arthur Anderson Johnston. So the son of a Scottish Baptist minister and a Scarborough shipowner's daughter carried the marvelous legacy of an obscure Shetland Islander who rose to great eminence and riches in Victoria's Empire. A.A. Johnston's uncle took a strong paternal interest in him, practically adopting him in his youth, providing a model of character far exceeding his command of shipping and commerce, or his lofty status in Britain's new entrepreneurial class.[6]

When Anderson died in 1868, leaving a large fortune, his namesake nephew Arthur Anderson Johnston was 17 years old. While Anderson bestowed much of his wealth on various charities such as educational institutes and widows' homes to help the Shetlands and the families of seamen, and he recognized a number of individuals in his will, his largest personal bequest by far was for £24,000 to be divided equally among the children of Hannah Johnston. Hannah's sister Mary Ann, his wife, had predeceased him. It seems likely that only three of Hannah's children, including young Arthur, became beneficiaries. Arthur, having been employed in P&O offices, might have ended up in shipping, but the sea and ships were not in his blood. Instead, he seemed musically inclined. At first he was oriented to fun and entertainment, using some of the money he had inherited to buy a skating rink located in the Croydon public gardens. When this didn't work out, he began wandering around Europe. His way toward the Croydon clock firm, heralding bells, was paved in France when he met a family called Brouneau, and wanted to marry the daughter called Amelie. Amelie's father Frederic said he couldn't marry his daughter unless he returned to England and got a partnership in some promising business.

Thus he entered William Gillett's clock firm in Croydon, and introduced bells to its production line. The year was 1877. With the birth of Cyril Johnston in 1884, the legacy of Arthur Anderson would in time ring out metaphorically—a hidden homage you could say—in Britain and around the world. The confoundingly

William Gillett, clock maker,
b. 1823–†1886

Arthur Anderson Johnston,
bellfounder
b. 1851–†1916

Cyril Frederick Johnston, bellfounder
b. 1884–†1950
as a Grenadier Guard 1914–1918

The Gillett & Johnston Bellfoundry, White Horse Road, Croydon, England, late 1920s

TELEGRAPHIC ADDRESS,
GILLETT, CROYDON.

Church & Carillon Bell Foundry

BELLS CAST TO ANY SIZE & NUMBER

GILLETT & JOHNSTON

ESTABLISHED 1844

CONTRACTORS TO THE GOVERNMENT

STEAM CLOCK
Factory & Church Bell Foundry
CROYDON

Church Turret House
& Musical Clock
MANUFACTURERS

EXHIBITION MEDALLISTS

Dec. 14th 1897

Dear Sir

We are at present engaged in tuning a small Bell and are in difficulties as to the exact note of it there being a diversity of opinion. Could you make it convenient to run up to our Factory and give us your opinion. Our Mr. Johnston will be at home next Monday. If this will suit you we shall be pleased to pay your expenses. We make this request as you have expressed your willingness to come here on many previous occasions

Yours faithfully,

Gillett & Johnston

per G.H.P.

Rev. A. B. Simpson

*Letter to Canon A. B. Simpson, December 14, 1897, from the Gillett & Johnston Bellfoundry
in behalf of Cyril Johnston's father, Arthur A. Johnston, showing early contact between Simpson and G&J*

Above, Fittleworth Church; below left, plaque inside church with incumbents from 1372 to present; below right, Canon Arthur Barwick Simpson, tenure 1876–1900

INCUMBENTS OF FITTLEWORTH

1371 ex Peter Dalton	1801 Charles Alcock LLB d
1372 John de Winchcumbe	1801 John Warner BA Mar–Apr
1513 William [Robert?] Darby ns	1801 Apl Thomas Hudson LLB d
1518 John Segar ns	1819 Jonathan Asbridge res
1522 William Draper ns	1826 Robert Tedcraft d
1523 Robert Bradman ns	1847 Henry Latham MA ns
1551 Thomas Mathewson	1859 William Goodenough Bayle
1557 John Emerson res	DCL d
1558 Richard Atkinson d	1860 Thomas Rompe Drake MA res
1570 Matthew Myers AM	1865 The Vicarage of Fittleworth
1572 John Burr curate licensed to	was raised to the status of a
celebrate divine service	Rectory under district
1581 Thomas Deane curate liansed	Church Tithes Act Aug.1.1867
to serve the cure	1868 Stephen Reed Cattley MA d
1590 John Leigh curate	1876 Arthur Barwick Simpson ←
1598 Arthur Hewsden MA d	MA d
1609 Christopher Greene MA Trans.?	1900 George Stuart Newbury MA res
1625 William Hinde	1920 Algernon Charles Lucey MA res
1655 John Walwyn minister by	1934 Bernard Foster Palmer res
letters Patent of Oliver Ld Protector	1947 John Edward Dieterlé d
1660 William Hinde restored Vicard	1951 Edward Maurice Sidebotham
1668 William Howell	1962 David E Shapland MA res
1668 Thomas Bidby d	1966 George H Handisyde MA
1706 John Pinnell AM d	1973 Vincent Strudwick BA
1745 Edward Prattenton MA d	1977 Keith Hyde-Dunn (p-in-c.)
1766 Robert Sandham MA d	1987 Francis Harold Doe
1776 Sir Robert Yeamans Bart d	1998 Anthony Irwin Smyth MA
1778 Joseph Francis Fearon ns	

The Whitgift School cricket team, back-row middle, Cyril F. Johnston, c. 1900

The Whitgift School, Croydon, England, c. 1950s

Arthur Anderson seated in tophat on one of his three steam yachts, the Eothin, *the* Norseman, *or the* Thule, *c. 1860; to his left, his wife, Mary Ann, née Hill; seated left her nephew, Arthur Anderson Johnston, age 10*

Arthur Anderson, co-founder of P&O b. 1792–†1868

Mary Ann Anderson, née Hill, wife of Arthur Anderson b. 1802–†1864

THE RINGING WORLD

Vol. I.   FRIDAY, MARCH 24th, 1911.   Price 1d.

OUR AIM.

It is customary, whenever a new journal makes its appearance, for those responsible for its birth to offer some explanation to justify its entry into public affairs, or to make an apology for trespassing upon the public notice. Little explanation, we feel, is necessary to justify the coming of *The Ringing World* into a sphere in which there is a demand for a journal which shall record faithfully and promptly the doings of those engaged in the pursuit of bell-ringing.

If little explanation be necessary, still less is there need for apology. We do not hesitate to say that the legion of bell-ringers throughout the country have long been awaiting a journal which shall be in the truest sense a " newspaper," which shall reflect their opinions, which shall keep them in touch, week by week, with the doings of their colleagues throughout the country, and which shall cater for all grades of the Exercise—for those who are struggling with the early difficulties of Grandsire Doubles as well as for those who have reached the goal of ambition in the achievement of London Surprise or Cambridge Maximus; for those who are only upon the threshold of those intricate mathematical problems in Composition as well as for those who are steeped in the science, and whose delight it is to revel in a maze of figures complicated enough to turn the brain of the uninitiated.

We fully recognise the service which has been done in the past by other journalistic enterprises. Efforts involving self-sacrifice have been made by men devoted to the Art, but there never was a time when ringers generally felt that their requirements were more inadequately met than they are to-day, and yet bell-ringing was never more in the ascendant than at this moment. Great feats are being accomplished, which a few years ago were undreamed of, composers are constantly conquering new worlds, yet the interests of ringers are being, to a large extent, neglected. It will be our endeavour, with the co-operation of the ringers themselves, to remedy this position of affairs, and it is because of the demand that exists, and of which we possess ample evidence, that we feel no apology need be proffered in stepping into the arena to-day and appealing for the support of church bell-ringers throughout the country.

What is to be our aim? We intend to use our columns for the information, the instruction, and, we hope, the elevation of all who take an interest in the Art of Change Ringing and in the business and social side of the organizations which promote that Art. There are two things in the

The first issue of The Ringing World, *March 14, 1911 with prominent advertisement display of Gillett & Johnston Bellfoundry*

GILLETT & JOHNSTON LTD · CROYDON · ENGLAND

Distinguished Visitors

The firm has been honoured from time to time by visits from many distinguished visitors, including :

	DATE
T.R.H. the Duke of Connaught and Princess Patricia (now Lady Patricia Ramsay)	1918
H.R.H. the Princess Beatrice	1922 & 1925
H.R.H. the late Duchess of Albany	1922
His Grace the Archbishop of Canterbury and Mrs. Randall Davidson	1927
The Hon. W. Mackenzie King, Prime Minister of Canada	1926
T.E. The American Ambassador and Mrs. Alanson Houghton	1925 & 1927
T.E. The Belgian Ambassador and Baroness Moncheur ...	1926
T.E. The Belgian Ambassador and Baroness de Cartier de Marchienne	1927

A brochure created for advertisement purposes, an example of Cyril F. Johnston's public relation skills. Photo shows left to right: Cyril F. Johnston, His Grace the Archbishop of Canterbury (Randall Davidson), HRH Princess Beatrice, the Duchess of Albany, Lady May Cambridge, and Lord Frematon

Top: Nora Johnston, and Cyril F. Johnston sounding the tenor bell for the Royal Exchange, 1920
Bottom: March 3, 1928, 2,400 ringers gathered for an All England Ringers Meeting
at the Gillett & Johnston Bellfoundry, Croydon, England,

Cyril F. Johnston with his mother,
Amelie Charlotte Johnston,
née Brouneau

From left to right: Cyril F. Johnston, His Grace the Archbishop
of Canterbury Randall Scott Davidson, his wife, the Right
Honorable Mayor of Croydon and his wife at the All England
Ringers' Meeting, *March 3, 1928*

Princess Beatrice, the
9th and last child of
Queen Victoria, and
Cyril F. Johnston

Left: In the G&J Bellfoundry, April 7, 1927, Cyril F. Johnston with Mr. P. C. Larkin, High Commissioner for Canada, inspecting the largest bell (or bourdon), 7 tons, destined for The Peace Tower carillon in Ottawa, Canada (this photo was in Olive Marjorie Johnston's possession at the time of her death in 1978)
Bottom left: Olive M. Johnston, née Crowe, the author's mother, in the Swiss Alps, 1927 around the time she and Cyril met each other
Bottom right: Olive Crowe, high school graduation photo, 1919

Top (left to right): Arthur Johnston, Cyril F. Johnston, Rosemary Johnston, 1949, at Conservative Party meeting in Brighton, England—photo was taken by Mrs. Mary Johnston
Bottom: Cyril F. Johnston and family's home in Croydon, England; the family lived there from 1930s till after Cyril's death in 1950

The Johnston family plot at Queens Cemetery, Croydon, England. Buried there: Arthur A. Johnston,
Amelie Charlotte Johnston, Cyril Frederick Johnston, Nora Violet Johnston,
and the family nanny Fanny Langford

successful, fabulously self-made Shetlander would reverberate in the lives of the Johnston family in many ways. The new bell-founder and his son became Trustees, one after the other, of Anderson's legacies in the Shetlands. A. A. Johnston had absorbed his uncle's lessons in social welfare; one of his charities was the provision of dinners every Christmas to Croydon's poor. A.A.'s father, Cyril's grandfather Robert Johnston, the Baptist minister, who died in 1895 at the age of 93, is buried with his wife Hannah in the London suburb of Norwood in the same plot where Arthur Anderson and wife Mary Ann are impressively memorialized by a tall obelisk. One of Robert's and Hannah's daughters, married to a Lyon, named her son Arthur Anderson Lyon, who in turn named his own son A. A. Lyon Jr. And Cyril of course called his only son Arthur. The name became as popular in two or three generations as John, Robert, and William had been in earlier Johnston families. An aura of greatness devolved from Anderson, enveloping his tribe of in-laws, in particular Cyril Johnston who would turn bellfounding into a celebrated profession—a rather unexpected outcome for a manufacturing firm.

He said it at his Royal Exchange bells luncheon in 1920. He wanted the world to know about the "great things and . . . problems mastered in the bell world during the last 20 years . . ." His ambitions evolved into business practices considered unacceptably flamboyant and competitive. Frederick C. Mayer, the American responsible for encouraging J. D. Rockefeller Jr. to hire Cyril as his carillon-builder, characterized him as aggressive enough to "rival the most radical American business precocity."[7] Cyril believed in the power of advertising and public relations, never missing a media opportunity to promote his work. In post-Victorian England, he was ahead of his time in exploiting avenues of support then considered ungentlemanly. I personally heard Cyril startlingly defined in 1984 when for the first time I visited the John Taylor foundry in Loughborough. Taylor's General Manager Alan Berry, a large imposing man, upon shaking my hand practically off, boomed out, "Your father was a celebrity." Then, taking my measure, if only through his knowledge of my

American nationality, Berry gave himself permission to broadside Cyril. Now I got my first earful of the undying bad blood between Taylor and Cyril Johnston. With Berry's litany of castigations— that Cyril unfairly underbid his rivals, that he "lived a champagne life on a beer income," that he didn't cast his very big bells himself (e.g. his 20-ton bourdon for Riverside Church in New York) because his furnaces were not large enough,[8] that he committed "industrial espionage" in acquiring tuning secrets—I should perhaps have felt defensive. But I think my mouth was hanging open a little and I must have looked a bit dumbfounded, unprepared for this gratuitous gift of insight into the savagery of business. Anyway I knew Cyril had put on a great show—a spectacle of social climbing, business opportunism and dramatic flair that can be admired and understood in perspective. The class that Douglas Hughes had disdainfully said Cyril aspired to: "higher than he was," can be identified as "fame." Alan Berry called Cyril a "celebrity." Although fame was not a class then the way it is now, it existed. And the attention synonymous with it was naturally anathema to competitors, whose work could suffer because of it. Cyril's meteoric career suggested the profile of a late bloomer. At his birth alone, the John Taylor Co. was already a century old. Whitechapel, the other English firm in 20th century contention, had been established as early as 1570. The Royal Exchange contract was fought over in 1919 by the three firms. It was a significant moment for Cyril. He was now sole proprietor of Gillett & Johnston, his father having died three years earlier. It was a year after the end of the Great War, when bell casting had resumed again (foundries having been largely converted to munitions manufacturing plants throughout the war), and a time when rumblings in America and Europe marked the new carillon movement afoot.

The Royal Exchange was opened in 1570 by Queen Elizabeth I. Bells of the Exchange have been heard since at least 1600. Along with St. Paul Cathedral's 16-ton Great Paul, the Bow Bells and Big Ben, the Royal Exchange bells are recognized as among the most famous sounds of London. The building itself, of historic importance, signified an end to the simple exchange of goods on the street, and the beginnings in Britain of modern commerce with traders exchanging bills, guaranteeing credit and raising loans, all taking place in a central structure. The Exchange's first two bells signaled the hours of trading. Subsequently the history of its bells is rife with difficulty and dissatisfaction, with the Exchange's official body, the Joint Grand Gresham Committee (after Thomas Gresham the financer of the original Exchange) giving a number of founders grief, rejecting their bells or demanding that they recast them. The building alone has suffered an inglorious past. It perished in the Great Fire of 1666. Rebuilt on the same ground, in 1838 it burned down again. In 1769 when the Exchange had fourteen bells in all, Thomas Pack of Whitechapel (the firm has traded in this singularly unlovely part of the British capital in just two locations, both on High Street, and diagonally across from each other, since 1570) was asked to recast the lot. Another Whitechapel founder, Charles Mears, was given the order for a new ring of bells for the third building, erected after the 1838 fire. In 1852, after yet another Whitechapel ring that the Gresham Committee didn't like, Taylor was given a contract to recast all the bells. In 1919, with history on the side of both firms, they felt they had a legitimate stake in any new contract.

In making his case, the upstart founder Cyril Johnston, echoing Canon Simpson, was quoted as saying, "All of London's bells are out of tune, even Big Ben which was cracked."[9] Big Ben indeed was, and still is, ignominiously cracked; the means were found to twist the bell around so the hammer would fall upon it in an undamaged area [See Chapter X]. Casting further aspersions on London's beloved 13-ton clock bell, which had been cast in 1858 by Whitechapel, Cyril said, "Its tones are enough to drive any good bellfounder into an early grave."[10] His judgment would be stated independently by Frederick Mayer, the American he didn't know yet, but a man soon to have the greatest impact, next to John D. Rockefeller Jr., on his career. Mayer, the West Point organist and choirmaster, while touring Europe educating himself to the tones of big bells, the better to advise JDR Jr. on how to select a founder for bells the millionaire wanted to install in a new church he was building in New York, heard Big Ben. In Mayer's opinion, it was the "worst large bell" he had heard—due to its fourth interval being too powerfully developed, at the expense of its third (i.e. the minor third above the fundamental note). Mayer could hardly have been versed in the bellfounding intrigues going on in England at that moment. Cyril's prestigious Royal Exchange contract was reminiscent of the earlier opportunity he had had, in 1911, to establish his firm and reap the rewards of a new reputation when he beat out his competitors to recast Wimborne Minster's revered old ring of eight. After 1906 and Elstree, 1911 was the next pivotal year for Gillett & Johnston.

In the interval, G&J had expanded its foundry premises, and notably, with the Elstree order introduced its first modern electrically powered tuning machine.[11] A bell of any larger size, always cast somewhat thicker than required, is clamped down mouth upwards to a vertical tuning lathe, and slowly revolved against a cutting tool fixed to a slide rest saddle, the tool following the interior contours of the bell. Any part of the bell can be reached and reduced in thickness as needed by turning off small amounts of metal. In this way, its partials are brought to the right proportions for their intended tones. With the tuning lathe and other new machinery and methods to master causing a slow-down in production, G&J burst forth in 1911 with thirteen orders. Of these, Wimborne Minster in Dorset, a magnificent big church dating in its earlier versions to the 1100s, was its most important. The old ring of eight, dating from 1629, was an aggregate of bells by at least five founders including Whitechapel.

In pursuit of this contract Cyril, 27 years old at the time, was relentlessly aggressive, pushing not only the Simpson method (yet to be adopted by Whitechapel) but a replacement of the old wood frame with a modern steel and iron frame—at that time a controversial innovation to reduce strain on the tower—and other accessories. Opposition developed especially over recasting the tenor (always the largest bell in a ring), cast in 1629, and hallowed by local history. In overcoming resistance, Cyril displayed the public relations expertise for which he would become well known, if not notorious, inviting the Vicar of the Minster and two members of the advisory committee to Croydon to see the foundry, afterwards entertaining them at his house overnight as guests. But Cyril also made an offer to recast five of the bells at cost. The Vicar became smitten, and strongly recommended Gillett & Johnston, saying, "It seems to me that the responsibility of rejecting such an exceptional offer would be [very] serious."[12] Cyril addressed the final meeting of the advisory committee at the Minster, then in a schoolboy gesture waited outside, sitting on the churchyard wall for the decision. He got everything he wanted, including two extra bells to make a ring of ten.

Once the ring was cast, he cannily persuaded the Vicar to arrange a dedication that would take place close to the time of King George V's Coronation date of June 22, 1911. So while there was general ringing on the dedication date, the true observance of the new bell installation occurred a week later on Coronation day with a peal by a band of famous ringers from various parts of the country. Keith Fleming, one of England's contemporary bell scholars, feels that Cyril must have organized the peal, that "only someone of his persuasive powers who knew these ringers" could have made it happen.[13] It sounds a bit like a crime, as if such amplified publicity achieved through the synchronous use of the King—which today might actually sound a little quaint—was an unconscionable way of doing things. Of course he would go on to do much worse, entertaining royalty in person, even the King himself, on many occasions at his works in Croydon.

The Royal Exchange bells were formally opened February 16, 1921, by the Lord and Lord Mayoress of London. In obtaining the contract Cyril had invited members of the Joint Grand Gresham Committee to his foundry, much as he had done in 1911 for Wimborne. The Committee had felt that some of the bells could be recast and others simply retuned, thus saving the latter for posterity, and saving extra expense as well. By having Committee members hear a peal comprising a mixture of retuned bells and newly cast ones, Cyril convinced them that only a recasting of *all* the bells would give them the musical effect they wanted. For the inauguration of the new bells, a superb celebratory six-course luncheon costing an extravagant £150 took place at Mercers' Hall, the Livery Hall belonging to the Mercers' Company, original owner along with the City, of the Exchange. Cyril, in a fine chance to expand his network and score for his social and business aspirations, had the opportunity to schmooze with 80 distinguished guests, including the Masters of some of the great Livery Companies and many other notable City grandees.[14]

While Cyril's careerism has made good copy, his critics have often praised his bells. Fleming, the Wimborne scholar, says, "Cyril Johnston's reputation will always stand on the Quality of the bells he made . . . We all regard him as a truly pioneering influence who moved the tuning of bells forward a vast amount in a very short space of time." Fleming feels "privileged" to ring on the Wimborne bells—"one of the best examples of [the founder's] work."[15]

In finding a clue to Cyril Johnston's surge to glory in his great-uncle Arthur Anderson's inspiring life, a comparison shows up between the roles of artist and tycoon. Arthur Anderson never made anything; he didn't design or build the ships he employed. His tremendous success never distracted him from what appears to have been his true calling as benefactor to his native land. His success seems almost to have been a means to accomplish that end. His great nephew Cyril Johnston had the artist's identification with his product, a compound so potent and overarching that where the fate of his bells was concerned, his very existence must have seemed to him to be at stake. A beautifully cast and tuned bell was an end in itself.

Such a man can be driven to extraordinary measures to assure a proper appreciation of his craft and art—the outcome of which might lead to the most auspicious contractual agreements and installation sites for his creations.

Chapter IV

THE MILLIONAIRES' CHURCH

I believe everything hinges on Mr. Johnston's courage now
—Frederick C. Mayer

It was a real thrill to hear these splendid bells for the first time
—John D. Rockefeller, Jr.

February 18, 1924, Anton Brees, a young Belgian carillonneur, sent a telegram "COMING AMERICA MARCH," to Frederick C. Mayer, John D. Rockefeller Jr.'s advisor in all things campanological. Brees said he would be leaving Antwerp March 12, and sailing to New York on the steamer *Mongolia* of the Red Star Line. Brees, a European wunderkind, was coming—soon to be employed by Rockefeller to play one of the first carillon instruments in the Western Hemisphere; it had first appeared in 1922 and would soon hit American shores in a big way. In the frenzy for gigantism that overtook the United States after the Great War—resulting in the longest bridges, the tallest buildings and the biggest boats ever built—bells would be a counterpart, though very few people would actually see them. Signs of the new American Empire abounded in the twenties. While this ascendancy would coalesce after World War II, it was surely in the making long beforehand, at least by the late 1800s when men like John D. Rockefeller, Sr., Andrew Carnegie, and John Astor were consolidating their industries and amassing their fortunes. More broadly in 1898 when the United States expanded its borders, annexing territories and acquiring protectorates abroad. In 1917, Rockefeller turned much of his wealth over to his only son John D. Rockefeller, Jr., to control or invest as he thought wise. JDR Jr., born in 1874, inherited from his father a double allegiance to business and to the Baptist Church, along with the belief in an obligation to use their assets to serve the public good. As steward of his father's interests, he continued to endow private charities and public-works programs. Junior also involved himself, as his father had, in ambitious building projects. He underwrote the restoration of Colonial Williamsburg in 1927, and by 1930, even as his fortune was withering to some extent from the stock market crash and ensuing Depression, he was beginning to erect what would become the spectacular midtown multi-building skyscraper complex called Rockefeller Center.

Unknown to people at large, JDR Jr. had another allurement: big bells, and having them in New York. More than that, by 1922 with his Park Avenue Baptist Church on 64th and Park in Manhattan built and dedicated, he was dreaming of installing there the largest carillon the world had ever seen. The arrival of Anton Brees from Antwerp in 1924 signaled an important step in his plan. Trained carillonneurs did not exist in the United States. The instrument was so new; in 1922 just seven carillons had been installed—two in Canada, the other five in the U.S., each one the minimal size for this instrument of 23 bells. Typically, it would be the organist of a church ordained somehow to receive one of these strange European installations, who would be canvassed to try his hand at its curious oaken-baton keyboard. But Rockefeller and his advisor Frederick Mayer were not going to entrust their imposing

53-bell carillon to any old American, organist or otherwise, not yet anyway. They wanted the best that could be had, and that could only be found abroad, in the land of the instrument's origins. On behalf of his employer, Mayer ever assumed a certain megalocentric interest. The success of carillon playing in America would depend, he was sure, on that first year of the Park Avenue carillon's existence. Writing to Mr. Rockefeller in September 1923, Mayer said, "It would seem to me that we want to bring over a man whose very blood is infused with the old artistic traditions of the Belgian School, which has been literally the cradle of the carillon world."[1] He quoted a New England authority on bells as saying "carillon music could only be made popular by bringing over a great carillon maestro like Jef Denyn (municipal carillonneur of St. Rombout's Cathedral in Malines) permanently."[2] Denyn however, a beloved figure not only in Malines (the Mecca of carillonism), but in all Belgium, aged sixty-one in 1923 was not going anywhere, except as an honored guest recitalist. The 26-year old Anton Brees had been raised to follow his father Gustav, who in Antwerp had the equivalent position to Jef Denyn in Malines. Brees had been a pupil of Denyn's, and was hailed by some as the next best to the master, the one in the making at least. And he seemed eager to leave his homeland.

In March 1924 when Brees arrived on the *Mongolia*, he was in New York to see the church, meet Rockefeller, discuss his income and scope out his living conditions once he came as it was thought for good. The bells for the carillon would not arrive until July the following year, with the dedication scheduled for December. A lot happened in the meantime between Brees and his two American sponsors. Rockefeller and his advisor had no idea what they were getting themselves into. They had secured an emotionally immature virtuoso musician, a young man with an artist's temperament. They had gone to a lot of trouble to get him, then were simply not equipped to deal with a problem import in their midst.

In acquiring Brees, one trouble they had had was in prying him away from Edmund Denison Taylor, head of the John Taylor

Co. during that time, and son of John William I, the man whose practical success with true-harmonic tuning paralleled Canon Simpson's directives. Denison, as he was called, born in 1874 the same year as Rockefeller, Jr., became the Taylor whom Cyril Johnston inherited in vying over the new exciting American market in carillons. Before Brees came to New York in March, Denison had corralled him, engaging him to inaugurate Taylor carillons at home and abroad. That March, Brees was in the U.S. not just to see Rockefeller, but to dedicate and show off Taylor's four small carillons here—in Gloucester and Andover, Massachusetts, Birmingham, Alabama and Morristown, New Jersey. Frederick Mayer, as emotional a man as Brees in his way, had been beside himself. He was sure he had Brees's commitment to play the Park Avenue carillon, and equally sure that Taylor "would rather that so brilliant a carillonneur did not play the finest carillon in the world, and made by his greatest rival [Cyril Johnston]."[3] A carillon, Mayer might have added more candidly, for which Taylor had failed to receive the contract. Taylor in fact had been the first serious contractual contender for the "Millionaires' Church"—so dubbed by journalists, but also called "Rockefeller's Church." Mayer and JDR Jr. were aware of Taylor by October 1921, when the instrument under consideration for the church was not a carillon but a 12- or 14-bell "chime."

North America's first carillon, made by Gillett & Johnston for the Metropolitan Methodist (now United) Church in Toronto, arrived in April 1922. On its heels came a Taylor carillon for a Portuguese church, Our Lady of Good Voyage, in Gloucester, Massachusetts, dedicated in July. In 1921, one year before these importations, Rockefeller remained unaware of the carillon instrument, or of its potential for Park Avenue. Though the bell world was right on the cusp of a carillon renaissance, with the U.S. shortly to become the instrument's new hub, Rockefeller could only look for a chime because the carillon was not here yet, and the chime was a very American collection of bells. Chimes were popular in American churches and colleges during the 1800s and right up through the 1940s. At least 650 chimes were made in that time. More than 200 bellfounders are known to have existed in the States since the 1700s, the vast majority of whom cast only single bells. One of them was Paul Revere, our famous patriot and express rider, by trade primarily a silversmith. Casting his first bell in 1792, in business with a son he would manufacture altogether 398 bells. Revere was too early for the chime movement. Just seven bellfounders became responsible for producing those approximately 650 American chimes.

Compared to the carillon, the chime is an ungainly primitive instrument. Requiring a minimum of eight bells, and tuned to the diatonic scale, with few or no semitones, it has very little expressive range. Set up similarly to a carillon, the bells are hung dead and suspended in heavy wooden frames (replaced by steel in carillon and change-ringing sets beginning in the early 1900s), with a "chimestand" of sizable wood keys in a single row situated in a room below. Likened to shovel or pump handles used on farms, some effort is required to "play" them—yanking them down fully a foot from starting position. With the notes corresponding mainly to the white keys of a piano, only melodies can be played, one note at a time, the way one might pick out simple tunes on a piano. The carillon by contrast, with a chromatic scale progressing through semitones in octaves ranging from two to six or seven, music of harmonic complexity and meaningful scope like that played by pianists Rubinstein or Horowitz, is possible. It was this kind of reputation that Jef Denyn had in Belgium and that it was hoped Anton Brees would generate in New York. In 1921, through Rockefeller's search for a chime, and information gleaned in the process in just a short period of time by Frederick Mayer about carillons that dribbled and finally poured in, a story reflecting a significant musical development can be detected. A European instrument would transform the American bellscape, superseding the indigenous chime.

Frederick Mayer did not actually enter the picture until the end of January 1922, three months before the Gillett & Johnston 23-bell carillon for Toronto, breaking North American ground, was installed. But Mayer came in with great strength, interest and authority. Before that, beginning August 1921, Rockefeller depended on several of his employees at the famous Rockefeller headquarters, 26 Broadway in Manhattan, to research chime manufacturers for him. A memo of that month lists seven American makers, and one foreign—John Taylor of Loughborough, England. Of this list, three were marked as "Okay"—one being Taylor, the other two: the McShane Bell Foundry Co. of Baltimore, Maryland, and Meneely & Co. of Watervliet, New York. McShane was soon ruled out. One of Rockefeller's informants had visited a McShane chime in Montclair in New Jersey, saying "it surprised him by its badness."[4] A Meneely chime at the West Point Chapel was found by contrast to be "by far the best" this informant had heard. And another advisor wrote to Rockefeller, "Meneely is considered the best maker in this country."[5] In fact Meneely of Watervliet (along with a brother competitor, Meneely of Troy) had made far and away the largest number of chimes in America—about 356 of the total 650. So the New York Watervliet firm was asked forthwith to submit an estimate for 12 bells of the same size and weight as those at West Point. Meneely was offering 12 bells at $22,000, or 10 at $16,000. By January, Taylor had become a strong contender. His prices—for number of bells and their weights—were compared favorably to Meneely's. And it was learned that Taylor had been selected for a chime at Yale. Had Rockefeller and company known of an early (1898) 10-bell Taylor chime in America at Iowa State College in Ames—of historic import for its five-tone Simpson tuning—the contest would have ended right there.

Chime bells in America had been tuned either roughly or not at all. Generally the founders knew from experience how to cast their bells—for size of diameters and thickness of metal—to come close to the desired pitch, casting more bells than needed, discarding the unsuitable ones following an application of tuning forks. Meneely drew ahead of the field in 1890 after becoming aware of an article on bell partials by Lord Rayleigh, a precursor of Canon Simpson's, in the *English Philosophical* magazine. Not until 1927 however would Meneely begin tuning according to the widely adopted Simpson method, but by then the firm was basically history (although they built four carillons during the interwar period), having been dramatically overtaken by the English founders John Taylor and Gillett & Johnston in the newly popular carillon market. Frederick Mayer played a large part in this. Coming on board with Rockefeller at the end of January 1922, he favored the English even before he heard their bells. And this despite the fact that the Meneely chime at West Point where Mayer held positions of organist and choir master was considered one of the best.

Mayer, informed of the Meneely bid and the Taylor counter-proposal for a Park Avenue chime, told Rockefeller that in 1917 when West Point wanted a chime, they were considering bells by Taylor or Whitechapel, but wartime conditions intervened. He wrote, "Personally I have never heard any of the English bells, but have a great curiosity to do so."[6] He had talked to William Gorham Rice, an American author and authority on bells who highly recommended Taylor. Fast educating himself, Mayer would soon be in a position to enlighten Rockefeller. For the moment, he revealed his ignorance by misidentifying Rice's classic tome, first published in 1914, *Carillon Music and Singing Towers of the Old World and the New,* as a work on chimes. Rice, a native of Albany New York, well known to the European carillon community before and after the Great War, would become widely credited for stimulating interest, through his books, articles and lectures, in the carillon in North America. He can be counted as one of five key figures in the carillon renaissance, along with: Canon Arthur B. Simpson, carillonneur Jef Denyn, and bellfounders John Taylor and Cyril Johnston.

An updated edition of Rice's book in 1925 would become famous with me because Cyril had given a copy to my mother July 8, 1928, as the inscription reads, presumably for her 27th birthday seven days earlier. The book entered my library when I first started having one, and is now a well-handled well-traveled piece of work. By July of 1922 Frederick Mayer was fully apprised of Rice's status and had become an authority on the carillon himself. Back in January all he could do was ask Rockefeller to put the Park Avenue contract on hold while they waited until Taylor's chime at Yale could be heard. No contract as it turned out would be signed until October. Cyril Johnston's name was not brought up until April, when his Toronto carillon, now installed, became another necessity for Mayer to hear. Soon, the Taylor carillon at Gloucester Massachusetts would be added to this pressing list of instruments. With Meneely out of the picture, chimes had been forgotten, a carillon was clearly in the works, a comparative study was underway, and the fierce competition between Taylor and Johnston in Britain was now wholly engaged in America as well.

A lot was riding on the Rockefeller contract. No one knew yet how big the carillon was going to get, but the prestige of signing with Rockefeller for New York's first carillon could guarantee privileged access to other donors and institutions eager to acquire the instrument as either a war or family memorial. Denison Taylor was a fair step ahead of Cyril Johnston, the way his father and brother had been at home. Cyril had exported no chimes as yet to America, and his single carillon was in Canada. But it was his Toronto installation that brought him to Mayer's attention, especially as it preceded Taylor's Gloucester Massachusetts carillon, if only by three months. Writing to Rockefeller in April, Mayer said, "I confess I have heard nothing about Gillett & Johnston's bells, and yet their Toronto Carillon swallows all other bells in this hemisphere in importance by way of size alone."[7]

Size alone! Here was Mayer's first mention of what would become his obsession in the months and years to come. Later in April he exults to Rockefeller that he has just received a letter from Taylor "now proposing a carillon of 35 bells for your church!"[8] Mayer's visit to the Metropolitan Methodist Church in Toronto had "converted [him] in less than a minute to the artistic advantage of a carillon over a chime."[9] W. G. Rice, a Taylor enthusiast, would surprisingly endorse the G&J Toronto bells, telling Mayer he was "delighted" with them and that "the general effect was equal to the best carillon music he had ever heard." Rice "noticed a mellow sweetness," Mayer reported to Rockefeller, "that he felt surpassed the Yale bells in quality . . . " [10] Rice was leaning with Mayer toward G&J perhaps because of the Rockefeller association. Fund-raising on behalf of Jef Denyn to help him open his school for carillon playing in Malines—the first of its kind in the world—he hoped for Rockefeller's contribution, and would get it.

Cyril received an additional boost after Rockefeller inserted himself directly into the picture, writing to Chester B. Massey, the donor of the Toronto carillon, requesting information on Gillett & Johnston. How had it come about that Massey had selected the firm? What had it been like doing business with them? How satisfactory had their relations been? And had Taylor been a competitor? No, Massey wrote back, Taylor had not been. Massey knew about G&J from his church architects who had been in touch with the firm over placing bells for another client. He had had his church organist, a "distinguished musician," visit the foundry in Croydon, and upon his advice, went ahead to sign with them. Massey advocated G&J strongly, saying he had found them "most painstaking, thorough and business-like . . . and most anxious to please." On the results, Massey said G&J had "succeeded in producing a tone quality which makes their bells so beautiful and different from others."[11] Still, Mayer held out for a "truer tone" from Taylor. Then he got a "bad jolt" upon hearing that a Taylor bell in California had "cracked badly." And when he heard the Yale chime, which Denison Taylor had brought with him from England, he didn't like it at all. Denison in person would damage himself while visiting Mayer at West Point and speaking scornfully of the Meneely chime there. Mayer informed Rockefeller of everything (his letters could ramble on for many single-spaced typewritten, typo-ridden pages, often flavored with malapropisms) and when JDR heard this he wrote back, "Mr. Taylor's comment on your bells at West Point seems a little uncalled for and does not increase my respect for his judgment."[12]

Denison was not dead yet. In June Mayer wrote to Taylor asking him to prepare a complete plan for his proposed 35-bell carillon. In case Denison was unaware of the importance of this contract, Mayer hyped the situation for him: "I wonder if you have been in America long enough to realize how totally unfamiliar Americans are with carillons? The entire country looks to the leadership of New York in a great many ways. Consequently, this proposed carillon in the newest church in New York, in a tower of architectural charm, located on the Avenue representing the newest and most fashionable growth or development in the city, with no street cars running by, presents an opportunity of rare potentiality to the Bell-founder. It is impossible to prophesy what this first carillon in New York may lead to."[13] Gillett & Johnston, approached for estimates at the same time, came in underbidding Taylor for 35 bells by 3,331 dollars—$14,400 against Taylor's $17,731. Mayer's comment was, "[G&J] is certainly anxious to take away this contract from Taylor Co."[14] Later, Mayer would say that Cyril Johnston understood the great advantage this contract would have for his business in America, "as Mr. Taylor did not." The noose was tightening around Denison, who might have wanted the contract badly enough but was assuming a misguided loftiness and superiority. He blundered again, damning his competitor in an unsportsmanlike spirit, writing to Mayer that Taylor bells were the only perfectly tuned bells in existence, denying the possibility that G&J could turn out anything but a weak imitation. Mayer said the "difference in attitude becomes somewhat noticeable at this time when we are able to judge for ourselves."[15]

The "attitude" of G&J had been most advantageously represented by Cyril Johnston's deputy R.F.A. Housman on a visit of his own to West Point. Housman had been in Toronto looking after the G&J installation there. He thoroughly impressed Mayer by inviting a critical test of the Toronto bells with those of Taylor. "He seemed so fearless of this test, making me promise to write him exactly what I thot [*sic*] . . . regardless of how the contract went. And he was fair and gentlemanly in acknowledging that Taylor's made . . . perfectly tuned bells [while] claiming their bells were as good as Taylor's and he would leave it to others to find out if they were better."[16] Housman further impressed Mayer with a disinterested history lesson, making Mayer aware of

Canon Simpson for the first time, and giving him a perfectly frank account of how Taylor had been the first modern bellfounder to adopt the five-tone tuning method. Answering to Mayer's anxiety over guarantees against bells cracking, Housman gallantly defended Taylor's cracked bell in California, saying that since the chime was cast during the war, the proper metals might not have been available. Capping his public relations coup, Housman praised the Meneely West Point bells, saying they were the best American bells he had heard. Cyril Johnston, who would not make his first Atlantic crossing until December 1925, could not have done better himself, and the table was set it could be said for the contract kill.

October 26, 1922, Cyril signed for 42 bells (!), with a total weight of 48,272 pounds, and a bourdon estimated at 10,640 pounds, to sound A flat. The carillon would have a purchasing price of £7,312, to be paid 80% on delivery, the remaining 20% upon completed installation. A hefty contract, nine pages on legal-size paper, it covered many specifications including tuning, fittings, frame, greasers, transmission wires, console, manual and pedal key action, and a delivery time of nine months after signing. This would be quite an optimistic forecast, as the dedication date kept moving up and was finally set for December, 1925.

A number of critical things would happen in those three years. Fourteen months after signing for instance, yet a new contract would be drawn up—December 4, 1923—for a further expanded carillon of 53 bells, with an E bourdon of 20,720 lbs. The Park Avenue tower would be found almost ridiculously small to contain such tonnage, its roof absurdly designated to hold some of the big bells, and its location aurally speaking a serious neighborhood liability, leading to plans for a new church to house the bells even before they arrived from England. And two romances of the business variety would be ignited and flourish until they exhausted themselves, as romances do.

The one between Mayer and Rockefeller and their protégé Anton Brees which began as a nice slow burning fire in 1922 would become a conflagration after Brees came to New York to actually begin playing the Park Avenue instrument. October 2, 1925 he gave his first concert, inspiring Rockefeller to write to him, "It was a real thrill to hear these splendid bells for the first time . . . for me, the larger bells are 95 percent of the pleasure of the carillon . . . I am happy indeed that I am carrying away with me the memory of the deep, melodious sound of these big bells."[17] Things went all downhill from there. Brees became desperately angry and unhappy over his living conditions and meager salary. He was expected to live at the West 57th Street YMCA and subsist on $250 a month. Mayer thought the young man should work his way up like any normal immigrant. But the two older men had treated him as anything but normal, building him up as a young genius, coming messiah-like to introduce the great music of the carillon to an unsuspecting New World. They even cast him as an authority on the very bells he was due to play, sending him to test them at the G&J foundry in Croydon whilst he was still conveniently in Europe, aggravating Cyril Johnston no end by his arrogance and peremptoriness. Once in New York to play, Brees must have felt abandoned, though his dislocation and isolation would never be adduced to account at least in part for the emotional chaos he created—hardly an unusual oversight for that era. After a confrontation with Mayer, Brees went simply ballistic, and endured what seems to have been a clinical breakdown. A great brouhaha ensued, with Brees writing outrageously insulting letters to Mayer and Mayer sending them on to Rockefeller and Rockefeller writing paternalistic reproving letters to Brees, taking righteous exception to the attacks on his advisor and defending him with devastating brio. At last in January, 1926, just three months after Brees had begun playing the Park Avenue carillon, and one month after the dedication concert, Rockefeller fired him. An official resignation was then agreed upon in order to save the musician's face at home in Belgium and with other potential employers.

The Mayer/Rockefeller romance with Cyril Johnston, of the founder/client type obviously, was engaged in England by Mayer in 1922, and sealed by Rockefeller in July 1923 when he visited the Croydon foundry himself with three of his sons. This was several months before Cyril signed the second contract, for 53 bells. Rockefeller told Mayer he and his sons had motored to Croydon from London and spent the afternoon. "We saw four bells cast, and about twenty that had already been cast and tuned. I liked Mr. Johnston and was pleased with all that I saw. Mr. and Miss Johnston [Cyril's sister Nora] very kindly gave us tea and I formed of Mrs. Johnston [Cyril's mother] the same favorable opinion which you had formed."[18] Mayer, a year earlier on an extraordinary Rockefeller-paid European tour to investigate bells and founders, had written, "Mr. Johnston very kindly asked me to make my headquarters at his home while at Croydon, and this was most pleasant. I liked his mother very much." Mayer had gone on to paint a rich picture of the bellfounder, saying he "could rival the most radical American business precocity—and with a good sporting spirit, as we already know."[19] He was impressed that Cyril personally tuned all his bells. R.F.A. Housman told him Cyril was often up till 2 A.M. tuning. But Mayer's most resonant encomiums came in 1923 while he was hatching plans and baiting Rockefeller for a still bigger carillon with an F sharp bourdon, more than twice the weight of the big Toronto A bell, which at 8,456 pounds or 4½ tons, was the largest Cyril had cast to date. The Toronto carillon of 23 bells weighed 17½ tons altogether; since 1922 it has been expanded twice and is now an instrument of 54 bells.

Mayer worried over the size of the English furnaces, the founders' lack of experience in casting big bells, and the reactionary English character. "I believe everything hinges on Mr. Johnston's courage now," said Mayer—who would not be disappointed.[20] With Cyril ready to go ahead, Mayer wrote Rockefeller, "It was a relief for me to learn that Mr. Johnston was not less progressive than I had believed, and that he had the courage to tackle larger things, even if they had not been done before. There is so much conservatism in the English nature that I did not know just what to expect."[21]

Chapter V

ONWARD TO RIVERSIDE

I am assuming there is no danger of getting the carillon too high
—John D. Rockefeller Jr.

If somebody puts a beautiful Steinway into a bad hall,
it's not Steinway's fault
—Richard P. Straus

There were many people, yet no one; many listened, yet no one heard
—Anton Brees

Sunday morning November 10, 2002, I arose with an unprecedented purpose—to find what was once the Park Avenue
Baptist Church and look at it. In my serious researches, engaged by
1981, I have no idea when exactly the Park Avenue church entered
my consciousness. But my literature on the subject long predated
this sudden urgency in 2002 to materialize it. A critical mass of ref-
erences had been reached. I am a fan of towers but not of mounting them. At one time, my elevator and subway claustrophobia
became more sweeping, and took in the enclosed spiral staircases

that a great number of towers feature. Since so many of Cyril Johnston's bells can only be reached and seen by going in circles mounting these phobic tunnel-like spaces, I have I suppose an interesting and ironic complex, not to mention handicap. The fear has never kept me from making the effort. And I haven't lacked for friends or carillonneurs who would try to coax me up. The occasional triumph has been duly registered with a certain pride and stupefaction. Of course once you have seen one bell you have in a way seen them all. It's been a number of centuries, in the West at least, since bells had curiously different shapes from the neck and flaring skirt with thickened hem or rim, the inverted cup-form, we now know as standard. But towers themselves vary considerably, determining by their size, shape and height the number and disposition of bells they contain. And the inscriptions on bells, along with their bands of ornamentation, are as special or aesthetic, also of olden interest, as the markings on tombstones can be. In the world of the carillon, the Park Avenue building is a historic site.

My knowledge of the church was so belated, with my data appearing exclusively on paper, I was not really sure the church physically existed. If it did, it had long had a different name. Approaching the northeast corner of 64th and Park Avenue that day in November, 2002, the building I saw there precisely matched a xeroxed picture of it I held in my hand. So there it was. And I had been so nearby all these years, no more than five blocks from my dentist's office on Madison and 60th, where I have been going for a quarter century. The time was 10 a.m., one hour before Sunday service. Only two workmen were inside, and I ran around excitedly as if I owned the place. Having felt proprietary about Riverside since childhood, here was the *mother* of Riverside to take on. Dedicated in 1922, it had functioned as the "Millionaires'" or Baptist church for only seven years when in 1929 it got its new name, the Central Presbyterian Church, having been sold by Rockefeller and his Baptist friends to the Presbyterians—for one million dollars. It had cost $1, 416,000 to build. In current monetary value, these figures are of course huger, but the church looks priceless to me.

Extending only 80 feet on Park Avenue, and going 100 feet deep on 64th Street, the length of the sanctuary, with a height of seven stories before the tower rises, the church is small, and elegantly apportioned. Pointed arched windows and buttresses show its membership in a species of Gothic Revivalist architecture that was popular then. The sanctuary is a marvel of both intimacy and Gothic grandeur. Classical fluted pillars, four on each side, ascend to support a vaulted ceiling 60 or 65 feet high, high enough to soar, not so high that contact is lost with a warmth and snugness below. Rows of dark wood pews lined with thick red cushions that can seat 800, face a simple altar discreetly adorned with some finely crafted carvings, floor mosaics and brass work. An unostentatiously rich interior, Rockefeller was not so much displaying his wealth as using it to create a communally comfortable space, serving not just the affluent, but lesser denizens of the neighborhood in a mile or so wide radius. Sixteenth century Flemish stained glass imported by Rockefeller from England where it had been in storage since the French Revolution, forms the East window. He had stone window frames specially made to size for the glass.[1] So why did the congregation move? The Rockefellers lived conveniently close by on 54th Street off Fifth Avenue, and other members or Trustees were no strangers to Park Avenue. Everyone loved the church, a cozy yet uplifting place, successor to the Fifth Avenue Baptist Church on 46th Street where John D. Rockefeller, Sr. had worshipped beginning in 1883 after moving with his family from Cleveland to New York. The tower was perhaps the problem.

If not the tower, it was Harry Emerson Fosdick, the hugely popular Baptist preacher whom Rockefeller had been trying to lure to Park Avenue to serve his congregation. It may have been both. The tower is lovely, the perfect size and architecturally integrated crown for its body. Narrow, 12 by 12 feet, yet octagonally shaped, some forty feet in height, the very top, made of delicate stone tracery, was clearly crafted to resemble the royal insignia of a diadem. Looking upward from the street, I could see the tower's beauty, but as a receptacle for 53 bells, the biggest 9¼ tons?—I didn't think so. This tower was built with a chime in mind, as my literature spells out. Once the chime idea was ditched, a carillon of 23 bells was well within reason. But Frederick Mayer was not reasonable, not at least after he fell in love with the sonorous deep-toned sublimity of the big bells he heard in Europe. And had surveyed the magnitude of Dutch and Belgian carillons, the better to know how they might be exceeded. He was questioning the size of the Park Avenue tower as early as February 1922, one month after his affiliation with Rockefeller had begun. Although he said it was "not within his province to ask why so small a tower was built . . ."[2] he proceeded as if it was, and to find a way of beating it, ultimately trying to squeeze something as big as a semi into something as small as a Volkswagen bug.

Issues involving size were raised frequently throughout 1923, until the unbelievable solution of having 45 bells, small and medium-sized, inside the tower, and the eight big ones outside on the roof was agreed upon. In March 1924 Mayer was urging Rockefeller to in effect build another church, or campanile, rising say 200 feet, to realize their dreams of enormity. And by May 1925, seven months before the Park Avenue Carillon dedication, Rockefeller was revealing his plans to Mayer of building a church perhaps 400 feet high, way uptown on Riverside Drive. At that very moment the Reverend Harry Emerson Fosdick was taking up the pastorate at Park Avenue, with the understanding that a much bigger church was in the works, a ploy that Fosdick says in his memoir Rockefeller used in snaring him for his church.

Perhaps the most gifted preacher of his time, and among the most radical, socially and theologically, Fosdick had turned Rockefeller down repeatedly. It was not just that the Park Avenue edifice "was situated," as he wrote, "in one of the swankiest residential areas of the city," where he would be "justifiably accused" of becoming a "private chaplain to a small group of financially privileged people."[3] Fosdick had sectarian objections as well. Baptism by immersion for instance was required for full membership at the Park Avenue Church. To Fosdick's surprise, in the end every separatist condition for membership was removed, thus opening the church to all Christians on equal terms, and paving the way for the model interdenominationality of Riverside, where Fosdick would reign as preacher for twenty years. In a well-known exchange between Rockefeller and Fosdick before the latter's acquiescence, the two men show ties that bound them across the gulf of riches and religion. While rebuffing Rockefeller, Fosdick had said, "You are too wealthy, and I do not want to be known as the pastor of the richest man in the country." To which Rockefeller replied, "I like your frankness, but do you think that more people will criticize you on account of my wealth, than will criticize me on account of your theology?" Their laughter at this, according to Fosdick, "helped to grease the way for the launching of the Riverside Church."[4]

He strongly implies here and elsewhere that Rockefeller built Riverside just for him. It's easy to see why Rockefeller pursued Fosdick, a man who championed the poor and oppressed—the very people struggling to survive the effects of America's industrial revolution brought on by such capitalist czars as JDR Jr.'s father. While the Rockefeller conscience may have been an issue, the genuine religious piety of the Rockefellers, father and son, might be shown to best advantage through a preacher known for his fervent dedication to the welfare of individuals. And his fame and popularity couldn't hurt. I don't believe however that Rockefeller erected Riverside just for Fosdick. My records indicate that Riverside was conceived, initially at least, to house an oversized carillon. With the new church in planning stages, and Junior courting Fosdick, he had at hand the ammunition of an expanded more metropolitan congregation along with enlarged capacities for community services to satisfy the preacher's social and ecumenical demands. The bells were not an item Fosdick would ever have been apprised of. In 1923 Rockefeller wrote augurally to Frederick Mayer, "I am and always have been desirous of installing the largest and finest carillon which physical conditions will permit."[5] Anyone entering the vast cavernous belfry at Riverside, 52 feet high, 40 by 40 feet wide at the top of a tower 392 feet up from street level, might wonder where this giant cavity in the sky came from. It grew of course from the imaginations of men frustrated by a container on 64th Street too tiny, and too low to the ground, for their ambitions. December 19, 2002, a month and a half after my first visit to the church on Park Avenue, I got to see the famously abandoned tower.

There had been obstacles. On the phone, a series of elderly volunteer ladies were dubious to discouraging about my proposed venture. At last the Reverend Douglas Grandgeorge, soon to be the Central Presbyterian Church's new pastor, called and arranged to meet with me in the sanctuary. From there, he and two maintenance men then escorted me to the tower. As always when approaching a tower, I worried about access, and whether a spiral enclosed staircase was involved. But we ascended seven floors by elevator, then a steep straight-up flight of iron stairs to the roof area. The trip is a miniature version of the way into the Riverside tower, where after a 20-floor elevator ride, you climb two open staircases leading to the tower door. And there on the Park Avenue roof was the graceful Gothic tower, as fulfilling architecturally up close as from the street, but inside looking like a body sadly deserted by all its bones and guts. The dirt and debris-strewn floor suggested a hasty evacuation seventy-three years earlier. Peering up inside the octagon, it was hard to imagine the dark cobwebby space full of gleaming bronze bells. Yet I have never found an empty derelict space so enthralling. The tall louvers are permanently shut tight. The door of a roomy free-standing closet, where Anton Brees would have hung his coat and kept his music, is swinging off its rusty hinges. And where oh where on the roof—consisting of several discrete areas—were those eight big bells situated exactly? They had been hung in a separate massive frame in a specially built campanile, a structure supported by an extension of the columns supporting the roof of the church. And how could they possibly have been mechanically wired to Brees's console, set directly under the 45 bells accommodated inside the tower? It must have been a cockeyed transmission system. Brees in fact, in the midst of his brawl with Mayer and Rockefeller, called the carillon the "most freaky installation imaginable." He also noted that it was impossible to produce satisfactory effects in the bell tower of a church surrounded by over-topping modern apartment houses.

Like giant sounding boards, these apartment buildings caught and threw back the bell tones, turning them into noise. Down through the great canyons of brick and concrete the sounds went echoing and reechoing. Across the street from the church the wall of a 14-story apartment building occupying the entire block shut off all sound traveling westward toward Fifth Avenue, and sent it back. Other apartment buildings also boomeranged the sound, resulting in such acoustic confusion that any semblance of harmony was ruined. The area around the church became a kind of chamber of reverberations. A few privileged areas existed where the music could be heard to advantage, but the neighborhood at large was of course a captive audience. One woman, it was reported in the newspaper, complained that it sounded like several bands at Coney Island playing different pieces at the same time, and all the clatter woke up her daughter. Many parents protested that their children were kept awake. Frederick Mayer had suspected something like this in March, 1924, a year and a half before the carillon was dedicated, actually urging Rockefeller at that time to abandon the Park Avenue site. Anton Brees was quoted as saying the church was so low and the echoing walls so high that "the carillon sounds to a man in the street much as a great organ would sound to someone standing among its pipes."[6]

Poor Brees! He had already been skeptical of his music's reception in America, noting much shallow praise on his earlier U.S. tour to inaugurate Taylor bells: "There were many people, yet no one; many listened, yet no one heard."[7] And at Park Avenue he was "heard" chiefly by outraged neighbors, who were circulating petitions to stop the bells from ringing. He did have an enthusiastic audience of three for his dedication concert at 7 P.M. December 27, 1925: Rockefeller, Frederick Mayer and Cyril Johnston, who had made his first trip to the States for the occasion. Staying at the Biltmore, Cyril had arrived five days earlier aboard the White Star Line's *Majestic* (formerly Germany's *Bismarck,* a 56, 550-ton luxury liner handed over to Britain as part of the 1919 war reparations). Cyril naturally knew all about the Park Avenue tower, its dimensions and disposition of bells, but he would never actually have seen anything like it—for its incongruity of architecture and bells—in England or on the Continent. No matter how the situation struck him, he could not have been too unhappy just then, with the Riverside carillon in the works. Though the contract was a few months away, he was the fairly obvious choice of bellfounder since all or most of the Park Avenue bells were due to be transferred to the big tower uptown, where the carillon would be augmented. The Gothic-Revivalist architect of the Park Avenue Church, Henry C. Pelton of Boston, would also design Riverside. A single maker for a carillon, as for any instrument, has always been considered desirable. But the carillon more than any other instrument has been subject to replacements and/or expansion of its complement of parts, i.e. bells, thus risking the dissonance of different makers' profiles. This would in fact infamously happen at Riverside in 1955, five years after Cyril's death, when all the trebles and middle-sized bells of his 72-bell carillon were removed and recast by a Dutch firm [See Chapter XIII].

In 1925/26 Cyril was very much alive and the Park Avenue and Riverside carillons were in a sense a single instrument, one moving seamlessly into the other. Park Avenue became a kind of depot or holding area for its expanded successor. However, not everything went smoothly. Cyril and Mayer would have a serious disagreement over International Pitch,[8] and Rockefeller would find the shipment of bells to Park Avenue "quite inexcusable," the bells having arrived without notation of sequence to facilitate their erection, and without the bolts with which to hang them. Money predictably became a matter of constant juggling and tussling as Cyril's bellfounding capacities were stretched to the limit. New demands for size, quantity, perfection, and for the developing experimental obsessions of Rockefeller's advisor, all ever pressing, necessitated advances for metal and other materials, and updated price adjustments that were often contested on both sides. Cyril would be taken ill, from stress no doubt, with a "severe gastric attack" as he wrote to Rockefeller in a letter appealing for advances, keeping him in bed for a month and unable to eat anything. The Park Avenue dedication that December 27th might have been a halcyon moment, but for the pitch dark and freezing cold conditions, and a wariness no doubt of the by then vaunted neighborhood hostility.

The donor, the advisor, and the bellfounder, the triumvirate responsible for this dedicatory eventuality, huddled in zero temperatures up against a door across the street from the church to listen. The musician must have been wearing an overcoat and a bear hat and playing with reinforced mittens. His program was not short; it included about fourteen numbers, some of them favorites of JDR Jr., and his mother Laura Spelman Rockefeller, in whose memory the carillon was lovingly dedicated. Typically for that time, Brees's program was a mix of popular music—folk tunes and hymns—and a couple of classical selections including a Minuet from Mozart's *E flat Symphony*, all drawn from compositions for other instruments, specially transcribed or arranged for the carillon.

Music composed directly for the carillon was still a rarity in 1925. In 1922 the Belgian maestro Jef Denyn listed just 25 compositions to that date written expressly for the instrument. *Eleven Preludes* by the Belgian Matthias Van den Gheyn (1721–1785)—municipal carillonneur of St. Pieter's in Louvain, and from a famous bellfounding family—remain classics in any carillon repertory. In America, a promise of concert music written just for the carillon, foreshadowed in Europe, would become a distinguishing feature of the instrument in its new home. The carillon in the Lowlands from the 1500s had been municipally built and owned, its musicians appointed by city conducted competitions and maintained on city payrolls, its audiences townsfolk serenaded on marketplace days by familiar national tunes. The carillon was in effect a marketplace instrument, forming a populist audio environment, and a thread in the social fabric.

In 1892, Jef Denyn created a revolution of sorts by introducing Monday evening concerts in Malines—the first time the carillon was presented as a recital instrument, encouraging people to listen to it actively and critically, undisturbed by market noises or religious processions. American carillonneurs, playing at privately owned institutions, educational or religious, would see a successful future for their instrument in creating its own unique literature, as Bach did for the organ and Chopin the piano. By the 1950s a body of work was beginning to exist, written by composers at large, composers particularly drawn to the carillon, or by carillonneurs themselves. But who was going to listen to it? An audience educated to this music may remain largely, even exclusively, among those who compose for the instrument and play it. The unique isolation of carillon musicians, holed up solitarily in their towers—a rather spectacular characteristic of this sort of concertizing—seems to have produced a self absorbed tribe, an ingrown extended family, the Guild of Carillonneurs of North America, who meet annually for Congresses at designated carillon sites where they play for each other. (There is also an annual international meeting). Granted, there are some distinctive listening situations, outstandingly the Bok Tower in Mountain Lake, Florida, set in the middle of a 250-acre park designed by Frederick Law Olmsted, Jr., planner of Central Park in New York City. Special concert series, fully advertised, are held at the Bok Tower, and rows of chairs holding programs are set before the 200-foot white marble campanile. The audience faces a large screen showing the carillonneur in action 160 feet high. This is where Anton Brees ended up, playing for 39 years, from 1928 when its Taylor carillon was dedicated, till his death in 1967.[9]

When Brees complained that "Many [people] listened, yet no one heard" he was speaking surely for carillonneurs generally. Before coming to grief with Rockefeller and Frederick Mayer in 1925, he told them he wanted his first recital to be a big affair, with a quartet of trumpets and trombones heralding the event from the roof. He hoped for a great crowd, imagining that a public demonstration of interest could offset neighborhood objections. Another brilliant musician, Daniel Robins, who would play the University of Chicago carillon, sister instrument to Riverside, throughout the decade of the 1960s, attracted tremendous attention through auxiliary extravaganzas involving tubas, drums and cymbals on the ground or on the University Chapel roof. Of course crowds never guaranteed real listening. Huge throngs flocked to carillon concerts during the 1920s (though never in New York), drawn by the novelty of the new "Singing Towers." The tower of Saint Stephen's Church in Cohasset, Massachusetts, with a Gillett & Johnston carillon installed in 1924, set in an ideal village location, attracted thousands for summer concerts performed by another Belgian, Kamiel Lefévere. Lefévere, carillonneur at Riverside Church, 1931–1960, was the man I found in the Riverside tower office after Cyril Johnston's death in 1950. People attending Cohasset concerts in 1924 brought picnic lunches and blankets and sprawled on the large village green below Saint Stephen's tower. Such multitudes did not apparently harbor the kernel of an informed listening public, or the likelihood of one developing.

Audiences or no, Lefévere had a more favorable start in America than his countryman Anton Brees. At Park Avenue on that frigid dark evening in December, 1925, Brees, alone against the elements, would have been hunched and overdressed at his keyboard, playing for his audience of three freezing in a doorway, trying to appreciate the beautiful bell tones of their European musician extraordinaire. Brees would have kept warm to some extent by his vigorous activity. The carillonneur at work has been described as looking rather violent, something like a miscast boxer or a gymnast—especially back then, with the keyboard action a lot stiffer, the transmission system much tighter than it is today. Rockefeller, it was reported, couldn't stand the cold, and soon scurried down Park Avenue, disappearing into an apartment house around the corner on East 63rd Street where a niece lived.

For Cyril Johnston, the important event of 1925 (and of his career perhaps), had already occurred. On May 12th, King George V and his consort Queen Mary had visited his foundry in Croydon to view the bells that would be shipped to the Park Avenue Baptist Church in July, and dedicated in December.

Rockefeller objected initially to having Cyril publicize the bells in England before shipment. He had "coveted for Americans the first opportunity to hear this great carillon." Writing to Cyril in February, he told him he and Mr. Mayer had thought it over and changed their minds. They realized that a "favorable and appreciative public opinion in England" could be "very helpful in preparing the American public [for this] . . . totally unknown musical instrument." Now he would like to see glowing reports of the carillon reach New York before its arrival. "Therefore we are entirely willing that such demonstration of the bells be given at the factory, together with as wide publicity as you desire and as is possible without delaying shipment . . . "[10] The King and Queen might have been enough, but Cyril, true to form, pulled out all the stops.

Yet he was hardly resting on any laurels. By his own account, in a press release May 4, 1925, eight days before the visitation by the royal couple, he had twenty-nine contracts in hand: twenty-one for British rings, the rest for carillons, in the U.S., Canada and Holland. Of the 383 bells thus on order and comprising rings and carillons, with total weight of 167 tons, a large number of them, organized for shipment, would have been on his foundry floor at once at any one time during that year. And that was just the beginning. By June of 1926, with the Park Avenue instrument still being played after Brees's departure, Cyril firmed up his contract for Riverside by once again outbidding Taylor, now for four new giant bells—52 tons of bronze, to anchor the carillon uptown. Mayer and Rockefeller had not been stupid about Taylor. They needed the competition to keep Cyril "honest," as any donor and his financial advisors would logically think. Mayer went out of his way to apologize abjectly to Denison Taylor for an errant note in the Park Avenue dedication program stating that Gillett & Johnston had rediscovered the art of bellfounding that had been lost since the time of the Hemony brothers, observing respectfully that it had actually been Denison's father John William I who had been there first. Under duress, Cyril revised his price downward for those four big bells, and came in with much more poundage than Taylor. Most tellingly, for the colossal Low C—at 20 tons destined to be the biggest tuned bell as part of a carillon in existence, and to epitomize an American dream for outstripping the size of any European bell, as well as creating an impossible standard at home, never to be matched or exceeded.

The Riverside bourdon, which would require pneumatic assistance to be played, became not so much an essential note—the Low C in a 72-bell carillon—as a tourist site, a monument not less interesting than, say, the fallen 220-ton Great Bell of Moscow. Cast in 1733, it fell in a fire, an 11-ton section breaking off and producing a large jagged opening—perfect for people to walk entertainingly inside. The bell never sounded. It lies in the Grand Square, as indispensable to see as was the tomb of Lenin. The Riverside carillon with its monumental bourdon would never be useless or unused, but it did turn out to be a type of white elephant, with problems opposite those that had afflicted Park Avenue, in height, location and tower architecture. Sound escapement from the tower of Riverside became as serious an issue, in its way, as it had been at Park Avenue. In 1925 while speaking of his new church under construction, Rockefeller uttered some famous last words: "I am assuming that there is no danger of getting the carillon too high."[11]

Chapter VI

THE KING'S BELL

There's no color that quite matches that!
—King George V (1925)

Knowing that Cyril Johnston had presented King George V with a souvenir bell when His Royal Highness visited the Croydon foundry May 12, 1925, in March of 2000 I wrote a letter to his granddaughter Elizabeth II, to make an inquiry. I wondered if the bell was still in her family's possession, and if so I would like to see and photograph it for a book I was writing about one of her late illustrious subjects. I said I "would consider it an inestimable favor" if she would "consent to being in such a picture [herself]." That I planned to be in London from April 1-10, but "for such an eventuality as I have proposed, I would come to London at any time convenient to Your Majesty." I enclosed a copy of the photograph that adorns the back cover of this book showing my father standing between her grandparents on the day that the bell in question had been presented as a gift. I had lived

69

with her grandparents for some time, the picture having become my apartment figurehead in the Orwellian year of 1984 when I had it enlarged from a negative to 50 by 38½ inches, then framed. The figures in the photo stand at half their actual heights. One friend who saw it commented, "You really are into those people aren't you." It's true. I had been "into them" since 1936 when my mother could speak of nothing but the scandalous love affair of Edward VIII with the divorced American woman Wallis Simpson, and Edward's subsequent abdication to marry her. You didn't have to be English or half-English to take notice or feel involved, since all of America was riveted by the story. My birth circumstance was not a necessary condition of my American Anglophilism. British royalty was simply a very potent American cultural reference, along with Shirley Temple, Charlie McCarthy or the Revolutionary War.

Three years after the abdication scandal, another opportunity arose to feel a part of it when Elizabeth II's father, King George VI, and mother, Queen Elizabeth, visited the United States—the first reigning sovereign to do so since the former colonies had rebelled against his great-great-great grandfather George III. The couple had arrived in Quebec in May, 1939, the eve of War, on the *Empress of Australia.* In June after visiting President Roosevelt in Washington they stopped in New York and passed by me and my mother and my mother's friend Bertha Hatch hanging out a window of Bertha's apartment on 116th Street between Riverside Drive and Broadway to glimpse them. A big crowd below lined the sidewalks. I remember only the excitement and the back of the Queen's white-gloved hand waving out the window of their slow-moving closed car. I don't remember seeing the face belonging to the glove, only the glove. What a thrilling glove! At that time, the couple's daughter the Princess Elizabeth to whom I would write decades later, was sixteen.

My third royal hit was the sighting of her grandparents flanking my father in the photograph I saw originally hanging on Kamiel Lefévere's tower office wall at Riverside Church. I was 20, and my father, recently dead, was beginning to come alive for me.

As a consequence of having a father who had lived for all the years I had thought him dead, once he actually died I would give him quite a grand afterlife. And anything he had to do with royalty would score high in this temple of posteriority. Nineteen-eighty-four, the year I came into possession of the photograph and enlarged it, happened to be the centenary of Cyril's birth, an event celebrated by carillon playing in many towers worldwide.

His birth date of May 9th, three days before May 12th, when in 1925 King George and Queen Mary visited his foundry, is close enough to make you wonder if he had calculated that proximity. Cyril had just turned 41. The King was 60. Off Queen Mary's left shoulder and behind her to her right in the back cover photo stands the partly obscured figure of Nora Johnston, Cyril's only sibling and unmarried younger sister, who in one year's time would be studying carillon playing in Belgium. For now, she played hostess along with their mother when notables came to the works. She and her brother, who would not marry until he was 46, still lived with their mother. On this occasion, Nora "received" the royal guests along with Cyril, as their mother, who would normally perform that service, was too lame to stand for long. Her condition was remarked upon two years earlier by Frederick Mayer when conveying messages to Rockefeller from a letter he had received from Cyril: "Mr. Johnston's mother is crippled almost hopelessly."[1] Born in Strasbourg in 1853, née Amelie Charlotte Brouneau, she would live another sixteen years after the royal event, until 1941, aged 88. Her son Cyril by his late 50s would in turn become seriously afflicted with arthritis. Her daughter Nora had problems as a result of being different for a girl, or one could say just being a girl and growing up as interested in the bells as her brother but having to watch him inherit their father's business. She was in any event very unlike her mother, who as mothers (and wives) go was emblematically beyond reproach. Yet Nora, an anomaly of her time, created a rich independent life, having a career in the theater as actor and producer, then becoming a pioneer as a woman in the man's field of carillon playing. In 1925, she was poised between careers, and at the Croydon foundry would soon find herself demonstrating new carillons, no longer simply receiving people or pouring tea. Not that she disliked this role, or being on the premises to greet prominent visitors. [See Chapter XI]

And on May 12, 1925, she was as proud and thrilled as Cyril to entertain Their Majesties. In a memoir she would write she said, "I shall always remember the graciousness of our much loved Queen, when Mother was presented to her. Seeing that she was lame, Queen Mary immediately sat down with her."[2] Nora also observed that this was the first time in many years that a King of England had visited Croydon. *The Croydon Times* created a pictorially rich Special Supplement in oversized pages to celebrate the event. It was a great day for Croydon. In the neighborhood of the foundry on Whitehorse Road throngs of adoring subjects, standing many feet deep, were managed with difficulty by the police. In the crush a few people had to be treated by medics on hand in ambulances. The crowds extended all the way from Brixton, waiting along the route just to watch the royal car drive by. The King was said to have "expressed a personal desire to see the world's biggest carillon in process of completion at Croydon."[3]

That part of the process called casting—the premier event in bellfounding—was the thing. I imagine it was the anticipation of seeing a casting that brightened the royal faces as they dismounted from their car at the entrance to the foundry, met by their host dressed to the nines in tails, vest, spats, striped pants, high starched collar and muted lavender silk cravat. Their Majesties, arriving at 3 P.M., saw the new carillon for Park Avenue in New York at 3:10, and at 3:20 a casting of bells for a ring at Great Haseley, near Oxford. A floral bell had been presented to the Queen. The couple witnessed also the casting of the bell—made from the same metal as the 9½-ton New York bourdon—that would be presented to them as a memento of their visit. The birthing of a bell is a lengthy and painstaking operation most of which would have taken place before the King and Queen sat down to watch the moment de resistance, when the molten metal—an alloy of roughly 77% copper and 23% tin—is liberated from the furnace. This is what people die to see. The furnace, a womb where the makings of the "baby" have reached a temperature of 1100 degrees Centigrade (copper melts at 1,980 degrees Fahrenheit and tin at 449, so tin is not added until shortly before casting) is tilted to let its glowing white-hot lava, its otherworldly incandescence, spill into a large cauldron, or crucible. "There's no color that quite matches that!" exclaimed the King when he saw it.[4] Workmen holding chains to maneuver the crucible were in the middle of an inferno of hissing sparks raining around them, and were not protected with helmets, fire-resistant gloves and transparent masks the way they are today. Crowds of visitors were allowed to stand pretty close too, whereas today they are judged a security risk and can only witness the proceedings, if at all, from a distant balcony—my own vantage point at the Taylor foundry in Loughborough in 2001, when I witnessed my first casting. The King saw the cauldron, now full to the brim, lifted with special tackle to make a short foundry-floor journey suspended on a traveling crane toward the site of conception—the standing or buried moulds, with openings at the top to receive the metal (See, Appendix 3).

The moulds, two for each bell—an inner called the core, an outer or cope—are what take so long to prepare for this brilliant moment. A bell is first worked up in a drawing; then patterns are cut and a profile created, with foremost attention to the diameter. The two moulds, differently built up with loam and brick, coke and clay and cow's hair or horse manure, are formed with a strickle board, or sweep or crook, revolved by hand, and correspond in profile precisely with the contours of the inside and the outside of the bell. Once assembled, the moulds are baked and dried, then in excavated pits (for the larger bells; for smaller ones the moulds are freestanding) the cope is clamped down over the core, the space between them obviously the "fallopian" receptacle for the blazing river of molten metal—the future bell. Cooling can take 24 hours or a few days depending on the size of the bell. Then as now, casting was rudimentarily close to how it was done in early Christian times when monks made bells, or founders were itinerant and their sites moveable (set up in church yards and utilizing townspeople); or when bellfounding became an established profession in the eleventh century. The sense of excitement and suspense at a bell casting is enduring. And Kings and Queens have not been strangers to the proceedings. King George V was in the middle of his reign, and presiding over an Empire hurting after the Great War but still going strong. He might not have wanted to miss seeing "the world's greatest carillon of 53 bells" as the program note for his visit read. Made after all in Britain by one of his subjects and paid for by the world's richest man, it would arrive invasively as it were, and ring out in the land of his ancestor George III's preeminently lost colony. It would have taken more however than the invitation that crossed the King's desk to get him to the foundry in Croydon. Cyril was not a friend of his. The King has no friends. So what were Cyril's royal connections exactly?

One has to imagine some lesser royalty as intermediary to facilitate a visit of the scope of May 12, 1925. Cyril's best royal link was undoubtedly with Princess Beatrice, born in 1857, and Queen Victoria's youngest and ninth child, thus one of King George's great aunts. Quite a few photographs, taken at the Croydon foundry beginning in 1921 feature Princess Beatrice, who had a special interest in bells. In that year she visited the works and received a souvenir bell herself. She had taken a leading part in the bell restoration scheme for a ring of eight at Carisbrooke Church on the Isle of Wight, of which she was the Governor, and had been responsible for the choice of Gillett & Johnston to do it. The old ring, dated 1770, was melted down and the metal used to cast the new bells along with the Princess's souvenir. On January 12, 1922 she visited the foundry again, this time with the Duchess of Albany, widow of Beatrice's brother Prince Leopold (Victoria's eighth, and hemophilic, child), to see and hear North America's first carillon, ready to be shipped to the Metropolitan Methodist Church in Toronto. *The Pall Mall Gazette*'s mention of the Princess's visit to "the famous works of Gillett & Johnston of Croydon" provides some idea of Cyril's success by then in drawing attention to both his craft and his business. The conjunction of "famous works" and "royalty" has a suggestive ring to it. After all, if important people came to the foundry, important things must be going on there. A week following King George and Queen Mary's visit to the foundry in 1925, Princess Beatrice came again, now to see the Park Avenue bells herself. The other personage on this occasion was American Ambassador to Britain, Alanson Houghton, of the prominent Houghton family—founders of Corning Glass, and donors of the Houghton Memorial Carillon at St. Paul's School in New Hampshire, a Gillett & Johnston instrument dedicated in 1933 [See Chapter XIV]. The elderly and one must say copious Princess was presented with a "beautiful bouquet of pink carnations, white roses and asparagus fern."

Cyril may have met Beatrice through another of Victoria's children, her seventh, Prince Arthur, the Duke of Connaught (1850–1942); or the Duke's daughter Princess Victoria Patricia, called "Patsy." Cyril and his sister Nora must have known Patsy, close in age to them, fairly well since on January 2, 1919, as reported by the *Croydon Advertiser,* they were present at an evening party given for her by Their Majesties at St. James Palace. The siblings also appeared at Westminster Abbey in February for Patsy's marriage to Commander Alexander Ramsay, one of her father's aides-du-camp, when she became Lady Ramsay. Patsy had fallen in love, thus saving herself from a fate as the Queen of Portugal, the Queen of Spain, or a Russian Grand Duchess, though by marrying down she gave up her royal title. She and her father the Duke had been in Croydon in 1918 to open a canteen built by Cyril for his employees in gratitude for their war effort in manufacturing hundreds of thousands of fuses for the government (largely undertaken by a force of women). For Patsy's wedding, Cyril presented her with a company gift: a special mantelpiece clock of glass panels at front and sides, set in a fine mahogany case with delicate satinwood inlay. It was the first in a line intended by G&J to bring back to England the high class household clock trade on which the Germans had a firm hold before the war. Somewhere amidst these royal connections was a communications line to King George. If it mattered, and I suppose it must have, bells had not been the only medium of attraction between Cyril and his royal friends.[5]

Descriptions of Cyril's looks and personality invariably say he was handsome to dashing and had a great sense of humor. My mother's favorite word for him was "debonair." She liked remembering dancing with him at Ciro's in Paris. "You should have seen him in his tails and white tie," she boasted. Charm, it seems, was one of his outstanding attributes. Thought to charm the pants off prospective clients—a descendant of his competitor Albert Hughes of Whitechapel, Douglas Hughes, told me, "I'm sure he was absolutely the most charming man, because he got away with murder; nobody made so many bells in such a short amount of time"—he had evidently plenty of charm left for the ladies. As Douglas Hughes added, "He was known to sweep the ladies off their feet."[6] My mother never recovered from being swept off hers. She said he was unlike anyone she had ever known before. Until he was 46, the age he got married (and the year after I was born), he was a keen bachelor. In 1984 I found a lady in Redlands California called Mrs. Donald Hunter who had known Cyril in his bachelorhood. She and her husband, an engineer involved in church architecture, lived in Detroit, a destination of Cyril's when Michigan carillon contracts were at stake. Mrs. Hunter said Cyril was "quite dashing."[7] He liked to dance, and he took her sister out. According to Mary Evelyn O'Leary, the woman Cyril would marry, and who lived on after he died as his widow for over forty years, "he had great fun [before his marriage] with American debutantes."[8] In the early 1980s, she wrote to David Cawley, Vicar at St. Mary's Church in Leicester, about meeting Cyril at some function, saying, "In came the tallest, most handsome man I have ever set eyes on."[9] His son Arthur, speaking at the centenary service for him in 1984, summed him up this way: "I personally shall always remember my father as someone with a tremendous sense of humor and a great capacity for enjoying life—but also for hard work." James Lawson, who played the carillon at Riverside Church for 21 years and had met the bellfounder, said he remembered Cyril's "cultivation." "He was a well processed gentleman . . . warm and extremely cultured."[10]

On a visit of Cyril's to Canada in June of 1927 the *Toronto Globe* described him as "an arresting personality; Mr. Johnston is at once a keen businessman, and an interesting conversationalist." It amused my mother that he kept a little book in which he jotted down American slang, a habit no doubt serving to aid him in chatting with his dates. On one occasion in Detroit, as Mrs. Hunter remembered, Cyril lost his "Grenadier Guard" silver cigarette case. The name of that illustrious regiment, in which the bellfounder had a commission as Second Lieutenant in the Special Reserve during WWI, must have been inscribed on the case. If he came across as "debonair" in tails, in his Grenadier outfit he had the "dashing" look.

It was as a Grenadier Guard, a regiment with origins in 1656 under Charles II and of great prestige and social standing that he met Patsy's father the Duke of Connaught, who belonged to the same regiment. A photo of the canteen opening in Croydon in 1918 shows Cyril and the Duke, both wearing the Guards uniform, sitting at a dais with Patsy. The Duke, named Arthur after his godfather the Duke of Wellington and hero of Waterloo, had had a distinguished military career himself. Cyril would not exactly. His first commission, in 1914 in the Royal Fusiliers was compromised by medical disabilities—appendicitis requiring surgery and some abdominal wall weakness resulting from straining himself, as he would report, "while pulling the rope of a church bell weighing two tons."[11] Discharged from the Royal Fusiliers in March 1916, one month later he received the Grenadier Guard commission. He was on the Somme after that western front offensive began July 1st, though abroad for only five weeks. Then in October he was recalled following his father's collapse and death from a coronary while playing golf, aged 65. Now head of the firm, Cyril had the sole responsibility for manufacturing munitions for the government. A Grenadier Guard till the end of the war, he sometimes rang in an officer's peal band. His record in service doesn't suggest a military aptitude or inclination, or any interest in dying gloriously for his country. Aged 32 in 1916, his calling had already been established; he was marking time until bell production could resume, and his foundry could again function as its own theater of operations.

Cyril's foundry has actually been described as a theater. He imported audiences and presented exhibitions and performances. He would talk or lecture, sometimes illustrating them with slides; tours were conducted; carillonneurs would come to play; he played himself sometimes; tuning was demonstrated; castings were featured, at which consequential people were invited to toss a coin into the molten metal. It was not reported that the King or Queen on May 12, 1925, acquitted themselves of this hallowed custom, perhaps because they carried no money on their persons. Or protocol precluded the invitation. How fitting would it have been for the King's own souvenir bell to have a coin embedded that he had tossed himself. At some moment during their tour, the Queen let herself go and performed a little tune on a row of small new bells they walked past on the foundry floor, tapping out with the point of her umbrella a few bars of *Rest, My Baby, Rest.* Their Majesties were highly amused by this unscheduled escapade, making them chuckle delightedly on their way to the reception room where refreshments awaited them. Before leaving the foundry, they heard the bells for Park Avenue played by Kamiel Lefévere, then being courted by Rockefeller to play the instrument in New York. A native of Malines, Lefévere was the first graduate, along with one other Belgian, in 1924, of Jef Denyn's new Carillon School, now called the Royal Carillon Belgian School Jef Denyn. On May 4, Denyn himself had appeared at the Croydon foundry to play for Cyril's elaborate day-long press conference. May 13, the day after the King and Queen's visit, another of Denyn's pupils, Clifford Ball (1899–1986), appeared to play for Princess Beatrice and the American Ambassador to Britain, Alanson Houghton. Ball was on course to become England's premier carillonneur—a rare position in a land of change-ringing, and paralleled by that of Percival Price, just two years younger than Ball, in North America.

Price and Ball led the charge to overcome the precedence accorded Belgian and Dutch musicians, and replace or at least successfully rival them in their homelands. Price, a Canadian, would also graduate from Denyn's School, enabled to go there through the financial assistance of the foresightful John D. Rockefeller, Jr., eager to have Price as well as Lefévere play in New York, and to encourage the development of native talent. Price too would play at the Croydon foundry, and would become a mega-star in the carillon firmament—musician, composer, consultant, scholar and author, teacher and organizer—one of the few who have been able to carve out a living exclusively devoted to the carillon. Clifford Ball, the Englishman who performed for Cyril Johnston's third big gathering at the works to celebrate the Park Avenue instrument, became the bellfounder's good friend, later facilitating an important contract for G&J in replacing a Taylor carillon in Bournville (suburb of Birmingham), where Ball played for many years [See Chapter XIII].

When Kamiel Lefévere rendered for the King and Queen, leading off with Schubert's *Ave Maria,* it turned out that the Queen had heard him before. Mentioning having been charmed by a carillon concert she had heard on the famed St. Rombouts Cathedral bells in Malines, and told it was Lefévere who had played on that occasion, she said she was "delighted to hear such a distinguished carillonneur twice."[12] He must have been thrilled. She was not Lefévere's Queen; but European royalty, still alive in the Netherlands as well as Britain, and whose members after all constitute one endogamous family, was and remains a mystique for its subjects that seems impossible for those raised without such figureheads to really grasp.

I can't imagine it myself, having been raised in America from the age of two. Our Anglophilism in any case is a pale interest next to the propitiatory sentiment of a sovereign's people. I'm quite sure though that if for some unimaginable reason I had to choose between an invitation to the Queen's palace or the president's White House, I would speed off unequivocally and with due haste to London. After writing to Queen Elizabeth in March 2000 inquiring about the bell presented by Cyril Johnston to her grand-parents in 1925, I heard from deputies of the Royal Collection. Yes, they said, the bell was still in the Queen's possession, one of about half a million or more royal gifts stored in dozens of places around Great Britain, and they would be happy to photograph it for me—at a price. The bell was tucked away at Sandringham House. Price or no, I wanted to see and photograph it myself. As for having the Queen in my picture, this mad dream was nipped in the bud when the first deputy who contacted me, Miss Henrietta Edwards, said she was sorry but the Queen unfortunately could not possibly make such an appearance. I could however, as it was finally determined, see and photograph the bell myself. I had a copious correspondence with the deputies before actually seeing the bell October 2, 2002. Advised at the beginning of 2001 that the Land Agent at Sandringham would be happy to receive me, secretaries at the House kept putting me off throughout 2001 because England was in throes of its bovine Foot and Mouth Disease, and it was thought perhaps that I might bring it in by my car tires or something.

Approaching Sandringham House the day of my appointment, having driven south with Ingrid from Yorkshire, I had no idea where to go exactly or what to expect. It was easy enough to find the Royal Estate, located near a town called King's Lynn in the northwest corner of Norfolk, that easternmost middling bulge of England, two hours north of London. A handsome high endless brick wall signified an important residence within. But I doubted we could just drive on in. And my only instructions involved a name and a time. The main gate, a huge black elaborately worked wrought iron portal, obviously the queen's own entrance, with her royal heraldry at the top circularly surrounded by that interdictory motto of the Order of the Garter, *Honi Soit Qui Mal Y Pense,* was awesomely locked. We were able to get through the wall after coming across a tourist refreshment center where a clerk looked at my appointment data and called a man who led us in his red pickup through a small guarded gate into the 66 acres of estate grounds. Now we were driving on the Queen's inner roads which she traverses herself in her Landrover when she comes every year to spend the end of December through February with her family.

Getting close to the Queen through my father's bell, or vice versa, was beginning to form a syndrome in my brain. Thousands of his bells exist throughout the world; I had never gone to this much trouble to see any of them. The symbolism here addressing a restitution of origins seems very freighted. Birth alone tends to be the presumed condition of membership in a state. But birth compromised by the missing imprimatur of the father sets up a contingency, raising strong doubts regarding admission or inclusion. All the histories of bastardy, the bar sinister, the dark side of legitimacy (unthinkable without it), bear this out. And royalty has served as a final court of appeal. England has its prototype in the improbable paternity of the mythic King Arthur, who had been required to prove he was a rightful heir by performing extraordinary feats. Modern England begins in 1066 with William the Conqueror, who spent much of his life on a horse, sword in hand, defending a birthright his father Robert I, the Duke of Normandy, had left in question upon departing for a Crusade at the age of 21, never to return. The Conqueror was widely known, in Normandy certainly, as William the Bastard.

A symmetry, or concordance, exists between the father and his sovereign. In my 1925 photograph the King and my father stand together in similar outfits, facing the same way and looking at the same thing—a bell, or bells. The bell fashioned especially for the King that day was now a figurative link between the man who made it (and made me) and the man for whom it was made. On his granddaughter's "inner roads" I seemed to be literally "on the path." A number of discreetly situated signs reading "no entry" indicated my fairytale presence within the "forbidden city"—or in reality: a walled fortress. At first, waiting at staff headquarters for Tony Parnell, the man designated to take care of my interests, it was imagined that I was there to see about a Labrador gun dog. Mr. Parnell, the Queen's Foreman of House Maintenance, raises these dogs and sometimes sells them in

America. He knew I was there about a bell, and was a bit stupefied that I had come, as he thought, all the way from America just to see it. Now when he produced it—in a small courtyard surrounded by quarters formerly housing pages and footmen—I could see it was nothing to get excited about. As "hidden treasures" go, it had no luster at all. Faded to nondescript grays, you can sense its once gleaming hues of bronze. Eight inches high, 9¾ inches in diameter and weighing 13½ kg. or 35 lbs., it is no longer even properly a bell since it doesn't sound off like one. Struck by its clapper or any metal object, it makes a noise something like a twangy thud on a rusty old washtub. Apparently the bell is cracked, though the crack must be internal since none is visible. Mr. Parnell said it was fastened for years to a wall on the staircase landing of household quarters long since destroyed by order of the Queen. I held the bell, a kind of abandoned child, in my arms, wondering if King George himself had ever touched it. He may not even have seen it, except in its molten form. Once it cooled and was removed from its moulds in the foundry following his visit that May of 1925 it would have been sent to Buckingham Palace and perhaps whisked right off by Royal Collection deputies into storage. It has a fine narrative inscription:

GILLETT & JOHNSTON CROYDON/ THIS BELL WAS
CAST IN THE PRESENCE OF/THE KING AND QUEEN/
DURING THEIR VISIT TO CROYDON/ TO INSPECT THE
NEW YORK CARILLON/ ON MAY 12th 1925/
PRESENTED TO THEIR MAJESTIES/
BY CYRIL F. JOHNSTON.

After beholding, handling and photographing the bell, we were given a private tour of the House by Mr. Parnell. As royal residences go, Sandringham is quite splendid, though I have not seen that many of them. I may have felt closer to the Queen when the day was over. Whether I did or not, I had not given up on seeing her—or I should add: seeing her about more than her inherited G&J bell.

Cyril F. Johnston

The King's Bell, 1925
8 inches tall x 9¾ inches in diameter
13½ kg or 35 lbs

The King's Bell at Sandringham House, 2003

Inscription on the King's Bell photographed at Sandringham House, 2003

Top: Nora Johnston and her brother, Cyril F. Johnston, May 12, 1925
Bottom: Cyril F. Johnston welcomes HRH King George V and HRH Queen Mary
to the Gillett & Johnston Bellfoundry, May 12, 1925

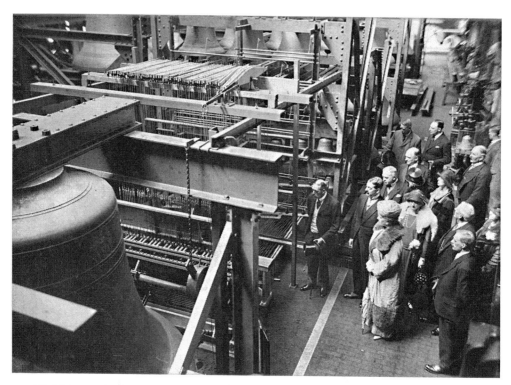

Top: HRH King George V, Cyril F. Johnston, HRH Queen Mary, Nora Johnston
and guests, May 12, 1925, viewing the carillon for Park Avenue Baptist Church, New York, NY
Bottom: Kamiel Lefévere playing the Park Avenue carillon for the Royal visitors

*HRH King George V, Cyril F. Johnston, HRH Queen Mary and Nora Johnston
at the Gillett & Johnston Bellfoundry, May 12, 1925*

John D. Rockefeller, Jr., December 1925

Tower and belfry of
Park Avenue Baptist Church

Belfry of Park Avenue Baptist Church

Park Avenue Baptist Church

Bird's-eye view of Riverside Church, New York, NY, 2002

Cyril F. Johnston with the 20-ton bourdon destined for Riverside Church carillon on display at Gillett & Johnston Bellfoundry, c. 1930

*The 20-ton bourdon being readied
for shipment to New York City*

*The 20-ton bourdon being hoisted onto
ship bound for New York City*

The 20-ton bourdon for Riverside Church being lowered into hold of the ship

BELLS CAST FOR RIVERSIDE
GILLETT & JOHNSTON BELL RECORDS, 1877 - 1957 (in abridged form).

LEGEND: C = Cast (weight). D = Description, i.e. N = New, O = Old, R = Recast. P = Peal Number. S = Single bell.

Vol /Page	Bell No.	Location	County/Country	P	D	Inches	Mm	Cwt QrLbs	Kilos	Note/	Hertz	Date	Remarks
5/1	1134	New York, Pk Ave Bpt Ch	USA - NY	53	N	98	2489	183 0 14	9303.17	E	167	06/04/27	[Bells t/frd to Riverside NY,]
12/1		New York, Riverside Ch.	USA - NY	72	N	122	3099	365 1 18	18563.70	C	133	03/01/28	[Bells t/frd from Pk Ave Bapt Ch with 28 recast. Now a carillon of 72 bells, 2 being added in 1995 by Van Bergan of Holland.]
12/1		New York, Riverside Ch.	USA - NY	71	N	109	2769	255 1 0	12967.29	D	149.5	04/06/27	
12/1		New York, Riverside Ch.	USA - NY	70	N	105	2667	235 2 9	11968.02	D$	158	26/08/27	
12/1	1134	New York, Riverside Ch.	USA - NY	69	N	98	2489	183 0 14	9303.17	E	167	06/04/25	
12/2		New York, Riverside Ch.	USA - NY	68	N	92	2337	162 1 7	8245.85	F	177	26/04/29	
12/2	1042	New York, Riverside Ch.	USA - NY	67	N	87	2210	130 0 0	6604.30	F$	188	14/02/25	[Nos 61,64,66,68,72 are swinging bells.]
12/2	1133	New York, Riverside Ch.	USA - NY	66	N	81	2057	101 1 6	5146.45	G	199	09/07/25	
12/2	1009	New York, Riverside Ch.	USA - NY	65	N	75 5/16	1913	82 1 13	4184.39	G$	211	27/10/24	
12/3	680	New York, Riverside Ch.	USA - NY	64	N	72	1829	73 1 0	3721.27	A	224	15/07/24	
12/3	804	New York, Riverside Ch.	USA - NY	63	N	67 15/16	1726	60 1 14	3067.19	A$	237	02/01/24	
12/3	872	New York, Riverside Ch.	USA - NY	62	N	64 3/4	1645	53 0 0	2692.52	B	251	12/04/24	
12/3	678	New York, Riverside Ch.	USA - NY	61	N	60 13/16	1545	43 2 25	2221.24	C	266	00/04/24	
12/4	677	New York, Riverside Ch.	USA - NY	60	N	56 13/16	1443	35 2 26	1815.28	C$	282	00/04/24	
12/4	676	New York, Riverside Ch.	USA - NY	59	N	54	1372	30 2 19	1558.09	D	298	09/11/23	
12/4	746	New York, Riverside Ch.	USA - NY	58	N	51	1295	25 2 12	1300.90	D$	316	28/09/23	
12/4	730	New York, Riverside Ch.	USA - NY	57	N	48 1/8	1222	21 1 8	1083.18	E	334	18/07/23	
12/5	673	New York, Riverside Ch.	USA - NY	56	N	44 7/8	1140	17 0 24	874.53	F	354	01/08/23	
12/5	672	New York, Riverside Ch.	USA - NY	55	N	43	1092	15 0 8	765.66	F$	376	18/07/23	and 13/2/25 [?]
12/5	671	New York, Riverside Ch.	USA - NY	54	N	40 1/8	1019	11 3 5	599.20	G	398	19/06/23	
12/5	670	New York, Riverside Ch.	USA - NY	53	N	38	965	9 3 26	507.12	G$	422	18/05/23	
12/6	1054	New York, Riverside Ch.	USA - NY	52	N	36 7/16	926	9 2 2	483.53	A	448	26/03/25	
12/6	668	New York, Riverside Ch.	USA - NY	51	N	34	864	7 2 20	390.09	A$	474	18/05/23	
12/6	830	New York, Riverside Ch.	USA - NY	50	N	31 7/8	810	6 0 27	317.06	B	502	04/03/24	
12/6	666	New York, Riverside Ch.	USA - NY	49	N	30 1/2	775	5 1 17	274.42	C	532	29/05/23	
12/7	665	New York, Riverside Ch.	USA - NY	48	N	29	737	4 3 12	246.75	C$	564	30/05/23	
12/7	664	New York, Riverside Ch.	USA - NY	47	N	28	711	4 1 18	224.07	D	596	15/05/23	
12/7	663	New York, Riverside Ch.	USA - NY	46	N	27	686	4 0 5	205.48	D$	632	18/05/23	
12/7	871	New York, Riverside Ch.	USA - NY	45	N	25 1/2	648	3 1 23	175.54	E	668	02/05/24	
12/8	824	New York, Riverside Ch.	USA - NY	44	N	24 1/8	613	2 3 19	148.32	F	708	03/03/24	
12/8	660	New York, Riverside Ch.	USA - NY	43	N	21 15/16	557	2 0 19	110.22	F$	752	10/02/25	
12/8	2909	New York, Riverside Ch.	USA - NY	42	N	21	533	2 0 18	109.77	G	796	27/03/29	C. Tunings = 26lbs.
12/8		New York, Riverside Ch.	USA - NY	41	N	0			0.00	G$	845		[No further details given.*.]
12/9	2193	New York, Riverside Ch.	USA - NY	40	N	18 15/16	481	1 1 18	71.67	A	896	26/11/27	
12/9	3163	New York, Riverside Ch.	USA - NY	39	N	18 1/8	460	1 0 24	61.69	A$	948	30/05/29	
12/9	3499	New York, Riverside Ch.	USA - NY	38	N	0		1 1 25		B	1004	16/01/30	C.
12/9	979	New York, Riverside Ch.	USA - NY	37	N	16 1/2	419	1 0 13	74.84	C	1064	18/09/24	C.
12/10	3602	New York, Riverside Ch.	USA - NY	36	N	16	406	1 0 9	56.70	C$	1128	12/03/30	C. Cast for Stock Carillon 19.
12/10	3626	New York, Riverside Ch.	USA - NY	35	N	15 1/16	383	3 19	54.88	D	1192	07/02/30	C. Cast for Stockgrove Park 1.
12/10	3107	New York, Riverside Ch.	USA - NY	34	N	14 1/4	362	3 7	46.72	D$	1264	17/06/29	C.
12/10	3559	New York, Riverside Ch.	USA - NY	33	N	13 5/8	346	3 8	41.28	E	1336	09/02/30	C. Cast for Chicago 26(2).
12/11	3335	New York, Riverside Ch.	USA - NY	32	N	13 1/8	333	2 25	41.73	F	1416	09/01/30	C.
12/11	3734	New York, Riverside Ch.	USA - NY	31	N	12 9/16	319	2 14	36.74	F$	1504	04/04/30	C.
12/11	3596	New York, Riverside Ch.	USA - NY	30	N	12	305		31.75	G	1592		[No further details given.*.]
12/12	3332	New York, Riverside Ch.	USA - NY	29	N	11 13/16	300	2 0	0.00	G$	1690	04/03/30	C. Cast for Stock Carillon 13.
12/12		New York, Riverside Ch.	USA - NY	28	N	10 1/2	267	1 16	25.40	A	1794	11/12/29	C.
9/108		New York, Riverside Ch.	USA - NY	27	N	10	254		19.96	A$	1896		[No further details given.*.]
12/12	3131	New York, Riverside Ch.	USA - NY	26	N	14 3/8	365	2 18	0.00	D$	1228	23/06/30	Sent to Beckenham, Ch Ch, Kent, (2)
12/12		New York, Riverside Ch.	USA - NY	26	N	9 1/2	241	1 3	33.57	B	2009.5	17/07/29	C. Cast for Experimental 9.5".
12/13		New York, Riverside Ch.	USA - NY	25	N	9	229		14.06	C	2128		[No further details given.*.]
12/13		New York, Riverside Ch.	USA - NY	24	N	8 1/2	216		0.00	C$	2260		[No further details given.*.]
12/13		New York, Riverside Ch.	USA - NY	23	N	8	203		0.00	D	2384		[No further details given.*.]
12/13		New York, Riverside Ch.	USA - NY	22	N	7 1/2	191		0.00	D$	2582		[No further details given.*.]
12/13	3271	New York, Riverside Ch.	USA - NY	21	N	7 3/8	187	18	8.16	E	2676	07/02/30	C. Cast for Chicago 12.
12/14		New York, Riverside Ch.	USA - NY	20	N	7 1/8	181		0.00	F	2832	00/00/30	[No further details given.]
12/14	3203	New York, Riverside Ch.	USA - NY	19	N	7	178		0.00	F$	3012	10/07/29	[No further details given.]
12/14	3269	New York, Riverside Ch.	USA - NY	18	N	7	178	14	6.35	G	3190	07/02/30	C.
12/14	3619	New York, Riverside Ch.	USA - NY	17	N	6 11/16	170	13	5.90	G$	3382	13/02/30	C. Cast for Chicage 8(2).
12/15		New York, Riverside Ch.	USA - NY	16	N	6 5/8	168		0.00	A	3586		[No further details given.*.]
12/15	3265	New York, Riverside Ch.	USA - NY	15	N	6 1/2	165	12	5.44	A$	3798	19/02/30	C. Cast for Chicace 6.
12/15		New York, Riverside Ch.	USA - NY	14	N	6 3/8	162		0.00	B	4019		[No further details given.*.]
12/15	2307	New York, Riverside Ch.	USA - NY	13	N	6 1/8	156	12	5.44	C	4264	00/04/27	C. Cast to Riverside 50.[?]
12/16	2086	New York, Riverside Ch.	USA - NY	12	N	6 1/16	154	12	5.44	C$	4520	30/04/27	C. Cast as Riverside 4(3).
12/16	2082	New York, Riverside Ch.	USA - NY	11	N	5 7/8	149	12	5.44	D	4776	30/04/27	C. Cast as Riverside 3(1).
12/16	3892	New York, Riverside Ch.	USA - NY	10	N	5 15/16	151	12	5.44	D$	4928	22/08/30	C. Cast for Chicago 3(4).
14/6	5679	New York, Riverside Ch.	USA - NY	10		7	178		0.00	G	3288	00/00/38	2nd cast. Sent to Morgan, Z.
12/16	2320	New York, Riverside Ch.	USA - NY	9	N	6	152	12	5.44	E	5352	24/04/27	C. Cast as Riverside 1(2).
12/17		New York, Riverside Ch.	USA - NY	8	N	0			0.00	F	5664		[No further details given.*.]
12/17	3648	New York, Riverside Ch.	USA - NY	7	N	5 7/8	149	15	6.80	F$	6024	27/02/30	C.*.[* = Estimated Hertz.]
12/17	3058	New York, Riverside Ch.	USA - NY	6	N	5 13/16	148	13	5.90	G	6374	24/08/29	C.*.
12/17	3145	New York, Riverside Ch.	USA - NY	5	N	5 15/16	151		0.00	G$	6760	27/05/29	C.*.
12/18	3359	New York, Riverside Ch.	USA - NY	4	N	5 5/8	143	14	6.35	A	7172	28/01/30	C.*.
12/18	3384	New York, Riverside Ch.	USA - NY	3	N	5 1/2	140	13	5.90	A$	7590	23/01/30	C.*.
12/54	3646	New York, Riverside Ch.	USA - NY	2	N	5 5/16	135	10.5	4.76	B	7840	07/10/31	4th cast. Sent to Chicago Uni(3).
12/18	3489	New York, Riverside Ch.	USA - NY	2	N	5 1/2	140		0.00	B	8037	22/01/30	C.*.
12/18	3796	New York, Riverside Ch.	USA - NY	1	N	5 1/4	133	12	5.44	C	8520	00/04/30	C.*.
12/10	3626	Stockgrove Park	Bedfordshire	1	N	15 1/16	383	3 19	46.72	D	1192	07/02/30	[Sent to New York, Riverside 35]

Printout of Alan Buswell's database of G&J bells for Riverside Church carillon, derived from the G&J tuning books, 1877–1957; Buswell's database encompasses 11,000 bells cast by G&J

Chapter VII

HEAVY METAL—
the MOTHER of *ALL* BOURDONS

Bells are fiendishly large, fiendishly expensive . . . [the carillon] is a sort of dinosaur of a musical instrument
—Douglas Hughes

The perfect bell does not exist
—Frederick C. Mayer

On June 7, 1926, Cyril Johnston wrote to John Rockefeller, Jr. saying he was ready to go ahead and cast the low C, at 20 tons destined to become New York's, and America's, actually the world's only tuned bell of such huge proportions. Only in 2000 was this to be exceeded. And even then not in a carillon. Its diameter is 122½ inches, its height nearly the same. Its inner clapper, the one that hits the bell's sound-bow when swung to create a tolling effect, weighs two tons. Outside the bell are two hammers, each weighing one-half ton—one for striking the hours, the other for striking the bell when activated by the carillonneur. Riverside Church would have the first carillon to surpass five octaves and is still the only carillon to have achieved a bourdon of pitch C, two octaves below middle C in the musical register. A few bells around the world are bigger, but were cast to stand or hang alone and therefore not tuned for placement with others in a chromatic scale. With his pronouncement in June, 1926, Cyril was unknowingly on course for a marathon run at one bell, and a severe test of his patience and his bellfounding expertise and ingenuity. His low C or bourdon for Riverside would not be declared carillon-worthy for another three and a half years—not until February 25, 1930, and only after three of these leviathans had been cast. On that date, JDR Jr.'s advisor, or "carillon architect" as Frederick Mayer had learned to call himself, cabled the donor from England that "Bourdon III" weighing nearly 48,000 pounds had a "sharper fourth" than the original and he needed authorization to revert to "Bourdon I"—a puny 40,926 pounds by comparison.[1] In the end, over a hundred and thirty thousand pounds of metal and a tremendous amount of money had been expended to subdue the pesky fourth. Often defined as the "wild fourth," it is commonly a mysterious and dominating tone in all bells weighing over ten thousand pounds. Frederick Mayer, in his efforts to get Cyril Johnston to tame the fourth in the Riverside bourdon, to have it consonant in other words with the other harmonics, was trying to get him to do something that had never been done before. The first, and ultimately chosen, bourdon was cast on December 2, 1927. In June the following year, Mayer rejected it. In October Cyril made a curious trip to Los Angeles, where he would stay until early December. Calling it a "health tour," he had every reason to be in his foundry at that time, with many orders for peals and carillons at hand and continuously pending decisions to make over the bourdon for Riverside. Of course not simply metal and money were being expended, but emotional capital as well. And not just over his business. By October 1928 when Cyril fled England, besides his pile-up of orders and his bourdon crisis and not so incidentally a looming contract to build the University of Chicago carillon, projected to be the sister-giant to Riverside, he was faced with an unprecedented personal crisis.

My mother Olive Marjorie Crowe, in England at that moment, was two months pregnant, and would have informed Cyril by then that she planned to go to full term, thus thwarting his wishes and declining his offer for the best most expensive abortion to be had on the Continent. His sudden and surprising departure for a "health tour"—six thousand miles away and to an area of the U.S. where as yet no carillon instruments were under consideration—suggests some type of breakdown, if not just panic. This was a man in his mid-forties who still lived with his mother, whose career was at or near its peak—the latter part of the twenties have in fact been called his "glory years"—and who had stumbled over a land mine. He may have hoped that if he went away my mother would too. She may have been a more serious interest than the women he dated or courted during his long-lasting bachelordom, but her pregnancy surely made her a lot more threatening. A close relative whom I arranged to meet in an undercover way in 2000 (much as I had met my half-brother in 1978) would laugh over Cyril's "engagements." And ask me if my mother had been engaged to him [See Chapter XVI]. I am quite sure she was not. She never said so, and her pregnancy seems to belie any pledge of marriage. So was this a woman hoping to snare a man she was crazy about who appeared not to want to marry her by getting pregnant with his child? I don't think so, consciously anyway. But once pregnant, her decisions and movements indicate the effort to use her condition to traditional advantage. After declining an abortion, she lingered in England both during the rest of her pregnancy and for another five months after giving birth. Then, leaving for America with me in October, 1929, we returned to England the following spring, and stayed another year before embarking again for America, this time for good. I wonder how intentional her time-honored strategy in catching her man was—a scheme simply culturally so old, practically a genetically inherited piece of knowledge, that there would be no necessity to think it out. It could have been purely reflexive. Just as reactively, my mother I believe would have wanted to make Cyril responsible, regardless of his serious attempt to absolve himself by urging her to abort at his expense. Refusing his offer, his own refusal after that to make her a proper woman by marrying her, or at the least to resume their intimacy, made her angry at him for life. Any remembrance of him caused her, except when forgetting herself in rhapsodizing over Cyril's dashing manner and appearance, to fall into a reverie of sadness tinged with suppressed fury over his defection and abandonment.

The ship he took from Southampton for New York, October 10, 1928, was the White Star Line's *Homeric.* Originally a German vessel, it had been the North German Lloyd's 34,350-ton *Columbus,* launched in 1913, and renamed the *Homeric* when Britain received it in the 1919 war reparations. Almost to the day one year after Cyril's embarkation, my mother boarded the same ship, the *Homeric,* with me to travel the same route: Southampton to New York. It was October 9, 1929. She had not given up on Cyril, as demonstrated by her return to England the following spring; but the time for a new mother to show her baby to her family was now rather overdue. At home however she faced another big issue: the uncertainty and apprehension over how indeed to present herself to her family. This could well have been an additional reason for her to linger abroad. Her i.d. for her *Homeric* journey on the Ship's Manifest for "United States Alien Passengers" proves that she had not yet put her story together, officially at least. Listed under her maiden name "Olive Crowe," with American nationality (b. Elizabeth, New Jersey), aged 28, her marital status was inked in as "Single." But she was traveling with a "Child"—called "Jill" aged 1 (an error, as Jill was 5 months)— with her own last name, however a different nationality: "Gt. Brit." And she said she paid for both passages. So she gave herself away, at least to any clerk or official interested in studying the data. Her plight was limned in the Manifest information. But she couldn't afford to arrive in America without altering at least two facts: our surname and her marital status. The *Homeric,* with its Odyssean reference, seems symbolically a not unarresting title of carrier for a woman and child now embarked on wanderings and adventures appropriate to their displaced, even outcast, state.

On Cyril's side, his troubles over the Riverside bourdon were already enough to drive him up his foundry walls. And even before the bell's rejection in June, 1928, he had plenty to deal with. A complaint over his trademark on the bourdon was not so worrisome. Rockefeller wrote to him in March and pointed out "the large size and prominent place on the bell of your trademark," saying that such a "commercial note seriously impairs the artistic beauty of the design, otherwise so satisfactory."[2] Cyril readily agreed to a new design, placing his trademark discreetly around the bourdon's lowest band. By "artistic beauty" Rockefeller had to mean the four archangels adorning the quadrants of the bell. It's easy to assume these archangels are identical, or for that matter that there is only one. Photographs prior to installation show naturally only one of the four sides. After the bell was installed in 1930, the only way to confirm, without access to original documentation, that there are four and they are different, is by clambering with difficulty around the bell in its tower position, wedged between its huge companions, notes G and F. Then you can see that two archangel heads, those facing north and south, are slightly tilted, while the east and west facing heads look straight forward. And each archangel holds a traditional symbol: the figure facing north a scroll, the one looking east a goblet, to the south a ball or sphere, and to the west a sword. An inscription around the base, just above the lowliest trademark band, records the fact that "for the first time in history a carillon compass of five octaves has been here achieved and exceeded."

The carillon's memorial inscription, to Rockefeller's mother Laura Spelman Rockefeller, can be found on the old Park Avenue bourdon, note E, transferred to Riverside in the enlargement scheme, and weighing a mere 20,720 pounds. That same month of the trademark question, Cyril was celebrating his soon-to-be-condemned 20-ton bourdon, and in the all-out style he had conjured up after completing his 53-bell Park Avenue carillon in 1925. He had started trying to set this up in December, 1927, three months earlier, the very day he informed JDR Jr. that the bourdon had been cast. In the same letter, he said the Prince of Wales wanted to see and hear the big Riverside bells before they left Croydon; that early March was the proposed time, and he wondered if the donor might be in Europe then, enabling him to be at the works too. What a heady scenario the bellfounder had envisioned: the meeting on his foundry floor of the richest man in America with the heir to the British throne. But it was not to be. Rockefeller wrote back saying, "It would be interesting indeed to be present when the Prince of Wales comes to Croydon to hear . . . the new bells," and he wished it were possible, however it seemed doubtful he would be abroad in March.[3] The Prince (later to become the hapless Duke of Windsor) was not able, as it turned out, to come either. But Cyril was resourceful.

On March 3rd, 2,400 English ringers came for tea—the event was called an All England Ringers' Meeting—for his worthy, Cyril had secured Britain's 96th Archbishop of Canterbury, the Scot, Randall Thomas Davidson, to be his keynote speaker. If the jumbo bourdon was Cyril's featured attraction, projected to anchor a great carillon in New York, and he wanted 2,400 of England's change-ringers, men who patriotically took a dim view of this keyboard instrument, to see, hear and appreciate it, he had to exercise care not to offend them. Thus he constructed a program catering to their devotional interests. A Ring of 8 he had made for Durham was on view; changes were actually rung on the bourdon and its three big companions. And in the course of the afternoon the ringers were bussed to two churches in Croydon, both with G&J ringing peals, where they could pull on ropes to their heart's content. A carillon concert to be sure was on the program—played by Nora Johnston and Clifford Ball. At the giant tea, Cyril tried to soothe the assembly over any fears English ringers had that carillons might supplant their methods of ringing, saying, "It would be a foolish bellfounder who tried to break the national traditions and established customs of bellringing."[4] The event was capped by dancing until midnight, to a band called "Goddard." Cyril said this was the greatest Ringers' Meeting ever celebrated. In photographs taken that day, the four-archangel bourdon is the backdrop—caged and obscured somewhat by its massive steel frame—for posed shots of the visiting notables. The Archbishop, aged 80, with deep sunken eyes under impressive Scottish eyebrows, looking somehow tragically soulful (he would die two years later), is holding a long rope. His wife, in a lengthy silk coat with fur trimmings and an indescribable hat, is beside him. Others are the Bishop of Guildford, the Duke of Argyll, the Mayor and Mayoress of Croydon, and Cyril and Nora Johnston.

Two months later, in May, the Riverside bourdon was on display again. This time another mighty company was gathered, ostensibly to appreciate probably Cyril's most important European carillon, for the Louvain University Library in Belgium: 48 bells, 31 tons in all, a 7-ton bourdon (called the Liberty Bell). While he built ten carillons for Holland during his career, this would be Cyril's only such order for Belgium. Created in five months, a record for such a large carillon, Frederick Mayer had been the advisor, while sixteen American Engineering Societies had donated the instrument, which cost $80,000, as a memorial for the hundreds of American engineers who had died in the Great War. Guests in Croydon included the American Ambassador to Britain Alanson Houghton, and the Belgian Ambassador, Baron de Cartier de Marchienne, their wives, and the Burgomaster of Louvain. They heard the Riverside bourdon and its companions, listened to a concert by the great Belgian carillonneur Jef Denyn, inspected a carillon in progress of 50 bells for Norwood, Massachusetts, and another of 49 bells for the National War Memorial Carillon in Wellington, New Zealand.[5] As if all that were not enough, a Commander and five officers of the British Navy along with the Civil Lord of the Admiralty, Earl Stanhope, were there that day also—to witness a bell being cast for a new battleship called *Kent*. One of the tuning rooms and an adjoining workshop, carpeted and bedecked with American, Belgian and British flags, were used as an auditorium and afterwards transformed into a restaurant where the visitors were entertained to tea. Exactly two weeks following this event in Croydon, the Riverside bourdon was deemed unfit, and there is some evidence that Cyril was as upset as a proper Englishman could be.

His parties, well covered by newspapers in England and abroad, functioned as advertisements for his big bell, and thus his firm. He had gone to the trouble, too, of having 2,000 postcards made of the bell. It would have been difficult to keep the failure a secret. One can guess that Cyril was embarrassed, but he was certainly angry. He issued one of perhaps only two protests he ever made to John D. Rockefeller, Jr., except when financially pressed. June 1st, after receiving the fateful cable from JDR saying his expert (F.C. Mayer) had rejected the low C, along with the low F, he cabled his objections right back, saying he was mailing a letter giving full details. These would include his feelings about JDR's "expert." Trying to soften his grievance, Cyril wrote, "We have been more than pleased to work with Mr. Mayer right through this great project, and appreciate his earnest endeavours to get the best possible results." Then, not holding back: *At the same time, I can assert confidently that no other living person but Mr. Mayer would have rejected these bells. I mean that he is forever trying for something hitherto unattained."*6 (My italics). The "wild fourth" was of course the problem. Cyril's full defense is instructive however futile in its effect on his client:

"For the low C the contract calls for the five principal tones to be correct with one another. I submit that this condition is fulfilled in the present bell. The contract specifies that the fourth above the strike is to be subdued as much as possible. Mr. Mayer cannot, I think, point to any existing bell of equivalent size that has a more or equally subdued fourth, and I believe he will admit that all the really big bells he has heard have much more prominent ones. That is my own experience. And no precedent or data is available in bells of this size for the fourth being more subdued. Mr. Mayer agreed when he was here that this big bell is the finest large bell that he has heard. This has also been the unanimous opinion of the thousands of visitors who have heard it, including many eminent musicians who have visited the works for the purpose. [Unknown to Cyril, Jef Denyn testified otherwise, having been hired by Mayer and paid forty dollars for the service]. The question revolves . . . round the 'upper fourth', which in order of sequence is the ninth note up the scale, counting the hum as the lowest and first. (There are nine tones that can be detected in bells of this size). The research work involved in manufacturing the four large bells has been of a most exacting nature, and the problems which confronted us in designing them made their production, with all consequent risks, *a matter of great anxiety* [My emphasis]. It should be borne in mind that in making these bells, something unparalleled in bell founding has been attempted, which removes them from ordinary commercial products into a category of highly experimental productions. Despite this the contract price was brought down to the rate of normal sized bells. In this connection I would point out that we were forced to reduce our original tender (for heavy work of this special and hazardous nature) by a large amount, in order to combat a rival bid [by Taylor]. Within limits of finance, health and ability, I concur with [Mr. Mayer's] aims, and realize that one's reputation is not damaged by aspiring to higher things."[7]

The bellfounder offered to make a special journey to New York to discuss the matter personally. He was not about to default on his Riverside contract by refusing to agree to new terms. Prior to sending his letter, in his cable he had already come around, offering a duplicate low C on Mayer's conditions—a loan of £5000 without interest for one year on security of the rejected bells—and a duplicate low F at his own expense. Completion of both bells he estimated would take seven months. Mayer, in writing to Rockefeller June 10, after having read Cyril's demurrers, was sympathetic and full of praise for the bellfounder's work, comparing him favorably to the Hemonys and even conceding, "The perfect bell does not exist."[8] But he was perfectly disingenuous when he said, "In my testing of bells made by Mr. Johnston I have been rather severe, in his mind, for I do not think more than a bell or two has ever been rejected by experts who have

91

examined current English-made bells of the best type." Mayer was in a good position to know, for on the two other G&J carillons he had served as advisor, both large ones—Ottawa's Parliament building Peace Tower, 53 bells, dedicated July 1, 1927; and Louvain's University Library, 48 bells, dedicated July 4, 1928—he had not required more than a bell or two each to be recast. With Rockefeller as donor however, Mayer was ready to spend his unlimited funds, or so they must have seemed to him, to experiment for perfection. Along with the low C and F, he made Cyril replace at least 28 ex-Park Avenue trebles for Riverside. Mayer had Rockefeller's confidence utterly. He held no doubt a special place in Rockefeller's heart from the beginning, in 1922, simply because he refused any pay or retainer fee for his work, only accepting travel expenses to test or investigate bells. Then too, he showed the most indefatigable zeal in leaving no bronze unturned to obtain the very best results, as he saw it, for the wealthy capitalist. A kind of trade-off seems to have been involved. If Mayer accepted no money personally, he must have felt he could spend lavishly for the sake of art. And he never forgot to flatter his chief as time passed. "I always feel like taking an occasional opportunity," Mayer wrote to JDR Jr. in 1930, "of expressing my great admiration for the scope and variety of your efforts to make the world better and living more inspiring. Your record is almost sufficient, single-handed, to refute the charges so frequently made abroad that America is materialistic and selfish."[9]

Bells of course have long been blessed or baptized by religious officials; they have performed in sacred observances associated with the church, as alarums or tocsins, as mediums of superstition in dispelling storms or other disturbance, and in rites of passage for the people. But the supersession of the materialism of bells by their historic sanctity didn't account entirely for the genesis of, say, the Riverside bourdon, perhaps arguably redeemed in any event by its insignia—the four beautiful archangels. In those heydays of American bigness, this bell emblematized the craving for size in one specialized department of possibilities. And Fritz Mayer, as he was called at West Point, a musician with a bent for technical detail, and the organist of an instrument he had famously built up to the unimaginable size of 14,195 pipes and 750 stop keys, was the man to make it happen. F.C. Mayer was West Point organist and choir master from 1911 to 1964. He died in 1973, aged 91. Over the Riverside bourdon, he seems to have been a man possessed.

During the rest of that June, 1928, and on through July, Cyril at Mayer's behest was trooping around Europe investigating other big bells said to have their fourth under control. A bell specialist, who has done frequency analyses of many bells, says the fourth which is often heard in such big bells is actually not present as a measurable frequency, but is a "virtual" pitch resulting from our ears being fooled by the combination of partial tones that are present.[10] If we wonder how coursing through Europe comparing big bells to his own struck Cyril, we could try to imagine how Stradivarius might have felt should a foreign buyer's advisor have sent him around Europe seeing if any violins by another maker were better than his! And adding insult to indignity, then made him participate, as Cyril would, in negotiations for having the sounds of his own and the other instruments turned into Movietone records that would be sent to the foreigner's homeland for comparative study. Not surprisingly, Cyril found the other bells worse or no better than his own. Anyway just one of them, the famed 7-ton "Salvator" in Malines, functioned like his Riverside bourdon, as the bass in a carillon. The others were single bells or parts of clock mechanisms. And only Cologne Cathedral's "St. Peter," installed in 1923, was close enough in weight, at 52,800 pounds, to bear a useful correspondence to Cyril's 20-tonner for Riverside. By the end of July, with the Movietone records made and investigative travels over for the time being, all correspondence mysteriously ceased between the donor, the advisor and the bellfounder. Throughout August and September, this blackout persisted. And August was the month, as mentioned above, that my mother became pregnant.

I have to believe that Cyril took off on a romantic escapade, submerging his troubles in an affair that had been in progress for a year but conducted until then in a rather desultory fashion. He had excellent lieutenants in his foundry to carry on his business, and he must have maintained close communications with them. He might even have been in and out. I'm not on evidential terms with his and my mother's movements just then. I know that at some point they were in Paris dancing at Ciro's, but that could have been at any time after June 1927—the month and year they met on a crossing from Southampton to Boston. By the time I got serious about interviewing my mother, in 1976, two years before she died, I was not an unknown author, and she was pretty certain I planned to embarrass her by writing about my father, her onetime paramour. I was never really able to properly interview her. Her undying position on her affair and its outcome—the shame and the mistake of it all—made her a most intimidating subject to the one most directly implicated, besides herself, in how things turned out. Unable to see her situation beyond its impact on her personally, my mother could never talk about what happened. Some education to the body politic could have helped, as it would help me in the late 1960s and early 70s.

Nonetheless I gleaned bits over the years. And in her last two years her fear of embarrassment was belied by certain disclosures she made—like the fact that Cyril had wanted to set her up in a flat in London; or that he saw me once when I was a baby and living with her in Worthing, a town on the Channel—indicating dim suspicions she must have had that the writer her child had become might have a more elevated mission than the mere debasement of her predicament. Who could vindicate her anyway, if not the victim of her secret? We had both left England *in the same boat* together. Once, asking me if I were not glad that she was my mother, I assured her I was, adding that inadvertently at least she had made it all very interesting. But where oh where was she exactly during August and September 1928? And what precisely was she thinking and feeling?

Curiously, except for the incontrovertible date of her pregnancy, my other parent, the one I never met, provides the best evidence I have for understanding the scrape they got into. My mother had one objective at that moment: my father. He on the other hand had his whole business, with worldwide interests—all-consuming and demanding—which during the course of 1928 overwhelmed him. For him, my mother was a consolatory dalliance. He may have cared a great deal about her, but she was not his objective. Over their liaison in its heightened dimension hung the shadow of the failed Riverside bourdon, swinging slowly, figuratively, fatefully, unprovidentially—a huge ego bust for the bellfounder. The solution to one emotional crisis can of course lead directly to another critical juncture. And that is what happened when Cyril's affair with my mother resulted in pregnancy. His curative diversion was over; he had to answer to my mother's interest in him and declare himself; he had to feel badly that a woman he cared about but with whom he saw no committed future was going to go ahead and carry his child anyway. If not, his abrupt departure from England October 10, on a lengthy "health tour," leaving behind a heavy workload, had a motive that is unaccounted for in my considerable documentation.

September 30th, Frederick Mayer wrote to Rockefeller saying he did not know just how Mr. Johnston's health and his proposed trip to California would complicate the upcoming demonstration in Croydon of a mechanism for swinging bells, but he trusted the G&J foreman could handle it. For months by then, Mayer had fancied having the five biggest Riverside bells capable of swinging electrically. It was one more technically challenging detail on the bellfounder's plate. And once he arrived in Los Angeles November 10, to stay at the Ambassador Hotel, Mayer lost no time getting in touch with him, wanting to meet him on December 5, in Chicago to discuss plans for the University of Chicago carillon. Mayer was not unsympathetic however. "I'm glad you are remaining longer in the west, and sincerely hope that the trip will be of great benefit to you." Or, "I am much distressed to hear that you are not so well. Do plan to stop off at the Mayo Bros. [Clinic], Rochester Minn., on your way east; they are great for removing ill-tuned harmonics."[11] What these "harmonics" were exactly, if not just a state of mind, remains uncertain. Cyril had taken the salubrious sea air for an entire month before arriving in L.A., boarding the Dollar Line's *President Monroe* in New York after coming in from England on the *Homeric,* to sail around through the Panama Canal and up the California coast. Upon arrival November 10, he told the *Los Angeles Times,* interviewing him off the ship, that he had come to southern California to study the history and tones of Spanish Mission bells.

"Health tour" was how Cyril described his trip, as reported by Britain's *Ringing World,* and in a cable he sent to the Archbishop of Canterbury, congratulating the Archbishop on his 50th wedding anniversary. Entraining to Chicago December 2, Cyril met Mayer as planned on the 5th, then moved on to the Hotel Ambassador in New York where he stayed more than a week, in part writing up his proposals for the Chicago carillon, before returning to England aboard the *Berengaria.*

Bourdon No. 2 was cast the following spring and declared unsatisfactory by Cyril himself in May, 1929, during the very week I was born. In February, 1930, after the third failed effort, bourdon No. 1 was redeemed; in August Cyril got engaged, and in November at age 46 he was married for the first time, to an Englishwoman. The same age differential existed between them as between Cyril and my mother: seventeen years.

Chapter VIII

NINETEEN EIGHTY-FOUR

I was told if I did marry Cyril Johnston, I would marry a bellfoundry
—Mary Evelyn Johnston

May 16, 1984, on the phone with my half-brother Arthur in London, an augural moment occurred when Arthur told me his mother—Mary Evelyn Johnston (called Mollie)—had said there was "not necessarily proof"—by which she had meant of my birth as her late husband's daughter. *Proof*!—I had never thought of it before. My mother's word had always seemed confirmation enough. And the fictional status she created, coupled with her colossal lie, killing off a man who was really alive, could seem unconvincing evidence that she was covering for yet another story. Then too, the truth she told, that the father she chose for me was a bellfounder, seems altogether believable. Practically nobody knows what a bellfounder is, and she would not have known herself until she met one. Anyway Arthur's mother, I hasten to add, also told him she knew of me, that Cyril had told her about me—"once."

Mary E. Johnston on her mother's side claimed ancestry through the Evelyns (including famed diarist John Evelyn) to Edward III and John of Gaunt. Both her children were given Evelyn as one of their middle names. I had been pressing Arthur to find out if in fact she knew of my existence. So by "proof" his mother must have been pointing beyond mere existence to the question of my legal rights. What did I want, and could I "prove" my identity to get it. The 1969 Act of Parliament by which all children (i.e. born in or out of wedlock) were accorded rights of inheritance, was not retroactive. So along property or monetary lines, Arthur's mother had nothing to worry about. Less materially speaking, of course she did. Having undertaken the traditional role of torchbearer for her husband's renown in the world of bells and beyond, she was duty-bound to protect his honor and reputation. Since Arthur had told her I was a writer, and was actually planning a book about the man whose memory she had until now irreproachably preserved, she would feel threatened indeed. And I had come to England just then to attend a public event for which she was responsible and that I could be viewed as crashing. Her son, in trying to discourage me from going, would describe the event to me in virtually exclusive family terms. He was especially concerned for his mother. Nineteen eighty-four, the centenary year of Cyril's birth, had provided a special opportunity for Mollie Johnston, then 83 and still hale, to star as devoted widow. She had organized a service at Croydon Parish Church May 5th at which the Speaker of the House of Commons, Bernard Weatherill, would deliver an appreciation. She had been in touch with a number of church dignitaries and many bellmasters around the world, the latter to request peals or carillon concerts in Cyril's memory.

Arriving in England May 4th, the day before the service, I had called Arthur to inform him of my plan to be in Croydon for the program. "How inopportune" were his first words. Then, organizing himself, he told me in high Englishese that he didn't want me to go. "This is very much a Mollie, Arthur and Rosemary [his sister] event," he explained without compunction. And he wondered how I had found out about it. He was brutal, but I was crossing an entrenched line. For six years until that moment we had been meeting "secretly" in hotels and restaurants for tea or lunch. Now I was proposing to contaminate his inviolate family space. And he could imagine my approaching one or another family member to try to introduce myself. Arthur felt like he was losing control. I was not unsympathetic, but determined to go nonetheless. My life was my book, and 1984 had turned out to be the year, or so I thought, for making headway toward writing it. This eventuality, purely coincidental with Cyril's centenary year, had been brought about by my having completed two volumes projected to be part of a trilogy, the third one on my father. Before leaving New York May 4th, James Lawson, the carillonneur who succeeded Kamiel Lefévere at Riverside Church and a man who knew Mollie Johnston and had attended Cyril's funeral in Croydon in 1950, had said to me, "The centenary could be wonderful material for your book." Jim was fully apprised of my story, and had become a collusive friend, even gratuitously copying letters for me that he received from Mollie Johnston.[1] When Arthur asked me how I knew about the centenary, I used Lawson's name as informant and told him that I was regretfully forgoing Lawson's commemorative concert in New York in order to be in Croydon. Here Arthur might have sighed or groaned inaudibly. My book, which he knew all about, remained something of an abstraction; the upcoming centenary was all too immediate and concrete. As things were left, understanding that I wouldn't be deterred from going, his voice trailed off while murmuring, "If you just don't speak to me or my family . . . "

Had Arthur known about my escort, he might have exhaled with some relief. The man I had asked to accompany me that day to Croydon—Stephen Trombley, an American expat living in London—was a surprise to *me*. I had not expected a "bodyguard" whose rather massive frame would be interposed like a moving Romanesque pillar between the family and me. Nor an American Anglified to such an extent that he viewed my venture as a potential assault on the remains of the empire. "I don't think you should do any guerilla warfare," said Stephen commandingly as we drove from London to Croydon in his car. Not noticing I suppose that my "guerilla" outfit was a conservative navy blue wool coat and that my hair though not coifed was perfectly arranged and my face garnished discreetly with makeup. We knew each other essentially through two books: one I had written, the recently published first volume of my imagined trilogy; the other his, on Virginia Woolf, titled *All That Summer She Was Mad,* a treatise on Woolf's four doctors. I had not read the book, but the catchy title alone might have warned me. Still, though all I had wanted on this occasion was a conspiratorial companion, my zealous chaperon did nothing worse than simply punctuate the resolve I already had to stay clear of the family, and try to observe them from afar. And he saved me from what might easily have been the mistake of attending the tea after the service.

Croydon Parish Church, or St. John's, of medieval origin, had 13 bells cast by G&J in 1936; they were clamoring appropriately as family and friends converged on the west doors, rung by the Surrey Association of Change-Ringers. With his 1936 installation, Cyril Johnston had vanished a Taylor ring of eight consecrated in 1867 following a fire that had destroyed much of the church. The Taylor bells had replaced a ring of eight by Whitechapel, dated 1738. St. John's had been the Johnston family church since Cyril's father took up residence in Croydon in the late 1870s. Arthur A. Johnston in a status move had abandoned his Baptist origins to join the Church of England. (His son Cyril's most important client, John D Rockefeller Jr., curiously never left the Baptists to enlist in the more prestigious American equivalency of the Church of England, the High Episcopalians). One of the 1936 G&J bells is dedicated to the memory A.A. Johnston, a gift from his widow and son. Hanging in the threshold to the nave of St. John's is a plaque commemorating Cyril, reading,

IN LOVING MEMORY OF/
CYRIL FREDERICK JOHNSTON/
FRIEND AND BENEFACTOR OF/
THIS CHURCH WHO DEVOTED HIS LIFE/

TO THE DEVELOPMENT OF THE ART OF/
BELLFOUNDING AND BELL TUNING/
DIED 30TH MARCH 1950

We sat in the last row of pews, and Stephen had us duck out during the last song. As we stood hesitatingly under the tower, he said we shouldn't go to the tea—it would be impossible not to talk to someone there. So my centenary expedition was a success. Nobody knew I was there, and I could say I went.

Afterwards, there was an unexpected collateral benefit. On May 9th, Cyril's actual birth date, having a customary lunch with Arthur, he was more forthcoming than usual—no doubt from gratitude over my prostrated profile May 5th. In the course of the Croydon service he had caught a glimpse of me, I know, because once when we were in a mutual sightline, I noticed him wheeling away exaggeratedly. May 9th we started off in comfortable chairs in the St. Ermine's Hotel lobby, went from there to a small restaurant with reproduction Breughels place mats and ended up in a small park somewhere, standing in a rainfall under umbrellas. Arthur saw me as being "in the unhappy position of an outsider to the family." In answer, I drew a specious parallel, "But you are outside my [American] family"—an oblique way of saying I didn't agree with his word "unhappy." Outsider yes, but as a birth position, the operative word should be "challenging." If presumed unalterable, unhappiness could be an expected chronic emotion. But even when my sweepingly supposed unfavorable birth seemed fixed, I was never a candidate for any misery over it. This may be because my mother protected me for so long from the truth—and all during those so-called formative years. Then once I was fully briefed, by age 25, the distractions of my studies and ambitions were functionally occlusive. Moreover, the marital conventions under which my mother had suffered remained something of a mystery to me. Further along, when my life became difficult (e.g. with the conflict of marriage/motherhood and career), inevitably my background became more visible to me; and by then I had read enough literature to place my story in historic mythological settings.[2] Now I was on track to view my origins as galvanizing. Even further along, in context of the women's movement, I had a moment of glory when so many women were leaving their husbands and condemning the fathers (as executors of patriarchy) and it appeared that my birth, far from having been a serious handicap, had actually been ideal! The moment passed of course, but not the residually exciting sense that my history had a compelling future. Or that "discovery," as the law expresses its intent, could point the way ahead. And here was Arthur Johnston in England, a perfect embodiment of the challenges posed in a redefined birth. He once told me he grew up loving all things Arthurian. I doubt that would have included King Arthur's dubious paternity, to me this legendary figure's most interesting attribute. Any comments my half-brother made on my origins— like his "unhappy outsider" idea— seemed especially serviceable. (His instrumentality, fortunate or not, was the natural outcome of my intrusion and his resistance). One great favor he did me was never to question, even from the first moment, that I was his father's biological daughter. Occasional, very occasional remarks he made about Cyril, I caught like raindrops in a desert.

If Arthur brought his father up, it was not to provide me with any useful information but rather to try to verify an assumed position, as much cultural as personal. "Would your mother and Cyril not have made a good match?" he had asked me three years earlier. My answer, "Definitely not," pronounced so instantly and emphatically, could have indicated to him that I had given the subject a good deal of thought. Arthur might have asked, "Oh really, why?" or something like that, invoking a real discussion; but he let it go, and I didn't try to elaborate. This was fairly typical of our encounters—a study in mono-phraseology. On May 9th, 1984, in answer to Arthur's renewed pursuit of the outsider theme in saying, "Blood is not necessarily thicker than water," I was moved to bring the subject up again. "My mother," I said, "was the wrong woman for Cyril."—Code for trying to tell him that in my opinion things had turned out for the best; also hopefully to imply that I didn't need his family to complete myself. And again,

Arthur let the remark go. The thing is had he really heard me, that is, entertained any truth in what I said, his underlying conviction—that I wished for a different outcome: *for my mother to have married Cyril so that I could have had Cyril too*—would have been imperiled. A received cultural understanding like this is not easily overturned. And my upsurge of interest in his mother at this point—not only wanting Arthur to find out if she knew about me, but to meet her as well—only reinforced his view. A view that, one way or another, in the long run was simply not to matter. Only my book truly mattered. My impossible approach to Arthur's mother just then was on its behalf. I had a relationship to it that was animate and twin-like. We consumed each other. In 1984 its long gestation seemed to be drawing toward a fruitful conclusion. But my desire, it turned out, was way ahead of certain realities. The carillon instrument alone for instance awaited my scholarly attention. That year in June, in between trips to England, I went to the North American Guild Congress for the first time, meeting members who were to become helpers in my researches and supporters in my cause.

The 1984 Congress was ideal for a maiden attendance since it took place on the site of a Gillett & Johnston carillon. On the beautiful campus of the University of Wisconsin in Madison, a few hundred yards from the shores of Lake Mendota, on a little knoll stands an 85-foot high campanile tower. Its cornerstone was laid in 1934. The knoll is called Blackhawk after Chief Blackhawk who crossed it in 1832, leading a small band of Sauk Indians as they retreated before an army of state militia and federal soldiers. A belfry within the campanile, a minimalist structure made of Madison sandstone, holds the remains of a G&J carillon installed 1936–37. I say "remains" because Cyril's original 30 bells were compromised beginning in 1963 when the French founder Paccard (in existence before 1796), added 27 bells, replacing six of the smallest G&Js. Then in 1972, the Dutch firm Eijsbouts (pron. Icebouts) replaced the 27 Paccards and added five bells in the bass range. The Continental founders, who had lost out in the great carillon reformation, had by now long caught up with the

English and the five-tone method of tuning, proudly reclaiming their heritage in the direct line of the instrument's 15th century origins. The Madison Wisconsin carillon, with donorship of the University classes of 1917–1926, like so many that started off small and have gradually accreted by fiat of new donors or carillonneurs in collusion with bellfounders, had become a medium-sized monster, here 56 bells, and not necessarily the better for it. One bellspert I know, Richard P. Strauss, holds the unpopular view that bigger is no guarantee of better. He says, "It's okay to destroy the musical integrity of a two and a half octave instrument [i.e. 23 bells, the required number for a carillon] to make it bigger. Yes, you can add a fish to a bicycle, but why?" He has never cared for additions by a non-original founder. "In the case of treble extensions," says Strauss, "it usually sounds like two separate instruments, one sitting on top of the other. It's like putting a VW Beetle fender on a Rolls Royce."[3] A carillon reconstruction specialist Peter Hurd feels that the addition of any Continental bells to an English instrument is a travesty, that the tuning and tonal concepts and weights and profiles are completely different. Bellfounders themselves would hardly find these outlooks agreeable. Alan Berry, while still General Manager of the Taylor foundry in Loughborough UK, once told me, "Bellfounders will remove everything they can until the bells are so big, it would be extremely costly to get them out." The carillonneurs tend naturally to defend the instruments they play no matter what. Lyle Anderson, at this writing the musician of the Madison Wisconsin carillon, says that both augmentations, by Paccard and Eijsbouts, were done with very careful attention to the sound of the original G&J instrument. And that the many visiting carillonneurs who have played it during his tenure have always given it fine reviews. In 1984, I would not have known the difference myself. Nor did I test my claustrophobic limits by trying to ascend the tower. I was paying foremost attention to Guild members and their opinion of me as the daughter of the bellfounder.

A startling incident at the Congress banquet, which always caps these events, gave me a disconcerting but useful idea of what

I thought myself of my status as the bellfounder's daughter. John Harvey, a white-haired gentleman and carillonneur at Madison since 1960, was now retiring, so his banquet doubled as a farewell dinner. Several distinguished guests sat with him at a long elevated table, one of them a daughter-in-law of William Gorham Rice, the carillon enthusiast from Albany widely credited with inspiring North American donors to import the instrument in the 1920s. A late edition of his seminal book, *Carillon Music and Singing Towers of the Old World and the New,* was given away as a prize when a raffle was held. An Irish carillonneur, Adrian Patrick Gebruers, was introduced as a "nut on the *Titanic* and the *Lusitania,*" and a man whose father had saved some people from the torpedoed *Lusitania.* An elderly man called Norris ("Curly") Wentworth had, according to Harvey, promised him that he wouldn't die before this Congress. Norris had been the head of the committee that planned the Madison campanile construction along with the original Gillett & Johnston installation. When Harvey introduced him, he provided a memory of Cyril Johnston, describing him as a "dramatic expressive Englishman— a big man."

I was sitting at one of the round banquet tables wedged between two Guild heavies: James Lawson and Wylie Crawford, the carillonneurs of Riverside Church and the University of Chicago, Cyril Johnston's notoriously mastodonic carillons, each of over 70 bells. If I saw myself as sitting in for the bellfounder, our threesome could appear somehow testicular. Bells themselves, I'm sure it escapes nobody, have their curiously phallic properties, their bronze skirt shapes providing shelter for their percussive noisemakers—the inner hanging iron or steel clappers. (The largest of the three clappers of the Riverside bourdon, each with a separate purpose, weighs a thousand pounds).[4] My partner Ingrid who had accompanied me to the Congress, and helped to uncover carillon archives at the University library, was also at the table. Margo Halsted, another longtime Guild member at our table, told me it had been rumored for some time that Cyril Johnston had an American daughter, and that she was at large somewhere. So here I was. "You're the daughter of a very famous man," said Margo, prompting Wylie Crawford to inform her that I had some fame on my own account. Suddenly I heard my name. John Harvey was introducing me, "We have with us the daughter of the man who made these [Madison] bells, and she's a writer." I stood up as required. Then just as I was sitting back down, I heard, "We're happy to have you whether you're Cyril Johnston's daughter or not." I dropped my jaw and opened my hands, almost falling off my chair. I imagined hearing a collective gasp. Wylie leaned toward me, hastening to assure me that Harvey had meant only that I would be welcome whether I was the bellfounder's daughter or not. Yes of course. It's a known social cliché. But in this instance it was just an incredible—I have no doubt unintentional—double entendre. Who of the present company, numbering no more than a hundred and ten, knew in any case what my filial status was exactly? Only Jim Lawson, so far as I was aware, had precise knowledge of it.

My confusion and dismay over the remark would come to seem educationally propitious. Though our Congress host had made it in innocence, I felt outed, exposed, by its inescapable hidden reference. And I wasn't prepared to take that on, to go public with a society so intimately associated with Cyril Johnston's work. If my inexpectancy reflected my readiness at that time to write this book, I can see how lucky I was that the project became deferred. Sixteen years later, after a long interim pursuing a career as critic of art and books, standing before the Guild of Carillonneurs of North America at their 2000 Congress at the Mercersburg Academy in Mercersburg, Pennsylvania giving a slide-talk on the life and work of Cyril Johnston, I rather suavely as I thought later, outed myself. A context had been created—a situation of my own making, thanks to an invitation of the Mercersburg Congress host. By then anyway it was hardly news. I was telling them something they already knew, or that had been well rumored. As for nineteen-eighty four, despite its representing a stoppage over the book, the year continued to be amazing for its revelations and findings.

Back in England in September and October, the way things would go, I seemed armed with a mission occasioned by two remarks: the confounding entendre in Wisconsin, and Arthur's challenging words earlier in the year, quoting his mother as saying there was "not necessarily proof," i.e. of paternity. For a while, I imagined digging up Cyril's bones at his Croydon gravesite to obtain a DNA match. But with the inexplicably new thought of applying for a copy of Cyril's will at Somerset House, my path toward material grounds became easier. In May I had made friends with a woman who kept the B&B where I stayed in Beverley, a lovely town in Yorkshire, close to the North Sea and south by 40 miles or so from Scarborough. I was on a genealogical tear then. It was in Beverley in 1833 that Cyril's grandfather Robert Johnston had started up a small Baptist ministry and a family of seven children. Mrs. Berna Moody, the B&B keeper, was an experienced ancestral researcher, and she liked my story. Returning to her B&B in September, I brought Cyril's will with me to show her. Drawn up in 1938, it had a mysterious clause in it, which Mrs. Moody interpreted with dispatch as pertaining indirectly to my mother and me. It comes on the first page at the end of the second paragraph in which Cyril bequeathed things like garden effects, plate, linen, china, glass and books to his wife "absolutely free of duty," along with the sum of one thousand six hundred pounds to be paid to her immediately after his death. Of this sum, Cyril designated one hundred pounds for his wife's immediate needs. Then the clincher: "As to FIVE HUNDRED pounds of this legacy I ask my wife (in the full knowledge that she will carry out my wishes as far as practicable but without placing any legal obligation upon her) to deal with this sum in the manner I have already indicated to her." The moment Mrs. Moody read this and said it had to be a directive concerning my mother, the number five hundred lit up in my brain like flashing neon. I remembered it vividly. If my mother was disturbed enough when Cyril died in 1950 to send me his obituary, thus informing me of the prodigious lie she had invented over his actual time on earth, she was apparently upset enough about the news of this money to tell me that too. She thought it a paltry sum, I guess for all her trouble during these years supporting a child Cyril had fathered (whether he had wanted it or not), and for living as a "hell hath no fury" woman; and she was having a solicitor in London look into it.

Now lo these thirty-four years later, I was looking into it too, if for different reasons. Returning to London from Beverley, I found the surname of one of Cyril's Trustees, Francis Clifton Hilbery, still listed in the phone directory, and under the same address: Henry Hilbery & Sons, Solicitors, 9 Grays Inn Sq., WC1. When I called, a Mr. Wate answered the phone and said that Francis was long dead and his son Henry retired. I told him I was a daughter of Cyril Johnston, who had been a client of Mr. Hilbery's. Could he tell me if any Trust papers had survived? Mr. Wate said he would look around and I should call him back in a couple of days. When I did, he said yes there were papers; did I want to come in and look at them? It was October 16th. At the Hilbery offices at Grays Inn Sq., I found a very gimpy and friendly secretary who ushered me into a conference room. On a long glossy table sat a tall, maybe three-foot high bundle of papers that had been inert so long that the cord binding it had indented and discolored the papers wherever the pressure was greatest. The secretary said I could look at the papers there or take them with me, adding that the firm didn't want them any more. Forthwith I staggered under the weight and size of the bundle out to the street, and fell into a taxi for the flat on Gt. Titchfield Street where I was staying. Spending the rest of the day vetting the papers, I struck gold—my mother's name listed three times next to that sum of five hundred pounds specified in Cyril's will. A typewritten Trust entry August 21st says, "Writing Mrs. O. Johnston of New York enclosing extract from Will and that we understood Mrs. M. E. Johnston intended to send her £500." Another entry August 25th, this one handwritten, reads, "500 pounds sent to Mrs. O. Johnston in U.S.A."

This was wonderful, although of course it did nothing for me—it would have no legal consequence—except to confer a measure of personal satisfaction. And it turned out to make a good story. Friends and family thought I made a great haul that day. My half-brother Arthur found my "proof" quite beneath his interest. He might even have learned of the transaction in 1950 between his mother and mine, the two widows! We were having lunch, October 17, at Bertorelli's on Charlotte Street. Now that his mother knew that he knew me, and her hostility was clear to him, he brought her shadow with him, and the privacy and potentiality that had existed between us were gone. He waved off my Trust paper extracts as irrelevant, his only comment being to wonder what the public would think if they knew how easy it was to obtain wills, implying that Cyril's will (the source of my proof) was none of my business. He said his mother was not happy that I had written to carillonneurs requesting that they observe Cyril's centenary. I might have pointed out that the musicians I had contacted were all in America, and added that Cyril's bells in America were exports to my own country. They kind of belonged to me. But I understood Arthur's mother's problem. And Arthur was quick to laugh when I quoted from two letters I got back, one asking me if "Mollie" was my mother, the other if Cyril was my grandfather. Familiar questions from Arthur came up. Did I resent my mother? Was I bitter? How did I feel about what Cyril had done?—with none of my answers fitting Arthur's preconceptions. No, I never resented my mother, no, I had never been bitter; as for Cyril, I never thought he had done anything wrong. My inferences were unfair perhaps, since I would never be able to explain to Arthur how I had turned my ignoble situation on its head. His hero King Arthur is a case study in the kind of historic disadvantage I had inherited. Arthur himself by entertaining these meetings with me had become a vital, if unwitting, party to a venerable questing tradition.

I had a lot of help in nineteen eighty-four. As unexpected as the Trust papers was another stash, this one turning up in Croydon. I had gone to visit Stephen Coombes, owner and manager of the remains of the Gillett & Johnston foundry. After Cyril's death in 1950, Stephen's father Cyril Coombes bought the clock side of the industry, and retained the G&J name. The bells died with the bellfounder, with orders and equipment absorbed during the 1950s by Taylor and Whitechapel. Stephen, boyishly disarming in his late thirties, and eager to please, produced a great number of photographs from boxes and file cabinets that he offered to let me take home. The pictures, of Cyril and his guests, his workers, his bells and clocks at the foundry, taken largely during the 1920s—a number of them from the illuminated visit of King George and Queen Mary to the works in 1925—would form the base of an extravagant personal collection. In May 1984, over another set of photographs I was not so lucky. But they would become at least the basis for understanding that when I got home I should buy a good camera. Tacked to movable screens on a broad landing at the top of the main Croydon Library staircase, they formed a centennial exhibition of family photos, portraits of Cyril, and a history of G&J, put together by Mollie Johnston. It would have been so easy to swipe them. But who would have taken them if not someone "calling herself Johnston," as Mrs. Johnston had described her son's American half-sister—a woman at that very moment known to be lurking around, trespassing, on British property. The pictures were very good, and the least I could have done was to have had a professional photographer take pictures of them. But this involved going to a lot of expense and trouble, and I ended up shooting them myself, with a pathetic sure-shot camera called Ricoh. The best computer photoshop program in the world would not be able to do anything with my results. Once home, I went with due haste to a Nikon store to buy an FE2 with flash attachment and a Vivitar zoom lens.

Early in 1984 I had had a dream that later seemed to foretell my immediate future in bells. There's a saying on Wall Street that goes, "Buy on cannons, sell on bells." Bells in wartime have of course traditionally been seized and melted down to make cannons. I have no particular interest in cannons or their counterparts, but I was about to sell on bells. In my dream I had myself in a holding pattern in an airplane that was inside a bell. Within the dream I told someone I was having this dream about being in a plane in a holding pattern inside a bell.

Chapter IX

COVENTRY

Mr. Johnston . . . is here today to witness the supreme triumph of his art
—The Chronicle of Quebec, June 2, 1927

*A bellfounder's calling in these days would seem to require many and
increasing qualifications. He must be versed in engineering, music,
bellringing, business methods, organization, finding his way by road
to a little village that is not on the map—and now, I am told,
in ecclesiastical law as well.*
—Cyril F. Johnston

May 5, 2002, I was approaching the tower and steeple of the
ruins of St. Michael's Cathedral in Coventry with Ingrid
when a great ruckus suddenly filled the air. A band of change-
ringers was making a noise I had never heard before. I knew
change-ringing well enough, but nothing like this. Notes were tum-
bling clamantly over each other, wildly, wantonly, swallowing you
up—a most stupendous ear-rending cacophony. A certain
monotony or predictability, a thinness even, about change-ringing

had been my prejudiced experience, with the tenor bell all too obviously punctuating or anchoring a sequence of notes. Now I knew change-ringing could produce one of the world's grand sounds. Location of tower, height of belfry, number of bells, the quality of their make, the skill of the band, are obvious factors in determining outcomes. And Coventry that day clearly had it all. A ring of twelve, the maximum convenient for rings, is ensconced together with two semitones in this tower, the spire of which rises 295 feet, the third highest in England. The west tower cum spire—only feature of St. Michael's Cathedral left fully intact after the infamous German firebombing of Coventry November 14, 1940—stands like a lone god-like sentinel, overlooking its impressive carcass of low, decimated walls and at its eastern end the surviving polygonal apse with tall arched open-to-the-air windows, their delicate stone tracery left preserved. Within the semicircular apse structure, a cross fashioned from charred beams that fell in the November, 1940, carnage stands on a reconstructed altar. Perpendicular to the ruins on the north, sprouting from its side and joined by porch, is the enormous hulking towerless modern cathedral conceived in the wake of the disaster and dedicated in 1962—a monumental phoenix risen from its ashes. A cross in the altar of the new cathedral was created from long nails found in the ruins. A large pink stone brought from Bethlehem was made into a baptismal font. It is said that people who come to these ruins are deeply moved. I became one of them when I visited the place in the nineteen seventies. Returning home, I couldn't stop talking about it.

The bells were cast, or rather recast, between February and April, 1927, in a maze of controversy. They belong to the conflict that was raging in that decade between English bell conservationists and Simpsonite founders and enthusiasts. Cyril Johnston, caught in the middle of these forces over at least three particularly nasty situations, including Coventry, seemed to relish the fight. Embattled at home, it could have been a relief for him to embark for the United States where he was hailed unequivocally as an innovator and a man of parts. On June 4th, less than two months after the St. Michael's dedication in Coventry April 16, he sailed from Southampton for New York for something of a triumphal tour. A number of newspapers noted his departure from England and/or his arrival in New York. Canadian papers were especially interested in his movements because he was due to be in Ottawa July 1st, Dominion Day, when 53 Gillett & Johnston bells installed in Ottawa's stunning new Peace Tower—centerpiece of the reconstructed Parliament buildings destroyed by fire in 1916—would ring out for the first time. It was Cyril's biggest carillon, and the largest anywhere to that date, slightly heavier than its sister, the 53-bell carillon made for the Park Avenue Baptist Church's flawed situation in New York, dedicated a year and a half earlier. And the Ottawa instrument would signalize a spectacular three-day celebration marking Canada's Diamond Jubilee, the sixtieth anniversary of the Canadian Confederation.

Before arriving in Ottawa, Cyril had visited Detroit, and attended the dedication June 17 of his 35-bell carillon for the Cleveland Tower at Princeton University. After Ottawa, he went to Toronto to see about an upcoming installation of a small carillon, 23 bells, at the Soldiers' Tower of the University of Toronto. Today, with its later additions by the Dutch founder Petit & Fritsen, this carillon consists of 51 bells. There are so few 23-bell carillons still intact in North America. They've become an almost extinct species—like Britain's pintsized funmobile the convertible MGB—and they are now seldom made. Those that are left are like precious scattered museum pieces. Any instrument under forty or so bells became vulnerable to corruption. Even the Riverside Church's 72 became 74 in 1955 when van Bergen of Holland, in what remains the carillon world's premier scandal, was permitted to melt down 56 G&Js, recast them and add two more for symbolic stature [See Chapter XIII]. The 53 at Ottawa, thanks to Gordon Slater the present Peace Tower carillonneur, have remained untouched. Slater says he has turned away constant approaches by founders to replace the bells or enlarge the carillon. Cyril Johnston would roll over I'm sure if he knew what has happened to some of his instruments.

I found 12 G&J bells, an octave's worth, in a remote Elysian corner of New York's Green Mountains near the Vermont border. Originally from a 36-bell Stamford, Connecticut carillon dedicated in 1947, and later expanded to 56 bells by a French founder, the twelve I saw in the Green Mountains had migrated mysteriously in 1977 to this foothill community called New Skete, a Russian Orthodox monastery of eight monks and a dozen nuns.1 Here the bells became part of a trezvon, a Russian type of ring, hanging in a charming little wooden, three-tiered, peaked Ukrainian-style belltower, and keeping company with four small Meneely bells and a bigger one from a French Roman Catholic Church in Hudson Falls. (Russian Orthodox missionaries first brought bells and their distinctive trezvon to America in the 18th century). The bells are hung dead like a chime or carillon, but rung by ropes knotted around the clappers and pulled at ground level by two or three ringers—a primitive system compared to either change-ringing or chime playing. In June of 1927, the carillon instrument, only five years old in North America, not surprisingly was still in a pristine state. No carillon bells were as yet under removal or dispersion or additive disarrangement. And the media was excited and intrigued by this new musical phenomenon. Of Cyril's upcoming appearance in Ottawa, the June 2nd issue of *The Chronicle of Quebec* declared, "Mr. Johnston . . . is here [in North America] today to witness the supreme triumph of his art."

The *Star of Toronto,* which headlined its coverage on July 4, VAST AUDIENCE SPELLBOUND BY CARILLON'S GOLDEN TONE, asked Cyril his opinion of the tremendous crowd that swarmed over Parliament Hill to hear the first concert, played by Kamiel Lefévere (by then a veteran inaugurator). "I think," he said, "it is the greatest carillon crowd ever gathered . . . " He also thought the location of the carillon could not be equaled anywhere, quoting "anywhere" figures: "There are 160 carillons in Europe, of which 40 are in northern France and 120 in Belgium and Holland." The *Globe* of Ottawa, with its headline, ORGAN IN THE SKY, reported that "Mr. Johnston stood at the foot of the campanile for the entire recital and was highly delighted." He was far more delighted I'm sure than when he stood freezing one mid-winter evening in a doorway in Manhattan listening to Anton Brees play an instrument dishearteningly opposed by its neighborhood's captive audience. The open setting of Ottawa's Peace Tower—standing nearly at the edge of a perpendicular cliff, commanding magnificent views over the Ottawa River and the Gatineau Hills extending for miles in each direction—was in fact compared to that of Park Avenue in New York, where the bells were imagined as "revolting against the riot of New York that has a strangle hold on earth, air and water."[2] Surrounding the Parliament buildings were gardens, lawns and terraces providing, it was said, a perfect auditorium. The belfry was at an ideal height of 180 feet, in a tower rising 280.

At the stroke of noon on the first day of Jubilee celebrations, uniformed RCAF trumpeters perched high on the battlements of the Peace Tower blasted a fanfare; the 10-ton bourdon of the carillon sounded the hour; massed choirs sang the national anthem, "O Canada"; and Prime Minister W.L. Mackenzie King, a champion of the carillon when the question of having one or not was under debate in Parliament, made a speech. One carillon bell bears the inscription: "Cast in the presence of the Rt. Hon. W.L. Mackenzie King, C.M.G., M.P., Prime Minister of Canada, November 19, 1926." By evening, a chain of beacons and bonfires and electrical illuminations chased the sunset across the continent in a fiery path 3,500 miles long. On the second day of celebrations Charles Lindbergh in his Spirit of St. Louis led a squadron of 12 U.S. Air Force planes in circling the Peace Tower, then flew south seven miles to a makeshift landing field where spectators had gathered to idolize the flier. One of the U.S. airmen was killed with his plane in a freak accident, causing Kamiel Lefévere to alter one of his carillon dedicatory recitals to include Chopin's *Funeral March*. One month earlier Cyril had seen Lindbergh in Croydon. He told Toronto's *Globe* that he had been within five yards of Lindbergh's plane when it alighted at Croydon airport, not long after the flier had touched down in Paris May 21st, where cheering thousands greeted him at the end of his solo nonstop trailblazing flight from New York. The Lindbergh connection could have resonated with Cyril, whose own cross-Atlantic journeys had a pioneering air about them. Back home in England, he was not so much introducing the wondrously new, as trying to overthrow the sentimentally established.

"Mr. Johnston," the *Ringing World* reported in its September 30, 1927, edition, "freshly home from the opening of the great Ottawa carillon and a successful business tour in the United States, made a speech referring to the recent happenings in the Consistory Court, causing much laughter . . . " A Consistory Court, an ecclesiastical sort of council or tribunal, was held on June 9, 1927 over a ring of six dating from 1729 at the Ickleton Parish Church in Cambridgeshire. The Chancellor of the Diocese of Ely was very upset that the Ickleton Vicar and churchwardens had allowed Gillett & Johnston to remove the six old bells without official permission. SPAB, the Society for the Protection of Ancient Buildings, became indirectly involved. It had all started in 1926 when the tenor bell cracked while being rung. It was decided to have it recast, and all the bells rehung in a new frame. A fund was started, and permission, or a "faculty" as it is called, was obtained in January, 1927. The trouble began after the six were removed to the G&J foundry where another bell was discovered to be cracked. Cyril Johnston then advised recasting the whole ring, and adding two more bells, saying he could arrange to give them a much better peal. The Vicar and churchwardens found this agreeable, but at the Consistory Court hearing in June where the Vicar applied to have the faculty amended to allow for the new expanded scheme, it came to light that the bells had already been recast. The Chancellor of the diocese was incensed, and refused to grant a confirmatory faculty, threatening dire consequences to the Vicar and churchwardens. But now the money had been spent and the tower at Ickleton was empty. Eight new Simpson-tuned bells with beautiful modern fittings, a lovely steel frame, and scrumptious ball bearings as one publication described Cyril's renovations, awaited the Ickletonians! What was the Chancellor to do—except issue various censures. He suspended the churchwardens, reported the Vicar to the Bishop, threatened the bellfounder with ostracism in the diocese, and meaninglessly refused the faculty.

The new ring was dedicated August 25, 1927. A month later at a ringers meeting at Ickleton, Cyril presented a speech, the one where he caused "much laughter," displaying, as one contemporary writer has put it, "a somewhat cavalier attitude to the legalities of the situation."[3] At the time, the *Ringing World,* always a champion of Cyril Johnston, who liberally advertised his firm in the magazine, was quite sympathetic. "The censure of the bellfounder is we think totally undeserved. It is not [the bellfounder's] business to apply for the faculty nor their responsibility to have one obtained before they begin the work entrusted to them. They merely carry out the instructions given them. *The position of the Chancellor is a threat to the whole progress of bell restoration and to the initiative of bellfounders.*"[4] [My emphasis] In his speech, Cyril celebrated the new installation with a few gentle ironies: He understood "the Vicar was a bad man, the churchwardens were not nice to know, and the bellfounders were not to be trusted in any tower in the diocese (laughter)." Ickleton's reply, he concluded, "was the best answer that could have been given. They added two treble bells, and the Vicar and churchwardens refused to retire (applause)."[5]

Two years later, Cyril made another large gathering of ringers laugh at the expense of church authorities. The occasion was the opening of a recast ring of eight at St. James's Church in the Clerkenwell borough of London. When St. James was built in 1788–92, replacing an old parish church dating from about 1100, a ring of eight from Whitechapel was installed. In 1925, with aging bells and appurtenances, and renovations generally in the air, a story similar to Ickleton's began to develop. Called in to inspect St. James's bells, Gillett & Johnston gave an estimate of £187 for repairs. The church felt it had insufficient funds, but with the matter reopened in 1928 and a new estimate of £180, the Vicar allowed the bells to be removed. That was in August. In September G&J, with St. James's bells in hand, now suggested recasting them. The firm's selling point was of course the new five-tone-harmonic or Simpson principle of tuning, the advantages of which they outlined in a letter. A new estimate of £345 for the work was accepted and a contract signed. It never occurred to the Vicar to secure a faculty. He looked at it as a question of repairs, for which he thought he was solely responsible. By the time the Chancellor of the Diocese of London called a Consistory Court hearing at St. Paul's Cathedral to challenge the removal of the bells, the bells had already been broken up, ready for the furnaces.

The Chancellor, Mr. F.H.L. Errington was appalled at the destruction of the bells before a faculty had been applied for. And he could not "altogether accept the innocence of faculty law alleged by Mr. Johnston in his evidence." However, he could not "leave the church without its bells," and he didn't want to "sue the bellfounder for the value of the bells unlawfully taken posses-sion of, and broken up by them." Thus he felt he had to "sanction a course of which [he] entirely disapproved." In granting the fac-ulty, he stood staunchly with the conservationists. "In these days, no part of the contents of a church is in greater danger than the bells . . . the interest in the preservation of old things which now happily exists has not yet spread to the bells, and they greatly need the protection of this court. They are frequently taken away and mutilated and put back without any reference to the court on the ground that these are mere repairs." Mr. Errington also called attention to the questionable practice of a contractor tendering a gift to soften his offer, making it more difficult for a client to refuse an estimate. He referred to a letter of the bellfounder in which while acknowledging acceptance of the £345 estimate, he wrote also that he "had pleasure in making a personal subscrip-tion of £35." This represented a deduction of about 10 percent on the contract price. While crediting Mr. Johnston, perhaps cynically, but no doubt ironically, "with the highest spirit of phi-lanthropy," the Chancellor warned that a "gift at the time of contract *should at least set [the church] thinking.*"[6]

At the St. James rededication April 28, 1929, a great gather-ing of ringers was on hand. The Lord Bishop of Stepney con-gratulated the Vicar, wardens and parishioners on the splendid results of their initiative. He especially complimented Mr. Cyril Johnston on the tone of the recast peal, which he said he much admired. It was noted in the Ringing World that the old bells had had an unenviable reputation for years, and that this was the first ringing peal in the city of London to be tuned on the Simpson principle. The St. James uplift was itemized, including its new cast iron headstocks and ball bearings, and an oak frame materially strengthened by corner plates and stout vertical bolts—"all the latest improvements evolved in recent years by the bell-founders . . . "[7] At the opening ceremony the G&J manufacturer once again addressed an appreciative company, here not omitting his run-in with the Chancellor. "A bellfounder's calling in these days," said Cyril, "would seem to require many and increasing qualifications. He must be versed in engineering, music, bellring-ing, business methods, organization, finding his way by road to a little village that is not on the map—and now, I am told, in ecclesiastical law as well (laughter)."[8]

Coventry was something else again. In 1926, fourteen years before the firebombing that destroyed all but the tower and spire of St. Michael's Cathedral, a Whitechapel ring of ten dating from 1774, under threat of replacement, would be fiercely championed by England's ringers as represented by the CCCBR—the Central Council of Church Bell Ringers. The debate between old and new received massive coverage in the national press as well as the Ringing World. The campaign to save the bells was led with inordinate passion by E. Alexander Young, secretary of the Central Council. Young, born in 1865, a ringer and historian, architect and district surveyor, often seen looking Dickensian in a frock coat and half topper, had written two pamphlets bitterly denouncing Simpson tuning. He and many others of his generation thought the Coventry peal one of the finest ever cast. "The bells came," Young pointed out, "from the well known Whitechapel Foundry, the oldest institution of its kind in the country, dating as it does from the times of Queen Elizabeth." "When they are melted," Young wrote to the Lord Bishop of Coventry, "we [will] have nothing left, but so much copper and so much tin. They [will] parallel the ashes after cremation. There is also the Association which can never be recovered . . . [for] with these very sounds and tones the whole life of the City of Coventry is interwoven for the past six or seven Generations . . . "[9] Young was fudging his Generations somewhat, for these Whitechapel bells had not actually been rung for fully forty years. In 1885 the celebrated bells of St. Michael's had rung out for the last time.

After the bells had been taken down and stowed away, a madcap (and unauthorized) experiment with the tenor bell involved hoisting it up into the octagon beneath the spire, fully 136 feet from the ground. An attempt to swing it caused the steeple to lurch and sway alarmingly, producing a sensation of giddiness. The bells were removed and stowed away. But this was hardly the first time that ringing at St. Michael's was suspended and its bells silenced. The whole situation had a Byzantine history. Even earlier than 1774, the pre-Whitechapel bells (by Henry Bagley Sr. and Jr., who in 1674 recast six medieval bells into a ring of eight) had caused concern for the safety of the steeple. Warnings were raised in 1774, and in 1782 ringing stopped. Once resumed, a new bell-frame in 1794 made the tower oscillate so badly, battering the walls, some thought it more dangerous than the original frame. By 1801, the bells had again fallen silent. Then it was proposed to lower the bells some 30 feet and rehang them in a new timber frame having no connection with the walls of the tower. With the bells now positioned just 80 feet above ground, restricted ringing resumed. In 1806–07 there was another restoration with an altered design to reduce strain on the tower. In 1817 ringing was suspended again. Things went on like this until 1885 when the bells were stored away pending an uncertain future. Weaknesses in the tower structure were identified: large openings in an insufficiently buttressed base or ground story; a deviation from the perpendicular caused by the original settlement (i.e. the tower was leaning); the great height of the interior, without floors or intermediate cross-bracing. Three courses of action were considered: to build a separate bell tower, or campanile; to rehang the bells as before; to rehang them as a chime.

In 1925 a chime was decided on, and this was where Cyril Johnston came in. The advantage of course of a chime was that the bells would be hung dead. It was the swinging after all that had caused the centuries of trouble. But now another adversity, and a novel one, faced every interested party—the possibility of losing bells beloved by ringers, and others, altogether through being melted down and recast. E. Alexander Young and the CCCBR regarded the proposed recasting as wanton destruction for commercial gain. Destroying the bells was seen to be akin to melting down ancient church plate of a similar age. Throughout 1925–26 Young fervently pressed his case against recasting. The bells were apparently like living beings to him, as close as close relatives. He told the Lord Bishop of Coventry that "in the process of recasting, some *fresh* metal must be added, leaving no room for any sentiment on the subject of the 'dear old' bells." He wrote to Cyril Johnston after the Consistory Court hearing in January 1926 when a faculty for recasting was granted, begging him to "hold off for a few days before throwing them into the furnace." Young had already tried to buy the bells and impound them on behalf of Coventry, until, say, a campanile might be built for them. Then when all seemed lost and the bells about to be broken up, he beseeched Cyril to keep out one of the smaller bells as a memento, to be enshrined at the British Museum. Cyril replied that the churchwardens intimated they couldn't possibly agree to that. At last Young requested "the Bells" at least be kept intact until the bereaved "Ringers" might have an opportunity of visiting the foundry to hear them ring for the last time![10]

It was the G&J chime bells that Ingrid and I heard on May 5, 2002, while approaching the steeple and ruins of St. Michael's, the very chime that rang through the terrible night of November 14th, 1940 when all around was in flames, and gave great encouragement to the people of Coventry. But what we heard was a change-ringing set. After years of use as a chime since 1927, in 1986 the bells were dismantled and delivered to John Taylor in Loughborough to be fitted for swinging. Tuned as a ring of 12 in the key of C sharp, with two semitone bells, a flat 6th and a flat 8th, one reason they sounded so stentorian and tumultuous was that they were pretty close to the ground, belting out their notes at a mere height of 50 feet. (So that's how they solved the swinging problem). Below them and just above the bookshop in the base of the tower was the ringers' chamber, 24 feet 6 inches high. Another reason for the divine racket we heard was that the bells had been cast to a chime or carillon profile. The English have tended to use the terms chime and carillon interchangeably.

Cyril himself would confuse this usage if the occasion suited. "I hope all ringers will understand," he said in defending the St. Michael's chime, "that we are not going to allow the ringers' interests to take second place to 'carillonitis,' as one frenzied correspondent to the *Ringing World* recently put it."[11] Another curious term, minted at the Consistory Court hearing, was something called a "Simpson howl." Albert Hughes of Whitechapel in testifying against Simpson tuning—therefore of course against the proposed replacement of his firm's 1774 ring of ten—said that with a heavy ring, like the chime in question, the harmonic overtones were greatly accentuated, producing a very disagreeable 'howl.'"[12] The "Simpson howl" was bandied about by bell conservationists to discourage tuning on the new five-tone principle, and thus the removal of any old bells. For Hughes, it was actually an awkward moment. In 1927 he was still resisting the tuning revolution in progress. Doing it in a limited way, the outcome at Coventry in favor of G&J must have persuaded him to resign himself to the inevitable, knowing his firm would have to change to survive.

Cyril would be pleased I'm sure to know that his chime eventually became a ring, even if Taylor his arch competitor made the conversion. Correspondence between E.A. Young and the bellfounder show that before creating a chime, the latter tried for five years without success to convince the St. Michael's authorities to let him cast, or recast, an English ring. I'm very pleased myself about the adaptation, because I don't care much for the diatonically scaled recital of tunes and popular melodies on chimes; and how would I have learned what an impressive sound change-ringing can make had I not chanced on St. Michael's that day. Two American men of bells, Percival Price the carillonneur and scholar, and Frederick Mayer the carillon consultant, became smitten in their own time by English change-ringing. Mayer had an experience at St. Paul's Cathedral in London similar evidently to the one I had in Coventry. He heard a ring of 12 with a B tenor, rung by a band that Cyril Johnston, who took him there, said was the pick of England. "Realizing," Mayer wrote home to Rockefeller, "that [in every cycle] the bells sounded in a different order, and that the great speed of the bells made it hard to even notice where the change occurred, and hearing them rung with such absolute evenness [i.e. without inflection] I felt it was almost unbelievable, and could have listened for hours. The result is a riot of tone. But it is a musical riot, and of a peculiar exhilaration and ecstasy that is unique. All England is devoted to this sort of thing . . . "13 Price too, noting that "a swing through a complete circle would give forth a fullness of tone not obtainable from a stationary bell," exulted in the "marvelously extended repetition of kaleidoscopic tonal sequences."14 They were echoed by E. A. Young who, while lamenting the loss of Coventry's 1774 bells and their replacement by a chime, said with pathos, "the full beauty of their tone would never be heard [again]. Such beauty is only attained when bells are swung throughout a complete revolution, and the tone comes from the upturned moving mouth."15 If I had stopped to think or try to analyze what was happening while walking toward the tower of St. Michael's in the year 2000, it was the bell tones piling up and overlapping with such speed and power that bowled me over.

Price compared change-ringing favorably to the simple chime, which became so popular in North America, raising the question why English-style pealing wasn't exported to the U.S. Though it exists here, it has never had any wide appeal.16

But had it taken hold, it is doubtful North America would have been receptive to the carillon—any more than England ever was. And I wouldn't be here to tell the story.

Chapter X

RODMAN WANAMAKER'S "BIG BEN"

Big Ben, the world's largest accurate clock, is a prime example of
"sublime" technology: an engineering artifact that inspires
public awe and fetishistic fascination
—Stewart Brand

In planning a suitable site for this new bell on the . . . roof of the
Wanamaker Store . . . I had my share of thrills
—Cyril F. Johnston

So saith anyway, Cyril Johnston's American daughter, for whom
his personal voice, never heard, became the utterances of his bells
—Jill Johnston

Cyril Johnston's first trip to America in December 1925 to attend the dedication of the Park Avenue New York carillon included a visit at the end of that month in Philadelphia to finalize a contract to build a huge bell for Rodman Wanamaker. Rodman, son of the "Merchant Prince" John Wanamaker, was said to have heard Big Ben broadcasting the hours on the radio while he spent a sleepless night in a London hotel in 1925. Hearing Big Ben inspired him to put a similar giant bell on the roof of his store in Philadelphia. He developed several ambitions for such a bell. He wanted to memorialize his father who had died in 1922. Nineteen twenty-six would be the fiftieth anniversary of the opening of John Wanamaker's first store, the Grand Depot (on the site of the Pennsylvania Railroad freight terminal) in 1876. His bell was intended also as a kind of extension to the Sesqui-Centennial Exposition commemorating 150 years of American liberty and the signing of the Declaration of Independence. To be called *The Founder's Bell,* specified to weigh 15 tons, one ton for each decade since 1776, it would function additionally as a counterpart of sorts to the Wanamaker store's great organ, under constant enlargement since its installment in the store's magnificent Grand Court in 1909. A special feature at the 1904 St. Louis World's Fair, the organ had gathered dust in storage when in 1909 John Wanamaker bought it for his "New Kind of Store." Rodman, like another millionaire John D. Rockefeller, Jr. (though hardly in the Rockefeller bracket), was not immune to the prospect of breaking a record, and going for big. By the mid-twenties his father's organ was the world's largest, with six manual keyboards, 17,285 pipes, 219 speaking stops and 293 ranks. The new bell, at 15 tons and exceeding the weight of Rockefeller's 10-ton bourdon for the Park Avenue Church carillon, would be the biggest in North America, the only tuned bell in the world of that weight, and the only single-voiced musical instrument of such dimensions. And it was going to be two tons heavier than Big Ben. Rodman desperately wanted it mounted on his roof by May 1926 in readiness to have it sound forth on the Sesqui-Centennial day of July 4th.

Comparison of *The Founder's Bell* to the 13-ton Big Ben would not have been lost on Cyril Johnston. This chapter could easily be headed "Cyril Johnston's 'Big Ben.'" There is some evidence that he did think possessively about Britain's signature bell. His comment that "the tones of Big Ben were enough to drive any good bell founder into an early grave"—made at a lecture he gave in his foundry in 1920—is one place to start.[1] An anonymous letter to the *London Times* proposing to have installed in the clocktower a carillon of 47 bells weighing over 50 tons, and "getting rid of cracked Big Ben and his cacophonous voice" sounds suspiciously like it was Cyril's. The writer noted that Parliament's clocktower was the same height, 300 feet, "as the grand tower of Malines [Belgium]," which happens to have a 47-bell carillon. Cyril knew the Malines tower and its municipal carillonneur Jef Denyn well. "Surely," said the *Times* letter-writer, "of all the towers in the land none would be better suited for such a set of [carillon] bells than the Clock Tower of the Houses of Parliament . . . Such an instrument would be worthy of the nation."[2] And whose would it be if not Cyril Johnston's? As for Big Ben by itself: from an anecdote once told to an interviewer by Cyril's widow Mary Johnston, it's clear her husband would have liked nothing better than to get the world's best known most popular clockbell out of Parliament's Clock Tower, take it home to Croydon, melt it down, recast it, tune it properly, and present it to England as his own. His widow said he was very friendly with a man called Bridges Webb with whom he worked hard over a period of time trying to get Big Ben down. An opportunity to extricate the bell arose apparently because of repair work on the tower. In May, 1941, the clocktower was struck by a small bomb or anti-aircraft shell, damaging iron and stonework to both belfry and steeple. The glass of the south dial (23 feet in diameter) was also shattered. But in the end according to Mary Johnston, the two men decided the world knew and loved the tone of this cracked bell, and with a properly tuned one, it wouldn't be the same thing, so they let it go.[3]

It was for the Western Hemisphere that Cyril would have his chance to cast a few of earth's Great Bells, and satisfy ambitions thwarted at home. The Liberty Bell, cast in 1752 by Whitechapel, at 2000 lbs. was hardly a contender in this field. But small and useless as it is—long irreparably cracked and on display in Independence Hall, now at the Liberty Bell Center in Philadelphia—it has some commensurate iconic status to Britain's Big Ben. The 1926 *Founder's Bell*, imported to celebrate not only John Wanamaker but American "liberty" after all, could be construed as competitive with it. It's a helluvalot bigger, it is Simpson tuned (a deep low D) and it still functions, tolling the time atop the 27-story Philadelphia office building now called One South Broad Street, its second home. One South is adjacent to City Hall. The renowned statue of Pennsylvania's founder William Penn that crowns the municipal structure is visible eighty feet away through a wide tall aperture in the bell's 40-foot high limestone tower.

Bell and statue are on aerial saluting terms. Unlike Big Ben, *The Founder's Bell* functions as a clock with no faces, only a mechanism, which lies in a room underneath it. New York's Riverside Church bourdon (and a number of other bourdons), perform the same way. Curiously, while Big Ben is famously cracked, it is not THE MOST FAMOUSLY CRACKED BELL IN THE WORLD, as a Liberty Bell story was once headlined. Of course nobody can see Big Ben. We see only his clock faces. To view the bell (and by the way also his four relatively small companions, the quarter-hour chiming bells) you need special permission to climb the 340 spiral interior steps of the Clock Tower, winding yourself to the belfry. The Liberty Bell on the other hand has been grounded since 1846, its final zigzag fracture, 12-15 inches long, on full view in its glass case. From any cracked perspective, both these bells have a tortuous history. And *The Founder's Bell* has a flawed past of its own.

Big Ben was first cast in May, 1856, by bellfounder John Warner whose firm would stop making bells in 1924.[4] Warner's had two 10-ton furnaces to do the job. Once cast, the ponderous mass, weighing more than 16 tons, was taken to London and mounted on a temporary gallows at the foot of the still unfinished clock tower, becoming an object of curiosity to thousands. The Houses of Parliament, destroyed by fire in 1834, upon being rebuilt were now for the first time to include a clock tower—an imposing Gothic structure that would support a clock of unprecedented size, a Great Clock, fit for all Londoners to tell the time by. While the huge Warner bell sat waiting for its tower to be completed, it was struck each week for a quarter of an hour by a six-hundredweight hammer. In 1857 almost a year later, unbelievably to all concerned the tone of the bell went flat. A man was sent inside the bell with a candle where he found a major crack, four feet long, stretching upward from the sound-bow. The damage was so extensive, the bell had to be ditched and recast. A large iron wrecking ball weighing one ton was brought to the site and dropped on the bell repeatedly from a height of 30 feet for a period of two days until the bronze was practically pulverized, then loaded into carts. Charles Mears of Whitechapel now entered the picture. Mears had been haughty originally, refusing to offer a tender, considering his firm above the competition (Taylor had been there, but he wanted to be paid in advance, so was turned down). Now Mears, realizing the tremendous prestige and sales value of such an order, became "delighted" to have the chance of "making the most famous bell in the world"—from the atomized remains of Warner's. All London was gripped by the bell drama. And a popular jingle circulated: *Poor Mr. Warner is put in the corner/ For making a bad Big Ben/ Good Mr. Mears as it appears/ Is to make us a new one—When?*[5]

April 10, 1858, the metal was poured. When the bell emerged, it was pulled on a flatbed from Whitechapel to the tower site by sixteen powerful horses—crossing London Bridge, along Borough Road and over Westminster Bridge. The new clock tower was still not ready, so new Big Ben was mounted on the same gallows where its predecessor had stood, and sounded by the same six-hundred-weight hammer. With a tone of E natural, it weighed 13 tons 1,219 lbs, had a height of 7 ft. 6 in., a skirt diameter of 9 ft., a hammer of 448 lbs., and a thickness at sound-bow of 8¾ inches. Apart from John Warner's original bell, it was the biggest ever made in England to that date. Its note was said to be superior in every way to poor Warner's. This one was luckier in any case. It had to sit only five months at the base of the tower before being hoisted up. And once it arrived, 205 feet to the belfry—a job that took eight men 32 hours working in relays pulling the bell on a strong specially made chain through an interior airshaft—something really terrible would have had to happen before removal would be contemplated as an option. The great bell had been designed to be short and narrow enough to fit into the shaft if turned on its side; for the 32-hour ride up, it was encased in a wooden cradle, and the shaft lined with planking. Then the terrible, the unthinkable, did happen. A few weeks after Big Ben struck its first hours, July, 1859, and the quarter-bells had started chiming (these four were Warner's—the ones he had made for the original contract), it too cracked!

Edmund Beckett Denison (1816–1905) who would become Lord Grimthorpe, designer of both clock and bell for Big Ben, and one of England's more interesting, multi-talented and difficult, 19th century men, had been blamed for the cracked Warner bell. When the Whitechapel cracked, he was blamed for that too. Mutual recriminations, resulting in legal action, were especially virulent over bell #2. The bellfounders in both cases claimed that Denison had specified too heavy a hammer, while Denison accused the bellfounders of producing a poor casting. The press was over the top in the controversy, publishing endless articles and letters largely denouncing Denison for a badly designed bell. Charles Mears's libel action against him for publicly maligning it was settled out of court. Denison demanded breaking up and recasting the bell. But the Office of Works and for that matter all those who had declared it a bad design, shrank from the enormity of the task of getting it out of the tower. Masonry walls and a number of other architectural elements would have to be cut or displaced at huge inconvenience. The manpower involved would be very expensive. And the crack was only some eleven inches long, and did not go right through the bell—a mere blip compared to the Warner damage. The Astronomer Royal, Sir George Airy, suggested turning the bell a quarter to obtain an undamaged striking surface, cutting down a small square to prevent the crack spreading, and reducing the weight of the hammer by one half. With this accomplished, the bell's tone was now deemed good, or good enough. Three years after the quarrels over the crack, the designer was vindicated when a famous analyst who examined the bell found a number of "blowholes"—cavities that can occur during casting, air bubbles leaving voids—and flaws in the metal.

Photo courtesy of Rebecca Reid

Band of change ringers at St. Mary le Bow, UK, 2007

Top: *The ruins of St. Michael's Cathedral,*
Coventry, England
Bottom left: *The cross in St. Michael's Cathedral,*
made out of charred beams
from the bombed-out ruins
Bottom right: *Memorial Plaque*

The night of November 14, 1940, the Luftwaffe headed for Coventry in what was code-named
"Operation Moonlight Sonata." Most of the city including St. Michael's Cathedral,
built in the 14th century, was firebombed. Left standing was the tower with its G&J bells intact.
In 1940, the bells were a "chime" of 14 bells, cast by Gillett & Johnston in 1927.
These replaced a Whitechapel ring dating from 1774. In 1986, the Taylor Bellfoundry fitted
the G&J chime for swinging as a ring of 12

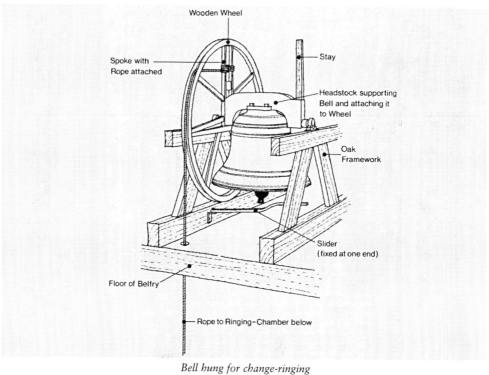

Wooden Wheel

Spoke with Rope attached

Stay

Headstock supporting Bell and attaching it to Wheel

Oak Framework

Slider (fixed at one end)

Floor of Belfry

Rope to Ringing-Chamber below

Bell hung for change-ringing

The bell is at hand-stroke. The stay presses against the pivoting slider. From this position every pull on the rope turns the bell through a full circle, first one way then the other

This bell is down and the wooden stay sticks up. The rope in the groove around the wheel leads to the ringing chamber below

Little Bob Minor

```
x  123456 ⑥
16 2\43/5
x  24\ /35
14 42/ \53
   4/2\35
   /4\253
   /4523
   \5432
12 /14523 ②
   \5432
   /5\342
   5\/42
   35\/42
3/52\4 -W
   /3254\
   /135264 ⑤
   3\256\
   32\45\
   234\ /6
   243/5\
   42/3/5
   4/2\35
   /4\253
   142\35 ④
   4\/253
   4\523
   /45\32
   /54\23
   5\/432
   5\/342
   /53\24
   154\342 ③
   5\3\24
   53\ /4
   352\ /4
   325/5\
   23/54\
   2/345\ -H
   /243\5
   12345\6
```

Little Bob Minor (continued)

	Bob		Single
	641253		641253
	23		23
	32		32
	23		23
	32		32
	641352		641352

144 or 288

	23456		23456
	64523		64523
S	32564		35264
	45632	−	64235
S	23645	•	52364
	56423	−	64352
•	34256		23564

Repeat twice. For 288
repeat five times,
calling single at * in
1st and 4th parts.

240 or 480

	23456		23456
	64523		64523
A−	23564		35264
	45623	−	64235
	36245	A	52364
−	45236	−	64352
B	62345		23564
−	23645		45623
	23645	B−	23645
	56423		56423
C	34256	C	34256

Each repeated twice.
For 480, repeat five
times, calling single at
A, B or C, in two places
240 changes apart.
480 changes is the
extent in this method
with the treble fixed.

26

Double Oxford Bob Minor

```
x  123456 ⑥   156342 ③
14 2\43/5     5\3/24
x  24\ 35     53\ 42
36 423/5      35\ 24
x  243/5      53\2\4
56 42 35      352 4\
   243 5,     53\24,
   42/3/5     352/ 4
   24/ 35     532/ 4
   42/ 53     35/24/
   4/2/35     3/52/4 -W
   /4\253     /3254/
12 142/35 ④  1352/4 ⑤
   4\253      3\256/
   4\235      32\5 4
   /42\53     235\ 4
   /25\3      3254/
   /4523      2345/
   4/253/     3254/
   452/3      2345/
   /5/23      324/5/
   /4/532     23/4/5
   /4523      2/345/ -H
   /4523 ②    /243/5
   \5432      12345/6
```

Bob
```
5\423
5\4\32
543\ 2
5\ 342
5432
5\34/2
5/342
5\/324
5\ 342
/53\24
156342
```

```
421653
35
53
35
53
421 35
```
Single
```
421653
4\ 35
4\/53
/4\35
4\ 53
421 35
```

```
421653
4\ 35
4\/53
/4\35
4\ 53
421635
```

St. Clement's College Bob Minor

```
x  123456 ⑥   156342 ③
16 2\43/5     5\3/24
x  24\ 35     53\2 4
36 24\53      352/4\
x  24\5/3     5324\
36 425\3)     3542/
   2453/      534/2
   4235/      35/4/2
   243/5      53/42
   42/3/5     35/24
   4/2/35     3/52/4 -W
   /4\253     /3254/
12 142\35 ④  1352/4 ⑤
   4\/253     3\/254
   4\/253     3\/254
   4\523      32/45
   /45\32     234/5
   /4\253     23/45
   4352/      325/4
   4\325      32/54
   423/5      235/4
   4/2/35     325/4
   /4\253     23/54/ -H
   154\32     /243/5
   5\342 ②   12345/6
   5\342
   5\3\24
   532\ 4
   5\234
   5243/
   5\42/3
   54/23
   5/432
   5\342
   /53\24
   156342
```

Bob
```
421365
53
53
53
421513
```
Single
```
421365
4\ 35
4\ 35
/4\35
4\ 35
421365
```

Callings for London S. Minor can be used for St. Clement's and Double
Oxford to give half the stated length. By calling a single at the end and
repeating, same length as for London is produced.

St. Clement's & Double Oxford Bob Minor

	96		144		168
	23456		23456		23456
−	64235	−	64235	−	64235
	26543		26543		26543
S	53264		52364		52364
	25436	S	34526	−	43526
	Repeat	−	65342	S	56432
	108	−	23654		45263
	23456		Repeat		24356
S	46235				Repeat
S	25463		**72, 216**		**180, 360**
	42356	S	46235	−	64235
	Repeat		24563		23456
	twice.		52346	−	64235
	144		23456		26543
	23456	S	36524	−	35264
−	64235	−	45362		Repeat
−	52643	−	23456		four
S	63524		For 216,		times. For
	56432		omit last		360, call
	45263		bob and		single at
	24356		repeat		end and
	Repeat		twice		repeat the
					whole.

Extents – 720 changes

	23456		23456		23456
−	64235	S	46235	−	64235
	26543		24563	−	52643
	52364		52346	−	36524
−	43526		35624	S	54362
	54632		63452	−	23546
	65243	−	24635	−	65234
−	32654	−	62543	S	24653
−	46325		56324	−	36245
S	35462	S	35462	S	25364
*S	42356	*S	42356	*S	34256

Repeat five times, Bob at *
half-way and end.

27

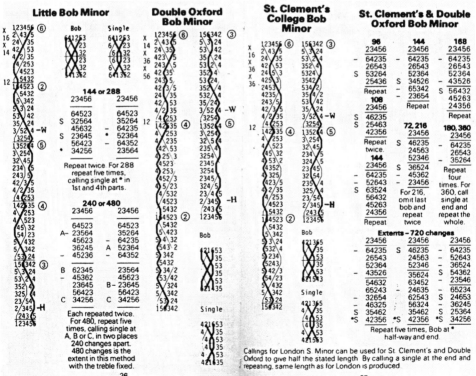

*Top: The new ring of ten bells cast for St. Andrew's church, Roker, Sunderland, Co. Durham on floor of
the Gillett & Johnston Bellfoundry, c. 1948
Bottom: Examples of Methods for change-ringing*

John Darwin, Engineer for the Palace of Westminster, standing inside one of Big Ben's four great dials

Big Ben with accompanying quarter-bells in the belfry of the Clock Tower, part of the Parliament buildings, London, England

*The Clock Tower with Big Ben clockfaces;
only Big Ben and his four quarter-bells
occupy this belfry*

*The clockface of the Peace Tower of
the Parliament buildings in Ottawa, Canada;
within the belfry are 53 carillon bells
(see diagram on opposite page) cast by G&J in
1927, with the bourdon at 7 tons, operating like
Big Ben as the city timekeeper*

*Opposite page: The Parliament Buildings in
Ottawa, Canada*

CLOCK
MECHANISM

KEYBOARD
ROOM

UPPER BELFRY:
47 BELLS

LOWER BELFRY:
THE 6 LARGEST BELLS

MEMORIAL
CHAMBER

Left: Cyril F. Johnston with The Founders' Bell on the tuning machine in the foundry of Gillett & Johnston, 1926
Bottom left: Clapper of Founders' Bell on roof of Wanamaker store in Philadelphia
Bottom right: The Founders' Bell at the Gillett & Johnston Foundry in Croydon

The Founders' Bell being hoisted onto ship in Southampton, UK, for transport to Philadelphia, USA

The Founders' Bell in transport from ship to train

The YMCA in Jerusalem, Palestine, surrounded by crowds in attendance of inaugural carillon concert by Nora Johnston, Palm Sunday, April 9, 1933

Top: Bells for the YMCA carillon arriving in Jerusalem, 1933
Bottom left: Nora Johnston, who inaugurated the Jerusalem carillon, at carillon practice console in the
Gillett & Johnston Bellfoundry, Croydon, England
Bottom right: The bourdon of the YMCA carillon, Jerusalem

Denison would say that the clock kept better time than any other public clock you could find. (He was in a position to know; it was his "double three-legged gravity escapement" invention that for the first time made a turret clock accountable to Mean Time within the second). But it's doubtful he approved of the tone of the bell. Years later, after he became Lord Grimthorpe, he could be heard saying, "Big Ben is a disgrace to the nation."[6] Time was the winner in the Big Ben sweepstakes. And how could it not be? Telling time is the purpose of any turret clock. "Time is to clock as mind is to brain," says Dava Sobel in her book *Longitude*. Guided by the time, we make and keep appointments, or break them, with self and others. Time as regulator is hardly as common as oxygen or the weather, but it makes civilized life possible. It's the state's call to work, the state's call for ceasing work, the state's requirement for prayer, for recognition of public affairs and events of passage. "Father Time is a Crafty Man/And he's Set in His Ways" go the words of an old song. The Clock Tower was designed for a surmounting visibility in association with government and crown—a command for order and regularity from on high as it were. The copper minute hands on Big Ben's four clock faces are 14 feet long. The gunmetal hour hands are 9 feet. The diameter of each face or dial is 23 feet, and each dial weighs four tons. The Roman numeral figures are two feet tall. There are 312 panes of opal glass in each face. Time is one thing, the aesthetic of the instrument telling it something else. And the Gothic structure of the Clock Tower, the work of architect Sir Charles Barry, is quite beautiful indeed—its proportions and detail a marvel of engineering and consummate ornamental design. The Time is Beautiful, it seems to say. With most of the citizenry now wearing wristwatches, telling time by public clock is no longer very essential, though passers-by and listeners to the radio still check the time by Big Ben. Still, given the spread of the personal timekeeper, the aesthetic or symbolic value of such a clock tower naturally began to supersede its expediency.

How might we account for the tone of its bell in this development? Unless a bell sounds really tinny in my view people are not going to notice much. The tone of Big Ben by expert opinion, both then and now, leaves much to be desired. The crack tells the tale. Its "true" sound in advance of the damage became difficult or impossible to determine, and that of course was before the 1896 Simpson revolution, when there was no guarantee that any English (or Continental) bell could be tuned to a harmonic precision. For the people generally it has never mattered. The tone of their Big Ben is sentimentally "beautiful." When a King or Queen dies, its tolling conveys a magisterial message. If it fails for some reason to register the time, as it has on occasion, the part of a Londoner's brain in which the sound has been stuporously instilled can be shaken, becoming disconcertingly conscious of an absence. In European countries occupied by the Germans during WWII, people will remember that listening to the radio was a punishable offense; and that the sound of Big Ben transmitted via the BBC came to symbolize hope and reassurance that the UK was still there and fighting to liberate them. To this day, Big Ben is unique in that, by means of "live" broadcasting around the world, more people in more places hear it than hear any other bell. In 1925, its tolling via radio waves in a London hotel room had such an impact on Rodman Wanamaker that he conceived of a bell as big or bigger to bring to the United States.

The Founder's Bell may have been a brilliant idea, but Rodman had only a dumb place to put it—on the roof of his 14-story Wanamaker store in Philadelphia. It seems unlikely that Cyril Johnston thought much of the spot himself. When he visited the city December 29th—two days after attending the dedication of the Park Avenue Baptist Church carillon in New York—his caper atop the building surveying his bell's designated location became a unique anecdote in bellfounder annals. Once home, Cyril gave an account of his rooftop exploit to the *Yorkshire Observer.*

> Adventure would hardly be associated with the work of a bell-founder . . . yet in planning a suitable site for this new bell on the . . . roof of the Wanamaker store, which not only holds gigantic wireless aerials but accommodates two fullsized ten-

nis courts and 'grounds' for other games, I had my share of thrills. The worst, or perhaps, best was when I crawled like a cinema 'stunt artist' beyond the protecting barriers right to the edge of the roof and looked over. After that experience, I felt that I had earned the contract which I have brought back to England.[7]

If that was all it took, he had reason in the succeeding months to remember it. Rodman Wanamaker was fairly obsessed: he wanted a Big Bell and he wanted it On Time. The time would come to seem as or somehow more important than the bell. By contract, the bell, to cost £6,780 or 33,000 dollars, had to be delivered in Philadelphia no later than May 30, in time to get it on the roof to boom out the July 4th Sesqui-Centennial. Certainly Rodman wanted no frills that might hold up shipment—not even the height off the roof advised by the bellfounder to ensure the tone being properly heard. But absolutely not a bell that could swing, or extra bells, like a carillon—ideas kicked around between Cyril and associates of Rodman's while Rodman was vacationing that winter at his exotic address in Miami Florida— aboard a Houseboat called the "Nirvana" at the Biscayne Bay Yacht Club. With threatened delays in April, a cable Rodman sent to Arthur Newson, his London Wanamaker Store manager and contact with Gillett & Johnston, made things quite clear: ABSO-LUTELY NECESSARY THAT BELL BE SHIPPED ON *ANY BOAT THAT WILL REACH HERE NOT LATER THAN JUNE 4 SO THAT IT CAN BE IN PLACE JULY 4, OR WE WILL NOT WANT IT.*[8] [My emphases].

In the end he wanted it, even after it was cast and "imperfec-tions" were found, requiring recasting. Rodman was "bitterly disappointed" to be sure, and he had to think up a new excuse for heralding its advent. With not much choice, given the five or six months now needed to cast, tune and ship a new bell, the New Year at midnight January 1st, 1927 was selected. The hapless bell-founder, who told Newsom he lost £8000 over the project (donor and associates expended no sympathy), was assisted no doubt by

Britain's serious transport strike during the month of May. His Wanamaker bell, weighing over 17 tons before tuning, was cast on May 6. The General Strike of 1926 threatened to disrupt law and order to the point of civil war. Arthur Newsom would write to Rodman on May 12, "I am advised that it will be utterly impossible to take such a weight by road to any port at the present moment . . . No cargo is being taken on board for outbound shipment."[9] On May 26, Cyril was able to make a 7-ton advance shipment of his steel girder work along with a case of bolts, nuts, disks, and washers. The bell, still to be tuned, was supposed to follow, but by June 1st, its "imperfections" had been discovered. Writing to Philadelphia, Newsom said he was "thankful" they showed up when they did—"otherwise no one knows what would have happened after the Bell had been hung."[10] It would surely have cracked. Just like Big Bens 1 and 2, and the Liberty Bells 1 and 2. When Whitechapel's Liberty Bell was hung in the Old Philadelphia Statehouse in 1752, it cracked upon the first stroke. A year later two American workmen, John Pass and John Stow, ingeniously—they were not bellfounders—recast it using the Whitechapel metal; so it was the "Pass and Stow" Liberty Bell that cracked in 1835, then irredeemably in 1846. The defects in Big Ben 2, the "blowholes" or flaws in the metal, were discovered three years after the crack occurred that had been caused by them.

The Founder's Bell was ignominiously late, but upon recasting remained intact, not to mention perfectly tuned, and was the heaviest single bell (i.e. a bell that stands or hangs alone) in America until 1998[11]—all perhaps to its detriment, since it is not nearly so well known as our cracked Liberty Bell and Britain's cracked Big Ben. Then too, as a clockbell without faces, its invisibility is more pronounced than, say, Big Ben or even the 10-ton nameless bourdon functioning as the bass of Ottawa's Parliament Peace Tower 53-bell carillon, but also as the tower's clockbell. With a face to look at, we can better imagine a brain behind it— a mechanism with its voice. If Cyril Johnston had to say which "voice" of his in North America best competes with Big Ben's, he might identify his 20-ton Riverside bourdon. *The Founder's Bell,* cast a year earlier, could have seemed a proper rival—until perhaps he saw the Wanamaker roof. Taking a bell and its entire environment into account, the Ottawa turret tower is I think the fairest comparison, and beats out Big Ben in at least a couple of significant ways.

For one thing, Ottawa's dials and mechanisms were designed and built by the Gillett & Johnston clock-works. Neither Warner's nor Whitechapel or Taylor ever built clocks. In this, the G&J firm had a distinct advantage; they never had to split their orders for clockbells. Taylor et al would have to order out for a clock mechanism and dials to accompany any commission they had to make a large strike-bell and four smaller quarter-chiming bells. Gillett & Johnston, known at first as Gillett & Co., dated from 1844 and produced only clocks until 1877 when Cyril Johnston's father Arthur bought a partnership in the firm and introduced bells, along eventually with his name. William Gillett (1823–1886), the founder, an itinerant clockmaker and repairer from Hadlow, Kent, moved to Clerkenwell in London, then to Croydon where he established permanent premises. Until 1877, one bell-manufacturing client of Gillett's was the John Taylor Co. Between 1844 and 1950, over 14,000 tower clocks were made at the foundry.

The Ottawa contract was among the most important of these. The Peace Tower's sistership to the Clock Tower in London housing Big Ben, is its most striking immediate aspect. If stood up next to the latter, the imitation is clear. Yet as a colonial appropriation, it was respectfully smaller, and in keeping after all with the size, relative to London, of the city it would represent. The history of its birth seems uncannily similar to that of the Clock Tower. Like the Houses of Parliament in London that burned down in 1834 and gave rise in the rebuilding project to a first-time clock tower, the same ravagement in Ottawa in 1916 led to a reconstruction with an equivalent outcome—a stunning Gothic-style clock tower. It was HRH the Duke of Connaught, then the Governor-General of Canada, who on September 1st, 1916, seven months after the fire, laid the cornerstone of the new buildings. Three years later on September 1st, the Duke's grandnephew the

Prince of Wales, later King Edward VIII, laid the cornerstone of the tower. London's Clock Tower, at 316 feet is 14 feet higher than the Ottawa Peace Tower. Measurements of the clock dial diameters, and minute and hour hands, show fair differences. Against London's dial diameters at 23 feet, Ottawa's are 15 feet 9 inches. The length of London's hour hands are 9 feet next to Ottawa's at 5 feet 3 inches. Minute hands of the former are 14 feet, with the latter 8 feet 6 in. The inner circles of both Tower clock faces, worthy of any mandala form, have schematic diamond motifs delineated in lead or bronze. The Clock Tower's interlocking and overlapping diamonds are composed of at least 120 of the 312 opal panes of glass in the face as a whole. Ottawa's "mandala"—of 30 panes—is simpler, its diamond shapes appearing within or as part of a Star of David design that touches the outer bounds of the innermost circle. The height of the Clock Tower to the center of its clock faces is 184 feet compared to Ottawa's 214—a difference that can be accounted for by what lies underneath the clocks at Ottawa: a 53-bell carillon, housed in a 50-foot tall belfry.

With his carillon for Ottawa's Peace Tower, Cyril Johnston far exceeded the limits of London's Big Ben and environment. He benefited of course from the changing times. The carillon instrument was virtually unknown in Britain until the early 1900s, and chimes were not popular, except in the form of the Westminster quarter-hour chiming accompanying many hour-strikers. Big Ben hangs in the middle of its four quarter-hour bells, the biggest of these weighing practically four tons, positioned in the four corners of the bell chamber. Their notes are the same as Ottawa's: G Sharp, F Sharp, E Natural and B natural. The London weights—1 ton, 1.25 tons, 1.75 tons and 3.5 tons respectively—are slightly heavier than Ottawa's. In Ottawa, the Westminster quarter bells hang above the carillon playing-room, integrated with 43 of its (carillon) companions. Below the playing-room are the six heaviest bells, among them the 10-ton bourdon, all hanging in a massive steel frame. Two floors below lies the machinery for striking the hours and chiming the Westminster quarters. Whether Ottawa is "Cyril

Johnston's 'Big Ben'" or not, its bourdon doubling as hour-bell, impeccably tuned by Simpson lights, and never impaired, has the tone that seems appropriate for the main time-teller and heraldic voice of a government and crown. So saith, anyway, the bellfounder's American daughter, for whom his personal voice, never heard, became the utterances of his bells.

The tone of *The Founder's Bell* in Philadelphia, the deepest D you ever heard, is a strangely disembodied note—in several senses. June, 2003, I went with Ingrid to hear and see it for the second time. One South Broad Street, the 27-story structure where the bell hangs, was built between 1929–1931 a block away from the original Wanamaker Store, which is now a Lord & Taylor's. Rodman's *Founder's Bell* arrived December 19, 1926, at pier 56 on the North River aboard a Cunarder, the *Ascania*. The Pennsylvania Railroad provided a lighter to transport it to their yards at Jersey City where it was loaded on a flatcar for Philadelphia. A great hoopla greeted the bell when it got to the store and was hoisted December 23rd—store and city officials in attendance, throngs of people choking the streets and stopping traffic, dozens of uniformed Wanamaker "cadets" in formation, blowing on trumpets. Much trumpeting was done also by the newspapers. The bell was bigger than Big Ben. It had a deeper tone than "the deep-throated" Great Paul at St. Paul's Cathedral. It would be the largest bell in America and the 10th largest in the whole world. It had been tuned "to form a perfect musical chord" on a principle perfected in the Netherlands three centuries ago and "rediscovered by the British bellfounder." It brought "a message of Patriotism, of Truth, of Love, of Faith and of Peace." And it would be heard from 30 miles away.

At the stroke of midnight, January 1, 1927, it was not heard at all. When Rodman Wanamaker pushed a button that was supposed to set it off, nothing happened. And when it did get going, it could barely be heard a mile away, much less 30. The eagerly awaited bell became a dud. But Rodman had not listened to the bellfounder about raising the height of the steel skeletal superstructure and jerry-rigged tower. Nor had he countenanced a swinging

137

bell, also advised by Cyril. But that was just as well because after Rodman died in 1928 and Wanamaker's managers built a skyscraper Men's Store a block away from the old store, with a 40-foot high limestone tower to house the bell, their efforts to make it a swinger were disastrous. The skyscraper was known as the Lincoln-Liberty Building. When the Wanamaker business was sold in 1986, it became the PNB, or Philadelphia National Bank. Now, as One South Broad Street, it's simply an office building—still an unlikely or ill-suited type of establishment to hold up a bell of such historic significance. Its proximity to City Hall and the William Penn statue may be redeeming features, but it doesn't seem to have lost its association with a commercial retail store. Ingrid suggests that a fantastic percussive instrument as token crown for mercantile America, is not such an irrelevant connection. At any rate, you can't see it, either up close or from any distance. It hangs in an awesome dark steel beam cage, through which its inscriptions and founder's trademark are fragmentarily visible. A large rusted wheel mostly hidden alongside it is a derelict reminder of its swinging days, which may not have lasted more than a minute, when it made the whole building shudder and shake.

We were standing with Herbie Schwagerl, engineer of bell and building, in the breezy limestone tower 425 feet up from the street, gaping at the cage, trying to make out a shred of the bell's inscription. Then we peered through a tall aperture of the limestone down at the roof of the old Wanamaker Store, a surface cluttered with water-tank and air-conditioning structures, the surface upon which Cyril Johnston had once had an "adventure." Then through another aperture at the Billy Penn, as Philadelphians call their iconic statue, at eye level eighty feet away. Before we left, Herbie most considerately asked us if we would like to hear one toll of *The Founder's Bell*—the depth of which we had experienced earlier on the street, sounding off eleven times, with long four-second waits between each roar. Saying yes, seeing him pull a switch on the clock machinery (in a glass walled room beneath the steel-swaddled bell), I stuffed my ears with my forefingers, and was quaked anyway by the huge din.

Later, sitting in chair #19 at the Historical Society of Pennsylvania on Locust and 13th Streets reading source material on *The Founder's Bell* from the Wannamaker Archive, I happened to look out the tall sunray window there, and saw the bell clearly in its limestone tower, maybe five long blocks away to the north. Or I should say I saw what I knew to be the bell, smothered in its dark, very dark, crisscross steel bandaging. A little excited to be able to "see" what I was reading about, I called the librarian's attention to it. He was standing close by at a raised counter, under the window, handling papers. He looked out and up, presumably saw the tower, and gazed back at me blankly. What had he seen except a black hole in the sky?

After talking to several men, including Herbie Schwagerl, and Curt Mangel, who manages the great Wanamaker organ in the Grand Court of what is now Lord & Taylor's, I concluded that the *Founder's Bell* is an object of pride to many Philadelphians. These men told me they love the deep D tone of the bell. They are aware of its special tuning. I suppose it means as much to them as Big Ben does to Londoners. Ray Biswanger, in his book about Philadelphia's historic Wanamaker organ, wrote, "For the past 70 years [the bell's] majestic tones have delighted residents and workers in the heart of Center City.[12] Another writer, Scott Huler, noting that "the city derives much of its image from the other bell [the Liberty Bell], the one that doesn't ring," and hailing the one that does, claimed that "Countless Philadelphians unconsciously cock their ears for *The Founder's Bell*'s hourly tolling."[13]

Chapter XI

JERUSALEM THE GOLDEN

I was born under the shadow of a bell
—Nora Violet Johnston

"As I went up into the belfry," Cyril Johnston's sister Nora Johnston would write in a memoir, "the sun was just rising on the Judean and Moabite Hills." She could see "a glint of the Dead Sea in the distance." "As I sat down at the keyboard, and played my first number of the programme, 'Jerusalem the Golden,' I realized that I was actually playing in the Holy City . . . "[1] It was April 9, 1933, Palm Sunday in Jerusalem. Nora was performing the inaugural recital on a 35-bell carillon built by her brother Cyril for the tower of the new YMCA building. Still one of Jerusalem's tallest and most beautiful architectural features, situated across the street from the King David Hotel, it was designed by Arthur Loomis Harmon, a partner of the same firm—Shreve, Lamb and Harmon—that had created the Empire State Building in New York. Until this time, the carillon instrument had not reached the

141

Middle East, nor has any since. Nora was excited to be in Jerusalem, and to be part of introducing something new to it. "When I came down from the belfry," she went on, "what a sight met my eyes! It was like a scene out of Arabian Nights. Massed against the gates of the building were . . . Arabs, Greeks, Orthodox Jews, Egyptians." It seemed to her that "every nationality in the world was there." She wondered what they thought "when they saw a female adorned in white shorts and socks, emerging from the belfry door."[2] The question was telling, but in the ensuing days she would have more serious things to wonder about. Before her six-week contract was up, Nora would lose herself in the Holy Land, though not to the degree that, say, the radical American Bishop James Pike would in 1969, perishing in the Judean desert while researching Christian origins, and/or having lost his mind. Nora must have been in culture shock; she was away from home for too long unattended by anyone she knew. And she had responsibilities. Sent there by her older brother, she was representing his English bellfounding firm; the money for both bells and building came from America; and Nora owed her training in carillon playing to Belgium. Her mentor and teacher at the school in Malines, the celebrated Jef Denyn whom she called "Papa Jef," saw her off on her first official engagement to inaugurate a carillon with the words, "Be a good girl, Nora, and do me the credit in Jerusalem."[3]

Nora was a 47-year old "girl" in 1933! Unmarried, still living with her mother, six years earlier she had abandoned her first career in the theater, acting in plays and producing them in London, and committed herself to the study of the carillon. In her memoir she never mentions the theater, which ended disastrously for her after she lost upwards of £2000 producing the Flemish dramatist Maurice Maeterlinck's "Bluebird," and her brother bailed her out. Her effervescent chapter on Jerusalem betrays not the slightest hint of the trouble she got into while playing recitals there. This is not to say that she should or for that matter could have. The proper form then was to put the best face possible on any account. And as a woman, a pioneer in a man's profession,

Nora was obliged to present a good model. She also left out the loaded political situation in what was then of course Palestine, under British Mandate since 1917—a climate that probably affected her indirectly. One omission in Nora's book really stands out—and that is her brother. If not for Cyril, her memoir, all about bells and carillon playing, would never have been written. Her brother's success in carillon building (beginning 1922) was naturally the force behind Nora's own entry to the field. Cyril had in fact made the formal introduction for her to study in Malines, writing a fatherly letter to Jef Denyn in 1924 asking him to accept his sister as a pupil at the school. Promoting Nora as having had "musical training since early childhood" and having a "good ear," he made sure also to apologize for Nora's gender. "Of course, this is a new idea, and we do not know if you have any objection to ladies invading the Art of Carillon playing . . . "4

Once Nora began studying in 1926, it would take her seven years (traveling between Croydon and Malines) to complete the requirements, passing her exams shortly before she embarked for Jerusalem. She was the fourth woman to obtain her diploma from the school, established in 1922, and the first Englishwoman. Just a year or so into her studies, during 1927–28, Nora made a startling tour around Belgium and the Netherlands, playing at least 23 concerts in various cathedrals. On the Continent and on her own, Nora seemed able to carve out a sense of herself as separate from her brother, perhaps even the grander sense of superiority as an artist. Between the siblings, two years apart in age, there must have been an unspoken pact: as the prized boy, Cyril got the best deal far and away, a privilege for which he would have to pay, sometimes literally. Then in 1930 when at age 46 he married and escaped his household of origins, his culpability magnified. No longer an "ally" at home, he now had a wife who would supplant Nora in various official functions, and disapprove of her to boot. Nora was or became a bête noire for her brother.

I knew something about Nora from my mother, who informed me at least once that Cyril had told her his sister was a "dipsomaniac." A term of 19th century origin, it's defined in the

Oxford English Dictionary as "a morbid and insatiable craving for alcohol." My mother, though not unlike Nora in at least one important aspect, never drank except for an occasional beer, nor smoked cigarettes (Nora much enjoyed the Belgian brand, Michels, and I've read that she favored Woodbines too), and in her looks she was quite fair with a mild countenance, while Nora was dark and sharp-featured. In my mother, Cyril was I believe finding a sister figure, not a mother or wife—someone he could have fun with, not settle down with. Like Nora, my mother was an independent woman with a zest for travel and adventure. Neither of them ever married, and they were both tall and lean in their youth. Both women had a good sense of humor, enjoyed people and made friends easily. A story Nora tells early in her memoir illustrates a family hilarity she shared with her brother, suggesting a close bond in tandem with their rivalry. So she does mention Cyril, but by his first name, just this once and in a private context, divorcing him utterly from his career in bellfounding—astonishing perhaps in a book of over 200 pages, considering the many carillon instruments he built that she played, either on demonstration keyboards in the Croydon foundry or at large. The siblings, in Malines together in 1923, spent an evening with the maestro Jef Denyn and his family. Trying to speak the native tongue, their "deplorable Flemish," wrote Nora, "in an appalling accent and no grammar," turned the dinner into an "uproarious affair."[5]

For my mother, an only child, seventeen years younger than Cyril, from a country often called Britain's offspring, Cyril was clearly like a father. She must have started looking for one sometime after her own beloved father, Frederick Herbert Crowe, died in 1920—at the age of 46. But did she really want to replace her father? Or could she? I hold that she couldn't, otherwise she would not have fallen so seriously for an unavailable man. I see her as the kind of resolutely father-identified woman who disdains the role of her mother, thus heads inevitably toward an unmarried state. And Nora surely had a similar orientation to her parents. The mothers in both cases made no effort to turn their daughters into versions of themselves. Or if they did, they were unsuccessful, with mutual disapproval, especially by the mother of her daughter, underlying an abortive transference. I know about this in Nora's case from early remarks in her memoir, and in my mother's from what she told me about the close bond she had with her father, and her father's contempt, shared naturally by her, for her mother—his domestic, relatively uneducated wife.

Daughters like Nora and my mother can end up left out of the nuclear scheme, devoted forever to their fathers, busy with careers, or as nuns worshipping a father in heaven. My mother nonetheless tried her best to go against this socially unalluring destiny, though she was bound as I see it to fail. Such a "disappointing" outcome seemed dictated by her meeting Cyril in the right place—aboard ship on a trans-Atlantic ocean voyage. Here, in mid-Atlantic, I find the trope of my birth: a couple suspended between ports, in the transitional medium of water, fated to live out the liminality of their meeting, never to make it to those symbols of permanence: land, legalities, home and family. They did find land of course, but only to resume their affair. Chance meetings with amorous results in such uncertain settings as ships' crossings, where secrecy tends to be the ordering principle, seem rather unlikely to find the common grounds or matching and complementary histories necessary for any real future.

Nora Johnston had a few romantic crossings of her own, never however meeting the kind of stranger who would change her life. Her voyage to Port Said in Egypt, leaving from the Tilbury docks in London, March 25, 1933, en route to Jerusalem, was quixotic in itself. And her ship of choice, the *Viceroy of India,* built in 1929 by the P&O for the Bombay service, was for this line a new model in magnificent opulence and comfort. Nora was proud to be the grand-niece of Arthur Anderson, co-founder in 1837 of the line upon which she was traveling: the P&O, or Peninsular & Oriental Steamship Navigation Company [See Chapter III]. And she seemed always capable, as her memoir attests, of having a great time and making a lot of friends. The *Viceroy of India* had a First Class Smoking Room done in period-design Scots baronial, replicating the Great Hall of a castle—

crossed swords decorating the walls, baronial arms hanging over a large fireplace, plush armchairs, rugs and tables. A built-in swimming pool, the P&O's first indoors, was surrounded by Pompeian reliefs. Ostentation altogether included an 18th century style music room and a dining saloon with blue marbled pillars. At 19,645 tons, the *Viceroy* was a benchmark ship, bringing new standards of speed, and the luxury of quietness thanks to her relatively untried turbo-electric machinery. Alas, she sunk only nine years after Nora's voyage, torpedoed off Oran in an Algerian harbor by a German U-boat. The *Viceroy* had been canvassed to be part of a convoy of 20 ships carrying troops in *Operation Torch*, the invasion of North Africa, which began November 8, 1942.

The day Nora sailed, Cyril Johnston wrote a letter to Mr. F. W. Ramsey, General Secretary of the YMCA to say his sister Nora was on her way and would arrive at Port Said on April 4th. She would be in Jerusalem well in time to play the inaugural recital. He added that he had succeeded in making arrangements for another carillonneur to assist his sister by playing alternate concerts: Captain van Geyseghem, an assistant instructor at the Malines Carillon School. At least eighteen recitals between April 9th and 26th had been scheduled for Nora and her "assistant." And the two musicians were slated also to teach one or more persons in Jerusalem how to play the instrument, ensuring that someone would keep it up after they left. Through van Geyseghem, Cyril apparently was hoping that the pressure on his sister would be minimized. It isn't clear whether it was Nora's or Cyril's idea in the first place for her to go. The Y in Jerusalem had been eager to have a name-value carillonneur dedicate the instrument. Mr. Ramsey was expecting the dedication of the Y itself to be "one of the most impressive and significant events in all the history of the Christian movement." On business in New York, he had met and befriended Kamiel Lefévere, then playing the Riverside Church carillon. Writing to Amelia F. G. Jarvie of Gloucester Massachusetts, the donor of the carillon (and niece of the building's donor James Newbegin Jarvie), Ramsey said he hoped she would kick in more money, beyond the total $15,617 cost of the carillon, for player expenses. In the end she did—but for Nora, whose expenses, a lot less than they would have been for Lefévere, were to be shared by Gillett & Johnston. With the question of carillonneur settled by July of 1932, Ramsey wrote a few "famous last words" to the firm: "We do not know of Miss Johnston's work and are trusting your judgment entirely in arranging for this service."[6]

As regarded Nora's work, he would have nothing to worry about—she would in fact receive very favorable notices, from Y authorities and others—but who could have guessed that England was sending out a lady with a serious drinking problem. Only Cyril and his mother perhaps, and by then his wife, but surely also one Fanny Langford, the family nanny since 1891 who would stay with them until she died in 1945, then to be buried in the Johnston family plot in Croydon. Fanny fussed over Nora, and played a surrogate mother role, a devoted caretaker, one much less critical it can be imagined than Nora's mother. Van Geyseghem was no doubt a good idea, and necessary for the number of recitals scheduled, but if Cyril had sent Fanny Langford to accompany Nora, he might have saved himself and his firm a huge embarrassment. After three weeks in Jerusalem, Nora was unable to hide or contain her alcohol dependency any more. March 25th, the day she sailed from London, in a letter to Waldo Heinrichs, General Secretary of the Y in Jerusalem, she sounded a cautionary note about herself. "Though I am quite fit now, I have been awfully overworked in Belgium, cramming three years of training into just over one year."[7] I wonder if Cyril had not made Nora having her diploma a condition of her going to Jerusalem. On April 23rd, having played the April 9th inaugural concert, the April 18th dedication concert, and ten concerts altogether (alternating with van Geseghem), she wrote to Heinrichs again, this time on site and complaining angrily about the tourists allowed in the belfry during recitals, making playing difficult. What she wanted was reasonable—to have the doors giving access to the belfry locked before and during recitals, and nobody allowed up in the lift without permission. But her tone was petulant, "I have come a great many miles to try and do the best I can . . . " and in the end threatening: "I shall most reluctantly be obliged to stop any of my future recitals even if I have started, until the belfry is clear."[8] Resolved or not, Nora did keep on playing. The day she wrote her letter of protest, her program included the hymn, *O God Our Help in Ages Past*—a sentiment, it turned out, she herself would soon desperately need. The next day, April 24th, Captain van Geyseghem played his Farewell Recital, and left for home. After that, Nora continued on her own, beyond the officially prepared program of concerts. May 8th, Heinrichs sent a startling cable to Cyril in Croydon:

> YOUR SISTER SERIOUSLY ILL SHOULD LEAVE PALESTINE IMMEDIATELY ARRANGING PASSAGE MAY REQUIRE MEDICAL ATTENTION DO YOU AUTHORISE ADEQUATE EXPENDITURE WIRE.

Cyril cabled back promptly:

> WIRE NATURE ILLNESS PROPOSE SHIP DATE SAILING PATIENT HAS RETURN TICKET PRESUME DOCTOR AUTHORIZING VOYAGE WHAT ADDITIONAL EXPENDITURES REQUIRED.[9]

Heinrichs' letter to Cyril that day provided some of the unhappy details. Soon after Nora arrived in Jerusalem, she left her quarters at the YMCA building, and went to a regular hotel, evidently because the Y didn't serve alcohol. "She made all her carillon engagements and [taught her] lessons regularly but frequently decidedly under the influence of liquor." When the situation grew worse, Heinrichs summoned medical attention in the form of one Dr. T. Canaan, who reported that Nora was having "delirium tremens," and was "in an abnormal mental condition"—that "she wept, cried, was excited, rough, and begging." A nurse was enlisted to be with her day and night to "prevent her from any rash conduct." "We consider her situation very serious . . . I am writing this letter with extreme frankness so you may be apprised of the facts . . . I am very sorry to have to terminate this contract under [such a] condition . . . "10

Nora's violent behavior on the 8th —and failure to be able to sleep even on large doses of luminal and veronal—had convinced the doctor that she should return immediately to England. May 9th, Heinrichs wrote to Cyril again saying he had arranged passage for Nora back to London the following day, May 10th, from the port of Haifa on the SS *Italia* of the Lloyd Triestino line. Her condition had improved from the day before, and she was giving a farewell concert on the bells that night. May 9th, as it happened, was Cyril's date of birth. The improvement was due—as Heinrichs makes clear in a letter of much greater disclosure to F.W. Ramsey—to the fear induced in Nora over Cyril learning the full nature of her state. She had refused even to leave Jerusalem, and when Heinrichs threatened to cable her brother all the particulars, she was "brought to heel and . . . agreed to leave May 10th." Heinrichs told Cyril he would see she was safely on board, and he had arranged for necessary precautions on the ship. To that end he wrote to the SS *Italia* Captain, commending Nora to him for "every possible courtesy," warning him that she would bear "careful watching," and adding the protective fiction: " . . . as she has been passing through a serious mental disturbance owing to tragic losses of relatives at home." On board the ship in Haifa, at the last moment Nora threatened to come ashore.11

The very day Nora left, May 10th, the donor Amelia Jarvie wrote to Cyril Johnston telling him she was "immensely pleased with the bells, the beauty of their individual notes and their harmony . . . it was a thrilling moment when I first heard them ring out over the Holy City and another when your sister played 'Jerusalem the Golden' as we were taking our farewell look. [Jarvie here was alluding to the May 9th concert]. Everyone spoke of the beautiful way in which your sister and Captain van Geyseghem played . . . "12 Waldo Heinrichs too, in his May 9th letter to Cyril, spoke warmly of his sister's artistry: "We have enjoyed Miss Johnston's concerts very much and they have made an excellent impression here. She has been well received by the

Jerusalem public." On a different note, stressing only Nora's condition, Heinrichs wrote to Mr. Ramsey: "The selection of Miss Johnston for the carillonneur by the firm has certainly not been a service without prejudice. Dr. Canaan believes her condition is one of long standing. The unfortunate thing is that she seems enamored of Jerusalem and wants to return to it. You may be sure there is nothing in our budget to provide for it."[13] Heinrichs was steamed.

Cyril was himself "much distressed" about what had happened, as he wrote to Heinrichs on May 24th. Without apologizing directly for sending Nora to Jerusalem, he was brimming with appreciation for the care taken of his sister, and the frankness with which he was informed of the situation. Beyond that, one could read into a request he made for more detailed data on Nora's flight into alcohol a certain confirmation of her condition as "one of long standing," the way Dr. Canaan had put it. "It would greatly help me," he wrote, "for our [family] Doctor here if I know full particulars such as the date of the first occasion on which any symptoms were observed and the date the attack commenced." Cyril concluded his letter, "I am sure you will understand my position as her only brother and indeed practically her only near male relative."[14] In reply, Heinrichs was admiring and respectful. "We greatly appreciate your courteous note," he wrote, "and the friendly way you have taken the situation." He hoped Cyril would feel they had done "everything possible to protect the reputation of your firm and of Miss Johnston who made a wide circle of friends in Jerusalem."[15] How was it finally, one might wonder, for Nora when she disembarked from the *SS Italia* at the Tilbury docks in London, to be met by Cyril? Or was she met only by her mother and/or Fanny Langford? Then simply swept off to the family doctor? And never perhaps contacted directly by Cyril?

I favor the latter conclusion. I doubt that Cyril ever confronted his sister in person. It wasn't the English way. And it wouldn't have done any good. He may not even have been angry. So far as I know, Nora never inaugurated or dedicated one of his carillons again. She would play G&J instruments, though not by recommendation of the firm. Her brother's great carillon-making days, or "glory years" as they've been called, were over by 1933. After 1932 for instance, he made only seven more carillons for North America—less than a fourth of the thirty instruments he built altogether, beginning 1922, for the U.S. and Canada. Just one of the last seven was installed in the Northeastern United States where Nora would make two tours, one in 1937, the other in 1938, giving a lecture she called "The Romance of Bells," and playing a "portable carillon" she had had custom-made for herself. The portable was her answer to the problem of not having a position as resident carillonneur, with no prospects of ever having one. Women at that time didn't have such positions. There was one, and she didn't last long. Gladys Watkins, a New Zealander, and only the second woman to graduate, in 1930, from Denyn's School, would play the 49-bell G&J Wellington War Memorial Carillon in New Zealand, perhaps because Denyn himself thought so highly of her. Her residency lasted from 1932, date of the instrument's dedication, to 1940, when she died. Nora called Watkins "quite one of the brilliant students at the School." One other woman had a position. In the U.S., Mary Mesquita Dahlmer played the 23-bell Taylor instrument at Our Lady of Good Voyage Church in Gloucester, Massachusetts, from the year of its installation in 1922 until 1945. Another American, and an esteemed carillonneuse—as the media liked calling any woman who dared to tackle the keyboard of "fistic combat"—was Ruth "Muzzy" Conniston, from a Waspish Connecticut family. Described as tall and stately, with a "morning smile," she had a music degree from Yale and was a concert organist when the carillon attracted her attention. In 1927 she substituted for Percival Price at the Park Avenue instrument in New York, then succeeded him after Price (who had been lured to the church when Anton Brees was banished) left to return to his native Canada, becoming resident carillonneur at Ottawa. Conniston was playing a virtually condemned instrument, due to be broken up, and parts transferred to Riverside Church the following year. She had additional work, frequently guesting at Princeton, playing the G&J Cleveland

Tower carillon dedicated June 17 that year [See Chapter XII]. And she was actually considered for the upcoming residency at Riverside. One of Rockefeller's assistants favored Conniston for the position, saying that while alternating with Price at Park Avenue, "no one has noticed the difference [in their playing]." R.F.A. Housman, GM of Gillett & Johnston, recommended her this way: "In my estimation she interprets simple tunes and airs in a way that sometimes gives more pleasure to the average public than the more elaborate and brilliant performances of the celebrities."[16] Kamiel Lefévere of course would get the Riverside job.

Nora Johnston was painfully aware of her disadvantage. I can see her, had her path led her there, at the suffragist barricades in London of that era. Her temperament, birth position and circumstances were suited for disruption. The challenging comment she made over her appearance in Jerusalem, wondering what the Arabs thought when she "emerged from the belfry door in white shorts and socks" echoed an earlier remark when she first went to Malines to study. "I was very conscious of my skirts," she wrote. Skirts, especially long ones, made negotiating the pedals of a carillon keyboard, sliding back and forth on the long playing bench, difficult indeed. Nora's solution was boy's attire. She tells us how this happened: Her fellow students in Malines tried to trick her, saying the automatic mechanism in the tower had broken down and it was the duty of the newest pupil to stay in the tower through the night and ring the big bell every quarter hour. "Messieurs," she addressed them, in unmistakable tones of manifesto, "tomorrow morning you will see me no longer in skirts, but in boy's breeches like yourselves. We shall be garçons together and I no simple miss to be led up the garden path by you strong, silent men."[17] The men at the school would call her "Mon vieux," a masculine term of endearment. She became "one of the boys," a phrase then unknown, but apt for the camaraderie Nora had with her male competitors, especially several English compatriots at the school.

She loved being "chaired" shoulder-high around a marketplace one evening in Belgium by eleven English footballers. The team had been listening to her concert near the Cathedral tower of Thielt. When she emerged from the belfry door, the captain and the rest of the team were waiting for her. The captain, with an "ingratiating smile," told her they had heard it was an English girl playing—"[so] whether you like it or not we're going to carry you round the marketplace."[18] In another story about herself, she became the victim of her lateness getting to Liège for a scheduled concert. Arriving at the Grande Place in the Cathedral vicinity, big crowds made her passage difficult. "A stalwart policeman," wrote Nora, "did his utmost to prevent me giving my recital. He put out his arm to keep me back and said I couldn't get through the crowds just yet as they were all waiting to hear an English girl play the carillon." Nora assured him in her "best French" that they would go on waiting indefinitely unless he let her through. At that moment, she saw the little red light go on in the belfry, the warning signal that a carillon recital was about to begin. "And there was I, more or less in the arms of a policemen! [Now] I told him in both French and Flemish so there should be no mistake, who I was and he let me through."[19]

A number of newspapers, from New Zealand to Britain and France and Boston in the U.S., covered Nora's Continental tours during 1927–28. A headline in the *Naval & Military Record* reads, "WOMAN FLIES 1,000 MILES IN FIVE DAYS."[20] The report had Nora making two round trips by airplane between Malines and Croydon in these five days, although according to her memoir, she made just one round trip.[21] She was studying at this time in Malines, but was in Croydon at Cyril's foundry, playing the new carillon for Belgium's Louvain University (1928). There she met an American man, Lucian Sharpe, who had flown to Croydon from Belgium on his private plane expressly to hear Jef Denyn, the honored guest player on hand. Hearing Nora play as well, Sharpe became "so intrigued," she wrote in her book, "to hear a woman handle this gigantic instrument" that he followed her to Malines the next day, when she returned to resume her studies, to hear her play the St. Rombouts instrument. Sharpe, his pilot, his engineer and secretary installed themselves at her own little hotel, the Trois Chevaux. Now Sharpe was evidently more than "intrigued." Hearing Nora play again, Sharpe pressed her to return by plane with him to Croydon where he planned to "discuss buying a carillon from [her] brother" to be installed in the tower at his works in Providence Rhode Island—a well known firm of American engineers, Brown and Sharpe. Nora was worried about going, but "Papa Jef" advised her to, for the sake of "business." She was wearing the wedding feast dress from a party that day in Malines when she left with Sharpe to fly to Croydon. She wrote, "I shall never forget the amazement of the family when we landed at home in time for Sunday supper [Croydon was still Britain's official airport], for only the day before they had seen me off to Malines at Victoria Station." The next day Sharpe flew Nora back to Belgium. The carillon for his works in Providence turned into a gift for Brown University of which Sharpe was an 1893 alumnus, but that never happened either. At least a dozen newspapers in the U.S. and Canada gave accounts of a carillon of 51 bells with a two-ton bourdon ordered by Lucian Sharpe through Atlantic telephone from Gillett & Johnston, an approach said to be without precedent. It's tempting to try and fill this story in a bit. Surely some kind of "bride price" or perhaps a sexual favor was involved, if never stated directly. And if so, Nora was not for sale.

If Nora could do nothing about Cyril and his indelible birthright at home, she could rebel abroad, or in a memoir that erased him. She could also invent a "portable carillon" that took her places where tower invitations might not be forthcoming. But with a lawless streak, and a serious addiction, Nora seemed unsuited to any permanent employment or position. Jerusalem alone, a kind of visiting artist's residency, lasted far too long. With her portable she could do hit and run gigs, more promisingly staying out of trouble. In New York in 1937, the base for her tour, she was on her own. From her writings, it's as impossible to tell if anything went amiss in America as it is from her chapter on Jerusalem. At the Hotel Astor (for five months!), her account of her stay there, and her forays to perform, is locked up tight with superlatives, unsparingly, unbelievably upbeat. Nora's first tour ended with a visit to Eleanor Roosevelt at the White House. "Mrs. Roosevelt was a most gracious person, very much interested in my portable carillon, and curious and amused as to why I alluded to it sometimes as 'he' and sometimes as 'she.'"[22] Nora thought of her portable as her child. When it was bad, e.g. got lost, which it did once, it was a "he," when good a "she." No bells per se were involved. Its soundmakers were metal bars or resonators, adapted from an orchestral Vibraphone; they were hit with hammers attached to the pedals and manuals of a regular carillon keyboard. Comparable to a practice clavier, the portable was four and a half feet square, and weighed about 700 lbs. Nora's idea clearly was to approximate the sound of a carillon. R.F.A. Housman thought her portable didn't come close. He was writing to Percival Price who wanted an evaluation. Price had been contacted by Nora or the manager of her American tour about performing in Ottawa. Housman indirectly discouraged Price from inviting Nora. He was afraid that if people mistook her portable for anything resembling the sound of a carillon, "it would affect us all adversely." He felt she would do well on her own, with her lecture and lantern slides. "She has good personality and address, and speaks well." Nora however was very proud of her pi or personal instrument. Whatever its efficacy, it served a vital compensatory need to feel active in a field that was in crucial ways closed to her. Eventually, toward the end of her life, while she was staying at a dry-out place near London called Manor Farm, she hauled her portable into meadows of cows, claiming the sound of her playing helped the cows give more milk.

I have long had copies of news clippings with photos showing Nora at her portable serenading the cows at Manor Farm. For longer than I can remember, I have heard strange things about Nora. Men have smiled crookedly over her, or spoken of her with disbelief, or shifted uncomfortably not knowing if they should say anything at all. In her memoir Nora describes herself as "that mad English girl." She never mentions the difficulty of being her. She loved bells and playing them and with the odds against her, she heroically you could say never gave up. If cows were her last audience, she was not too proud to have them. Nora may not have been the kind of genius Virginia Woolf had in mind for the fictional sister of Shakespeare she wrote about in her feminist nonfiction book *A Room of One's Own.* But Nora had a brother who was Shakespearean, i.e. Stradavarian, in his field, and she claimed a piece of it to make a great run of her own.

Chapter XII

THE BELL(E)S OF ST. MARY'S

An institution is the lengthened shadow of one man
—Ralph Waldo Emerson

Things make reparation . . . and therein due justice to one another
according to the order of time
—Maximander

During the late 1940s while Nora Johnston was writing her memoir, which I was able to unearth in 2001 from the archive of the Carillon School in Malines, and have published in 2002,[1] I was finishing up my years at a very English prep school in Peekskill New York. Nora signed off her memoir with the date of October 14, 1947. Four months earlier I had graduated from St. Mary's School with fifteen classmates. Beginning the fall of 1941, a few months before Pearl Harbor and President Roosevelt's official declaration of war, I had lived there for six years. In June, the very month I graduated, Nora's brother Cyril was in the U.S. seeing to a carillon installation in Stamford

Connecticut, his last trip to America. Upon his death two and a half years later, I would begin to learn just how close by he had often been. St. Mary's was a High Episcopal school, run by the nuns of an order called Sisters of St. Mary. Eighty-five girls, directed by a cadre of nuns whose convent was nearby, and taught by a resident lay-faculty, lived and studied in a single structure—a truly beautiful building. Red brick, studded with French windows, ivy-clad when first I went there, surmounted by two castellated towers, proportionally breathtaking, it sits gloriously on a high promontory that was called Mount Saint Gabriel, overlooking the Hudson River facing south. If you take the Metro North train from Grand Central in New York City that runs along the river, 40 miles north at the Peekskill stop you can see the building by peering out a river-side window diagonally upwards. The train veers westward right after Peekskill, rumbling along way beneath the school (it used to make our windows rattle in their lead frames), crossing a trestle and rounding the Military Reservation of Camp Smith before snaking north again, progressing beneath the eastern end of Bear Mountain Bridge, on toward Garrison and Cold Spring. Our soccer field was a steep walk down from the school premises through wooded land halfway to the railroad tracks. It wasn't just the soccer at St. Mary's that was English; our English classes took their name seriously, rarely touching on American literature. History, after the Ancient stuff, was updated quickly to England, mysteriously if you happened to think about it and I never did, leaving out the country in which we lived. And the extraordinary building we were so fortunate to inhabit was designed by an American architect famous for his Anglo-Gothic Revivalist style.

It wasn't until I heard his name—Ralph Adams Cram (1863–1942)—in connection with buildings and towers accommodating carillons by Cyril Johnston that I learned he was the architect of St. Mary's, built in 1910. I had walked or climbed in a number of Cram structures including St. John the Divine in New York City, and on behalf of carillon researches before realizing I had spent six years living in one. Nora Johnston visited a

Cram tower in Richmond, Virginia—playing the World War I Memorial Carillon of 1929 by Taylor—while she was on tour in America in 1937. Architects in general seem as anonymous to the occupants of their erections and to people at large, as the founders of bells are to everyone except those who play them. In the world of carillonneurs, bellfounders are integral to their small society. As the daughter of one, I was invited to speak at the Mercersburg Academy in Pennsylvania in 1993 about Cyril Johnston, founder of the 43-bell, 1926 Mercersburg carillon—the first in Pennsylvania and second largest in the U.S. at that time. Here, not knowing it yet, I was speaking in a Ralph Adams Cram tower cum chapel, dated the same year the bells were dedicated. This commodious tower, reached from the splendid chapel by convenient open staircases, was built obviously to provide for a carillon.

While at Mercersburg in 1993, at the "Fourth Annual Mid-Atlantic Carillonneurs Conference," celebrating 100 years of the Academy, I learned that a plan was underway to add bells to the carillon. And I was asked, in Cyril Johnston's name, to give my opinion on the widespread practice of replacements and/or additions to carillon instruments. Cyril was called "Your Dad"—a most disconcerting attribution. I had no way of speaking for "My Dad," and I was ill-informed back then on the merits of tearing instruments apart. Nor did I know the stunning extent to which carillonneurs and bellfounders are in each other's pockets. Under the impression that bell casting itself had improved, not that commercial interests entered in, or that the integrity of an instrument could be at stake, I offered the lame thought that as time goes on the old bells might remain but in some token or "historic" way. I felt proud somehow that the Mercersburg carillon, its bells hanging in the floor above where I was talking in the tower playing room, had lasted intact since 1926. It was considered one of the loveliest sounds in the carillon argot. Three years later, in 1996, six trebles would be added (by Meeks & Watson of Ohio), making it a 49-bell instrument. Alas, that would hardly be the end of it. At current writing, only 31 of Cyril's original 43 bells hang in

Mercersburg Academy's Cram tower. Other carillons have been mangled or dismembered beyond recognition.

Both buildings and carillons are subject to changes and enlargements, but *some* buildings become protected as historic or landmark sites, while the carillon, in the United States anyway, has never enjoyed such a consideration. Unfortunately my beloved school St. Mary's, a small Cram jewel, was not protected, and during the 1980s its entire interior was gutted to make way for condominium apartments in a tragic sale to Peekskill developers. The sale was expedited by George E. Pataki, then the Mayor of Peekskill, later the Governor of New York. Virtually the only reason a carillon has survived intact is ironically through neglect. Another R.A. Cram tower accommodating a G&J carillon is at Princeton University's Graduate College. Here, a history of both neglect and interference would leave an instrument altered unrecognizably. Transmission systems (linking keyboards to clappers) once attended to, have been a harmless actually enlightened focus for doing something good for a carillon. These systems have benefited greatly from overhauling because they fall out of repair, and the modern ones are mechanically more efficient. Keyboards have also been extensively replaced, especially as developed under the North American Keyboard Standard agreed upon by the members of the Guild of Carillonneurs in 1966. *Bells themselves, once tuned, never lose their tone unless they crack.* (Acid rain, also industrial pollution, can be factors, eating away metal and eventually, after say fifty or a hundred years, affecting the pitch). But bells themselves are the premier targets of bellfounders, or of musicians eager to compete with other towers in making their instruments as big or hopefully bigger, certainly "better."

As if by magic, an entire carillon once disappeared from the campus of a school in Nashville, Tennessee. In this way, ironically the instrument remained historically intact. It was an astounding sort of heist—a 23-bell carillon built in 1928 by Gillett & Johnston for the Ward-Belmont School ending up on the lawn of an electronic company called Schulmerich Inc. in Sellersville, Pennsylvania. Like St. Mary's in Peekskill, Ward-Belmont had roots as a girl's school in the 1800s. Now Belmont University, with a co-ed student body of 2,800, the land was originally a private estate of 640 acres dating from 1850. A Water Tower, over a hundred feet high, fed by two springs and supplying water through a network of underground pipes to every part of the estate, ultimately became the receptacle, the campanile, for the G&J carillon of 23 bells in 1929. During the Civil War the structure functioned as a signal tower or lookout for Federal troops. The fund for bells, started in 1921, was an Alumnae effort. Costing $13,000, the carillon was installed in November 1928, during the time Cyril Johnston was "resting" in California, and drawing up plans in Chicago and New York for the University of Chicago carillon [See Chapter VII]. The Ward-Belmont instrument was to be the second in the south, the 25th in North America, and the first in a girl's school. I can imagine how special it would have seemed to me if St. Mary's had had Cyril's bells in it. My school certainly had the appropriate towers. The school was built in 1910, twelve years before carillons were exported to the U.S.

The only bells we had were metal concave spheres fastened to corridor walls that sounded off electrically, running our lives, telling us when to go places; and sanctus bells rung, i.e. shaken, at chapel services by our two resident and alternately presiding priests. A little dinner bell was rung by the Sister Superior at her head table after every girl had filed into the refectory, nodded to her, marched to an assigned table, and grace had been sung (in Latin in two parts)—the signal to sit down and begin partaking.

It's conceivable that one of our school's two castellated towers had a chance to become the vessel for a carillon. Princeton University's Cleveland Tower, in memory of President Grover Cleveland, centerpiece of the Graduate College, was built in 1913, three years after St. Mary's. Not until 1927 would it accommodate bells—a 35-bell Gillett & Johnston instrument. A much richer architectural compound at Princeton—the stone tower, grand at 40 square feet, 173 feet high, rising from the southeastern corner of the Graduate College: two linked four-sided building structures surrounding courtyards or quadrangles—was more favorable altogether for the extra expense and size of a carillon.

The single building of St. Mary's was constructed like the two that are conjoined at Princeton, on four sides enclosing a quad. In the middle of ours was a small rectangular lily pool. Our yearbooks were sometimes called Quad-Angle. Many Anglo-Gothic features of our red brick building are reflected in the stone of Princeton's Graduate College: the French and bay windows or clustering of windows within masonry walls, pointed arches with multiple ribs including Sally Port facades, stone mullions separating panes of glass, the various castellated elements.

Overall, it was Cram's design for intimacy and community that made these buildings so distinctive. At St. Mary's we were living virtually in a mandala, of rectangles within rectangles, all rooms and corridors giving necessarily on the womb of the quadrangle, which was entered and exited through two large Sally Ports facing each other from the quad's northern and southern ends. At any point, all students within the four sides of the building surrounding the quad were more or less equidistant from the center of the lily pool. The harmoniousness of life at St. Mary's, its routines and rituals and architecture inextricably mixed, was its notable characteristic.

Visiting Princeton's Graduate College on a mild sunny afternoon, I imagined the smiling students I saw wandering in and out of their quarters existing in a similar kind of thrall. The idea Princeton got for a carillon around 1925 came from a member of the class of 1892 after traveling abroad and hearing the instrument in the Lowlands. Someone at the Ward-Belmont School in Nashville got the same idea, though it is not known how exactly.

The Princeton carillon would become one of the most neglected and messed-with bell assemblages in our history. Ward-Belmont would enjoy their rare percussive concert instrument intact for two decades—before it was grabbed up and spirited north by some unusual highwaymen. Schulmerich Electronics Inc. has made among other tinklers a spurious bell product called "Carillonic Bells." Tuned bronze rods weighing just ounces, struck by solenoid from a keyboard or automatically by a "roll," are electronically amplified through speakers located anywhere but most egregiously in a tower. In 1951–52 Schulmerich waged an aggressive campaign to talk Ward-Belmont out of its 23 cast bells in exchange for one of their "Carillonic" devices. The school had just been bought by the Tennessee Baptist Convention, becoming Belmont College, a co-ed junior college. George L. Schulmerich, president of his electronics company, wrote a letter in 1951 proposing to install a complete "Carillonic Bell" instrument costing $10,000, but free of cost in consideration of receiving the 23 cast bells in full payment of same. Schulmerich claimed that "the value of the cast bells" was not very much to his firm but that they wanted them for a museum they were planning of cast bells gathered from all parts of the world. Press releases and letters abounded with sales mumbo-jumbo confusing the legitimate concert carillon with their "Carillonic" contrivance. At the same time they would clearly compare the two, promoting the saliency of an automatic device over a hand-played instrument. Schulmerich boldly inflated his product, e.g., "Our 25 bells [not bells really, but notes] will have considerably more sonority, color, timbre, and carrying power."[2] But the electronic firm was able to play on the difficulty at that time of finding and keeping, heck hiring, anyone who could perform on a carillon keyboard. Especially in the provinces, where a man like Rockefeller, eager to locate and fund a trained, resident player to justify his investment, didn't exist. As Schulmerich truthfully argued, " . . . there are few people today who are interested in, or know the technique of playing cast bells, for they are played from a claviar [sic] that requires considerable physical activity and exposure to the elements."[3] Belmont College, writing to Percival Price, (then collecting information on North American instruments for a book he would write on the subject) excused turning in their carillon by saying that their carillonneur, who doubled as their organist, was getting too old to climb the tower. There was, apparently, no one at the college at that point interested enough to look for a player young enough to make the climb. Nor anyone obviously who understood the *expressive* value or potential of what they had, and could tell Schulmerich where to go. Proudly, and naively it would turn out, Belmont told Price that their instrument would be placed (as Schulmerich had led them to believe), in a "museum of cast bells gathered from all parts of the world."[4]

In July, 1954, only two years after their amazing and uncontested "theft," Schulmerich, far from having any museum plans, wrote to a man in Massachusetts proposing to sell him the Ward-Belmont 23-bell instrument! "This beautiful little carillon," Schulmerich put forward, could be had in its steel frame and equipped with clavier, for the price of $10,000. And he promoted the firm that made it. "Gillette [*sic*] & Johnston, Croyden [*sic*] England, enjoys as you know a very favorable reputation."[5] Cyril Johnston was four years in his grave at this time. What would he have thought? Would the Ward-Belmont annexation have happened had he been alive? The bells were not sold, but Schulmerich had more proverbial aces up its sleeve. Years later, in 1973, two Belmont College faculty members, having learned that their former bells were in Sellersville, paid a visit to Schulmerich to make an inquiry. Told that the Ward-Belmont carillon had been maintained in good condition, and played from time to time by visiting carillonneurs, they were offered the instrument at "fair value price"—for $17,000! Belmont was interested in reacquiring the original bells but they couldn't afford them, and no donor was at hand. A trade-in request by Belmont—to give the cast bells back to them in return for their "Carillonics"—was dismissed out of hand. I suppose the Sellersville company found the suggestion outrageous. Their records showed that for 15 years their electronic device in Nashville had not been serviced, thus would probably be of no value to them, and they were not interested anyway in donating the bells back to their original home. More years passed, and in 1982 Schulmerich submitted a proposal to Belmont for returning the bells, with upgraded features, for a mere $124,550. Schulmerich evidently now thought that the folks they once ripped off would pay any price for sentimental reasons to get their bells back.

To this day, the 23-bell carillon rests on Schulmerich grounds in Sellersville, while all trace of the Carillonic device in Nashville has long disappeared. If the Sellersville firm originally wanted the Ward-Belmont carillon in order to turn it around and sell it, they ended up with a token museum piece on their lawn, the real thing fronting for a fake product behind the scenes. Here it has not been neglected as a concert instrument, serving to attract audiences who might incidentally notice the firm it advertises. In 1979 Frank Law, carillonneur for Washington Memorial Chapel in Valley Forge Pennsylvania, gave a recital observing the fiftieth anniversary of the dedication played in 1929 by Percival Price at Belmont. The Price program of April 12, 1929, had naturally included Ward-Belmont's alma mater, curiously called *The Bells of Ward-Belmont*. The program was high-minded, representing more classical composers than was usual then, with selections by Beethoven (*Ode to Joy*), Händel (*The Harmonious Blacksmith*), Schumann and Mozart. *America the Beautiful* was the opener. Another patriotic air and a couple of folk melodies were included, and at the end, *The Bells of Ward-Belmont*.

Set to the tune of *The Bells of St. Mary's*—the song that would become so popular in 1945 when Bing Crosby sang it in the hit movie of that title and co-starring Ingrid Bergman—Ward-Belmont's use of the tune could have dated from 1917, when it came to the United States from England. Composed in 1914, with music by A. Emmett Adams and lyrics by Douglas Furber, it was a World War I song inspired by the bells of St. Mary's (a peal of a single octave), Southampton's mother Anglican Church, ringing out "in sight and sound of the sea." Since Ward-Belmont had no carillon when they started using *The Bells of St. Mary*'s tune, they were perhaps referencing the kind of electrically sounded bells that directed our lives at St. Mary's in Peekskill. Or they were casually pointing to the "Bel" in Belmont. Most likely, someone at the school had fallen in love with *The Bells of St. Mary*'s and decided to appropriate it for Ward-Belmont, prefixing the school's name with "The Bells of." The question rings changes for me on my school St. Mary's, whose alma mater was sung to *Danny*

Boy!—"St Mary's School," the song went, "Thy name we'll ever cher-ere-ish/ As Times go by/And closest friends must part . . ." During the 1940s at St. Mary's Bing Crosby was big (as were Frank Sinatra, the War, and Thanksgiving soccer games). We had no fancy bells, and I have identified with Ward-Belmont's possession and subsequent loss of them. In a postscript to this story, in 1985 Belmont University purchased 23 new bells cast by the Dutch firm of Petit and Fritsen. The price was $115,464, for bells, keyboard, and a console for programmed automatic play.

Like people or buildings, every carillon has its intricate individual history. The Princeton carillon is interesting for its location in a Ralph Adams Cram tower, but also for its various renovations, sometimes unconventional, beginning 1941. Its neglect was foretold from its inception when the Class of 1892, donor of the carillon, spelled out conditions for having it played minimally as a concert instrument. Three times annually were specified: Christmas Day, Alumni Day, and June 15th, the Class of 1892 graduation anniversary. After the handful of musicians in America who were carillon trained took their turns at Princeton (e.g. Anton Brees did the dedication June 17, 1927; Jef Denyn was imported to perform a series; Ruth Conniston guest-played), the interest in maintaining even those provisional dates languished. The carillon cost the Class of 1892, $60,000. From an endowment fund of $5000 for upkeep of the instrument, just $400 a year was allotted for concerts. The men of 1892 seemed really to want nothing more than an automatic mechanism equipped with favorite tunes. A letter from one classmate to another right after dedication reads, "I fail to see the use of going to the expense of a carillonneur. I think a daily ringing of the bells at some appointed time by automatic device is all that is necessary."[6] One year later, in 1928, William Gorham Rice, author, lecturer and indefatigable publicist for the carillon who appeared to take a proprietary interest in every carillon installed in the U.S., wrote to Charles Hart of the 1892 class. Rice had just visited the Cleveland Tower, and "found great regret expressed by a number of people that carillon recitals did not occur there weekly." He warned

Hart, "Your carillon will lose its flexibility if it is not played upon at least once a week, and all the wires and keys kept in proper tension."[7] But Hart and his classmates wanted essentially to hear the bells "ring out the strains of *Old Nassau* in glorious celebration of our many future [football] victories over Yale and Harvard."[8] The automatic system was also programmed to produce tunes every evening at 6:30 as the Graduate College students filed into their refectory, Proctor's Hall, for dinner. The carillon in the meantime gradually became unplayable.

Then in 1941 Arthur Lynds Bigelow showed up. Bigelow, a man of various talents and ambitions like the versatile Percival Price, has along with Price become a hallowed figure in American carillon history. That year, Bigelow was hired by Princeton to be its "bellmaster," in effect its first carillonneur, as well as assistant professor in the Graphics Engineering Department. Born in Springfield Massachusetts in 1909, Bigelow became interested in bells and carillon playing before leaving home to study engineering at the University of Pittsburgh, 1928–30. Upon graduation, he went directly to Malines in Belgium to study at the one and only Carillon School in the world. Passing his exams in 1932—only the second North American, after Percival Price in 1927, to gain this rare diploma—Bigelow stayed on in Europe, playing many Lowland instruments, holding down a position at The Collegial Church of St. Pieter's in Louvain, getting married, and cutting his teeth as an engineering consultant on major carillon projects before returning to the U.S. in 1941. Accustomed to playing the grand Continental carillons in the four or four and one half octave range—47 bells on average, the scope of any important Dutch or Belgian instrument—Bigelow immediately wanted to extend the three-octave G&J instrument at Princeton.

Cyril Johnston's bells at Princeton, neglected until 1941, were now in the hands of a man whose training as both engineer and carillonneur, and new plum appointments as engineering professor cum bellmaster at a university outstandingly uninterested in its carillon instrument, made him ideally situated to do pretty much what he wanted with what he found there. The Class of 1892, its members now old or dead, had turned down an offer by Gillett & Johnston in 1925, two years before casting was completed, for a 43-bell carillon, the same size as Mercersburg's, and much closer in magnitude to the Continental assemblages seen by Bigelow as standard or exemplary. Now in any case, perhaps the Continental resentment toward the English bellfounders who had come to master an art their own had once dominated, indeed invented, and subsequently lost, had rubbed off on Bigelow. By the time Bigelow was through, the Princeton instrument was no longer English but in effect French. In 1967, the year he died, he left a 58-bell carillon: 25 G&Js basses, 33 Paccard trebles.[9]

The first thing Bigelow did when he arrived on campus in 1941 was to disconnect the automatic playing mechanism, signaling his intent to return the bells to concert status. Then he removed the upper 18 bells from their steel girders and rehung them on massive fir beams, reverting to the style of the old Lowland frames. Next he cast about for bronze detritus to create 14 bells of his own to add to the 35 G&Js. Nineteen-forty-one was not a great year for trying to refurbish anything made of bronze. A time when Wall and Fleet Streets and their governments were "selling on bells" and "buying on cannon." Fortuitously perhaps for Bigelow, he could not be faulted for not approaching G&J to expand their instrument when the Croydon firm was (for the second stretch of time in the 20th century) producing munitions for a war effort. Then after the war, Cyril personally, along with his business, was in serious decline. In 1941 Bigelow was resourceful, finding bronze bearings in the Cleveland Tower belfry, more remarkably a locomotive bell unearthed in a Trenton junkyard, and other deserted or obsolete bells he scavenged the countryside for. If after metallurgical analysis a bell or bearing was found to have the carillon-prescribed composition of copper, 77%, and tin, 23%, Bigelow would buy it, have it melted down, the forms made in a university masons shop, recast in an East Newark all-purpose foundry, finally turned and tuned in the Princeton Engineering Department. At length, with his jerry-built 14, he had a 49-bell instrument, the same size as the one he had played for a decade in

Louvain. "Knowing what effects could be produced on 49 bells," said Bigelow, "I was naturally anxious that Princeton's belfry be as complete."[10] In the 1960s, now in close association as paid designer and advisor with the Paccard bellfoundry of Annecy in France, ultimately the majority founder in Cleveland Tower, Bigelow ditched his 14, and ten of Gillett & Johnston's 35—perhaps in consolation for getting rid of his own.[11] There were reasons of course. There are always reasons. It is not known what was wrong with Bigelow's 14, but Bigelow himself had avowed that all the G&Js were 100 percent pure in tone. "The 35 G&J bells," he once said, "are of excellent tonal quality and in themselves leave nothing to be desired as to trueness of pitch or fullness of tone." Bigelow, not so incidentally, was hired as "consultant" by Schulmerich Inc. for 10 years. [11]

Once a carillon is seriously dismantled, who is to mourn the loss of what it was? Bellmasters or carillonneurs, the ones closest to the instrument, are most frequently the agents of its loss. No audience such as can be built up for a symphony orchestra exists to protest or lament its end. Very few extant recordings of North American instruments exist that predate the rage since the late 1970s to renovate them. The sound is as dead as the interior of my old school St. Mary's.

One great and indestructible looking thing at Princeton is their Chapel, like the Cleveland Tower cum Graduate College and many other architectural features on campus, the work of Ralph Adams Cram. Although Cram's Mercersburg Chapel is a lot smaller, it has the same exquisite Gothic detail and proportions of length to width and height. The Princeton Chapel, a cathedral if a few more inches were added, looks like a sister to Cram's West Point Chapel, the structure wherein Frederick C. Mayer, carillon advisor to J.D. Rockefeller, Jr., reigned for so many years as organist and choirmaster. These places, all incidentally wealthy with stained glass, are still going strong. As is another site where G&J bells hang, but hang intact: St. Paul's School Chapel in Concord New Hampshire. A Henry Vaughan masterpiece (1886–1894), Vaughan was an early Anglo-Gothicist, creator of an impressive architectural patrimony of New England Episcopalianism, which is to say America's most prestigious private boys' schools. And a major influence on Ralph Adams Cram who in fact would later enlarge the historic Vaughan Chapel. St. Paul's 23-bell G&J Carillon was dedicated in 1933. My chapel at St. Mary's, built by Cram right into the school, lovely however simple and diminutive, the same size and high ceiling as the refectory which lay one floor below, was vaporized by Peekskill developers in 1984 to make way for their condominium apartments. Ward-Belmont lost its bells; the alumni of St. Mary's and a host of future schoolgirls lost a whole institution. Ward-Belmont survived a critical late 20th century transition in American education: from single-sex schools and colleges to co-ed ones.

St. Mary's did not. In 1973–74 during the tail-end times of social convulsion, the nuns of the Episcopal order of St. Mary handed over the reins of their 105-year old girl's school to a Headmaster, an Episcopal priest, ushering in an enrollment of boys. This lasted for just three years, when the Board of Trustees who included the Headmaster voted to close the school. The excuses were that they needed more money and more student enrollees. One member of the board, a graduate of the class of 1948, reported that she had found alumni not interested in supporting a school which had become different from the one they knew. So why didn't they revert to being all girls? A malaise in the Sisterhood itself was perhaps the crucial factor determining the fate of the school. If the so-called sexual revolution was then at its height, so was a lesser known apathy for joining celibate organizations like nunneries and monasteries, with their satellite schools. The Sisters of Saint Mary were seriously decimated in numbers by the end of the 1970s. And they lacked leadership. My own six years at the school had been spent under a majestic and inspiring nun called Sister Mary Regina, once an enthusiastic 5-year student at St. Mary's herself. With her death in the 1960s and the end of the glorious garb of starched white wings the nuns wore and that had become too expensive to maintain, the order was on its way down.

The school, shut tight for seven years, was said to be up for sale. No trustees or alumni seemed aware that its architecture qualified it for preservation as a historic landmark. In the meantime the town of Peekskill had been going downhill, and the new Mayor George E. Pataki, later of course Governor of New York State, saw progress in real-estate opportunities, especially four moribund church-owned institutions that sat on large tracts of land and paid no taxes. Pataki earned big brokers' fees from developers. In a *New York Times* article headlined "Pataki and Peekskill: Reviving a City, Then Profiting in a Realty Boom," the then Mayor is himself pictured against the southern façade of St. Mary's—the side facing the river—smiling triumphantly, arms akimbo, in shirt sleeves and tie.[13] Now a condo called the Chateau Rive, consisting of 56 apartments, after two decades one need only tour the unkempt grounds and interior with its hodgepodge design and unfinished junkheaps of rooms to hear the despairing cry of a 1912 graduate when she learned of the school's closing in 1977: "There are many broken hearts all over the world."[14] The photo of Pataki leering before the building in 1983 reminds us of how often public enterprise and venturism can obscure private pain.

As I appear to lobby for history over the vaunted musical improvement of carillons in their dismantlement, I identify clearly with origins, which in the case of Cyril Johnston's bells were so implicated with my own.

Chapter XIII

RIVERSIDE REDUX

Disaster struck [the Riverside Church] in 1955
—Joseph Clair Davis

*The proposed renovation of the Riverside Church carillon should be
regarded as the loss of a cultural monument [1955]*
—Adrian Hamers

*Of course I guess that Antiquarians and musicians will always be
at odds, to some degree, over changes in any carillon*
—Richard Mathews Watson

In April 1997 I heard that Harry van Bergen owned a small
Gillett & Johnston bell left over from the 1955 removal of 56
altogether that had hung at New York's Riverside Church. I had
wanted a "redundant" G&J bell for some time, and one from
Riverside seemed ideal. It seemed also fortuitous that I might be
able to get one from a member of the Dutch van Bergen family of
bellfounders that had replaced those 56 back in 1955, while the

16 G&J basses were left hanging. I considered that it might even be free, given the pall that still hangs over the 1955 transaction. In the North American carillon world, the dismantlement of Cyril Johnston's trailblazing 72-bell instrument dedicated in 1931 remains its liveliest, most enduring scandal. But Harry, whose Uncle Andries had been the hapless bellfounder in Heiligerlee, Holland, was not interested in giving away his G&J souvenir. He wanted 5,000 dollars for it. Like his father Harmannus before him, Harry is a bell salesman in South Carolina. Harmannus brought Harry to America in 1939 when Harry was four, one year ahead of the German invasion of the Netherlands, settling in Greenwood, and resuming representing his brother Andries' firm from this side of the Atlantic. It was Harmannus who negotiated and drew up the contract for Andries for the 56-bell Riverside conversion in 1955.

One shadiness still clinging to the van Bergen/Riverside business deal has been the question of what happened exactly to the 56 Gillett & Johnstons that were removed. By contract, they were sent to Heiligerlee to be melted down and recast. Now I knew that one of them was not, and with Harry wanting to sell it, I wondered if perhaps others had been sold as well. He told me his father had given him the 10 lb. (F Sharp) bell. Wherever they all went, they went quietly. In the year 2000, the van Bergens, along with two extras they had cast to make 58, were themselves dismounted, to be replaced with bells by Whitechapel, returning the carillon to England, as it were, and satisfying those bellsperts who believe that only English bells should be added to an English instrument.

Most carillons go quietly. No one protests their depredation. Towers are secret places, and bells, their prisoners, are subject to trials and disappearances as imperiously decreed as ancient royal prerogatives disposing of humans. "Crimes" of bells are designated by people with very specialized knowledge, and/or interests; the bronze bodies are removed by caretakers or workmen who cannot know what is wrong with them. Many falls from grace of carillon assemblages in the 20th century are, I have discovered, due to their trebles, the highest and smallest in any tower. "It's the trebles, stupid," any member of the Guild of Carillonneurs of North America might have been tempted to say to me as I corresponded with some of them, looking deeply into this matter. A carillon consists rather obviously of basses, mediums, and trebles, in ascending order of size and weight from the heaviest at bottom to the lightest at top. The specialists sometimes refer loosely to all the bells above the heavy basses as trebles. In a four-octave instrument, the first octave can be called basses, the second the mediums and the top two octaves the trebles. According to Richard Watson—since the death of the Meneely foundries in the late 1940s America's only bellfounder, operating out of Georgetown Ohio—there is no hard and fast rule about which bells can be called what. Watson says "the names really only serve to indicate in a general way the function of the particular register of bells within a given instrument, not the actual range of tones within the whole spectrum of possible carillon bells."[1] However, it is certain that any uppermost octave consists of trebles. And that these bells have been a problem since at least the 17th century, even in the work of François and Pieter Hemony, the brothers who spearheaded the first golden age in carillon building.

Trebles historically have been cast too thin, their sound thus tending to be drowned out by the bigger mediums and sonorous basses. They can be tuned perfectly to desired pitches, but if lacking in proportionate volume to their larger companions contribute to an unbalanced instrument. In many cases the treble tones have simply not been able to get out of their towers. At the Riverside Church in New York, with a tower 392 feet high and the trebles near the very top, hung skyward above streets that hum with city traffic, this was notoriously the case. In 1931, very soon after the time that Cyril Johnston's unheard of 72-bell carillon was dedicated, Frederick Mayer was writing to Rockefeller about shipping the upper 35 or 37 bells back to Croydon for re-tuning. Mayer and Cyril Johnston already had treble history behind them. During 1928 when the 53-bell Park Avenue carillon was under removal to Riverside Church, and decisions were being made over which bells to keep, Mayer was having his captive bellfounder recast the 28 upper bells or trebles taken down from Park Avenue, to install at Riverside. While volume was a serious concern, Mayer was preoccupied chiefly with another issue involving re-tuning—one more specialized and scientific. He was bent on the importance of "stretch-tuning" in upper octaves, making the bells progressively sharper than what would be technically accurate in order to compensate for a perceptual deficiency of the human ear. Cyril's trebles were considered individually pitch-perfect, and superior to Taylor's and to the Hemonys and other old classic makers; however not sharp enough in tonal intervals—the proportionate ratios between vibrational frequencies of the notes. Whether "sharp" or not, the lightest bells at 10 and 12 lbs. were not going to be heard on the ground without more metal on their bodies. A carillon of this size, with total weight of 100 plus tons, had never been made before. The undertaking was an experiment.

One trial Mayer and Rockefeller couldn't afford or survive was the 392-foot high tower, housing its 52 feet high, 40 by 40 feet wide belfry. They had to live with it. Unless they moved on again, abandoning yet another bell home the way they did Park Avenue, this time splitting the instrument up—an option that was actually given a little thought at the end of the 1930s. As things would turn out, Mayer and Rockefeller, and Cyril Johnston until he died in 1950, concentrated wholly on the trebles, neglecting things they could do in the tower, short of busting apart stone to create more or bigger openings, to help free up the sound. Not until the year 2000 when the Whitechapels were brought in to replace the van Bergens would the entire tower be reconfigured: the playing cabin moved, bells resituated, the machine room with its awesome contents of motors, generators, compressors, quarter-barrel or drum and electro-pneumatic pistons jettisoned completely; tons of steel, masonry, wood and seaweed (yes seaweed) thrown out. The centerpiece of all this—the bells—would endure two colossal disembowelments.

Remarkably, it may be thought, with 58 bells by a different founder, and just 16 G&Js left, the instrument is still considered

Cyril Johnston's. But these 16 include the famed 20-ton bourdon, which together with four other mighty basses are hung for swinging, creating a sight and a sound the likes of which when set in motion the nation's biggest city, perhaps the nation itself, has no equal [See Epilogue]. Also, in the aggregate the 16 G&J basses weigh 103 tons compared to the 58 Whitechapel (formerly van Bergen) upper bells at 7½ tons. It's conceivable that even had the 16 been deposed (and they could not be, without a fortune being spent rupturing masonry at high levels to get them out), the carillon would be seen overshadowingly as Cyril Johnston's. Protests in 1955 when his original 56 were taken down and sent to Holland included a letter from Bonaventura Eijsbouts, head of another Dutch firm, Eijsbouts, saying that the proposed renovation of the Riverside Church Carillon "should be regarded as the loss of a cultural monument." Eijsbouts hailed it as "the most important work of the late Mr. Cyril F. Johnston . . . one of the two [English] bellfounders who recovered the bell art about 1920, after a period of decadence lasting two hundred fifty years."[2] Another protest, by Gillett & Johnston itself, limping along trying to produce bells after the death of the founder, had holes punched in it by the Rockefeller office in New York. G&J's Managing Director, A.M. Craig, had written to Frederick Mayer, "We learn with the greatest regret of the decision to retune . . . the bells of the Riverside carillon. We feel very strongly about this, as we have at no time received advice that this master creation of the late Mr. Cyril Johnston was not almost perfect, even in the light of the most recent scientific advances in bell founding and tuning, and we feel sure you will appreciate our position as this affects our dearly won international reputation."[3]

Rockefeller's business manager, George Heidt, hearing from Mayer about the Craig letter, wrote to Rockefeller expressing great surprise, saying the present G&J firm could not have very good records if they were unaware that Cyril Johnston was himself involved in plans for recasting a number of Riverside bells.[4] Indeed, he had been very involved. And had he been able to renovate his own carillon, there would have been no outcry in 1955.

Rockefeller's business manager was dodging a nice distinction between self-renewal and outside corruption—here an imminent adulteration by van Bergen. By 1939 the number of bells bandied about for recasting (and thus retuning) was sixty-one, of which the five heaviest would have no chance of making it out of the tower. When Riverside's sister-giant carillon at the University of Chicago was dedicated in 1932, Mayer heralded Cyril's improvements on the heels of the more experimental Riverside, saying "the sharpening of all the Chicago trebles turned out to be a splendid stroke, musically speaking," and telling Rockefeller the bellfounder had signed a letter while attending the dedication in Chicago saying he would correct any Riverside trebles they wanted him to.[5]

But the decade of the 1930s from thereon out was a difficult time for Cyril and his business. With the Depression wasting America and overtaking Europe, his orders for peals and carillons fell off dramatically. His "glory years" of the 20s, when the United States in particular was to his benefit reveling in its new money, were over by 1932. In this year the last of his bells under contract in the preceding boom decade had left his foundry floor and were installed and dedicated. Recasting bells was not a priority at Riverside or anywhere else. Of Cyril Johnston's 30 carillons built altogether for North America, the orders for 22 of them were placed in the decade of the 1920s. Only six were allocated during the 1930s, and thereafter two in the 1940s. Cyril's carillon business in other countries during the 1920s was correspondingly brisk, with a dozen instruments on order, half of these for Holland. In the 1930s he cast just four: one for Jerusalem [See Chapter XI], one for South Africa, and two for Great Britain.

Of the latter, his 1934 contract to reconstruct a 1906 Taylor carillon atop a small red brick school in Bournville—the model suburb of Birmingham built by chocolate manufacturer George Cadbury for his factory workers—is a classic all-English remake, examples of which dot the North American carillon towerscape. Richard Watson, American Midwestern bellfounder, who has done a number of renovations, is one specialist who believes in

*The Gillett & Johnston Bellfoundry, Cyril F. Johnston standing in the middle in front of the
49-bell carillon, hanging in its steel frame, destined for
the Wellington War Memorial Tower, Wellington, New Zealand, 1932*

In Gillett & Johnston Bellfoundry, 1922, Cyril F. Johnston playing the Massey-Drury Memorial Carillon of 23 bells destined for the United Methodist Church in Toronto, Canada, the first modern carillon instrument in North America

Top: Percival Price demonstrating the carillon for guests and Cyril F. Johnston
at Gillett & Johnston Bellfoundry
Bottom: Jef Denyn playing the Laura Spelman Memorial Carillon, circa 1930
at the Gillett & Johnston Bellfoundry, standing Cyril F. Johnston

A 1898 print of a carillonneur at keyboard of a carillon

*Kamiel Lefévere playing the Park Avenue Baptist Church 53-bell carillon
at the Gillett & Johnston Bellfoundry, 1925*

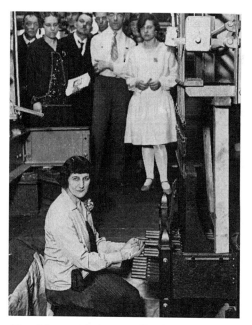

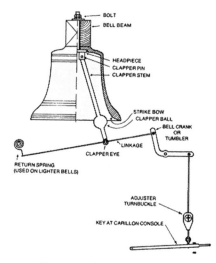

BOLT
BELL BEAM
HEADPIECE
CLAPPER PIN
CLAPPER STEM
STRIKE BOW
CLAPPER BALL
BELL CRANK
OR
TUMBLER
LINKAGE
CLAPPER EYE
RETURN SPRING
(USED ON LIGHTER BELLS)
ADJUSTER
TURNBUCKLE
KEY AT CARILLON CONSOLE

*Diagram of a carillon bell with its
transmission system to keyboard*

*Nora Johnston playing a carillon for visitors at the
Gillett & Johnston Bellfoundry*

*Right: The 23-bell carillon for
Canterbury School, New Milford,
CT, 1931, hung in its steel frame at
the Gillett & Johnston Bellfoundry,
with keyboard attached*

CANTERBURY SCHOOL
NEW MILFORD
CONNECTICUT U.S.A.
CARILLON OF 23 BELLS
WEIGHT OF BASS BELL 1120 LBS
TOTAL WEIGHT 6608 LBS
GILLETT & JOHNSTON
BELLFOUNDERS & CLOCKMAKERS
CROYDON ENGLAND 1931

this configuration. Peter Hurd, responsible along with his brother Timothy for the 2000 Riverside restoration, blankets the subject unreservedly: "Never add Continental bells to an English instrument because the tuning and tonal and weight concepts are completely different."[6] Hurd has called the 23-bell G&J Mayo Clinic carillon in Rochester, Minnesota, installed in 1928, and enlarged in 1977 by Petit & Fritsen, with 33 new bells on top, *a train-wreck of connections.*" The Hurd brothers did more to ensure a compatible Riverside re-make than employ an English founder to replace the van Bergens. They were party to a connection between Whitechapel and Alan Buswell, an Englishman and longtime change-ringing enthusiast who has created a rather amazing database from the Gillett & Johnston tuning books, which contain detailed records of each of the 11,000 plus bells G&J ever cast.[7] With tuning and casting information provided by Buswell on the 56 G&Js removed and lost to posterity, Whitechapel could create new bells that had a good chance of synchronizing with the originals and thus with the 16 that were left. (The Hurds also conducted physical and acoustical measurements of G&J bells at Chicago, Ottawa and of Riverside's 16 big ones as the basis for a new design). If there is any doubt how important an all-English recasting was, you can see the inscriptions around some of the biggest new bells: "WHITECHAPEL, LONDON, 1999, AFTER GILLETT& JOHNSTON, CROYDON."

In a case like Cyril Johnston's own reconstruction of the Bournville UK carillon in 1934, the Taylor bells under removal were ready at hand to examine, but considering what little Cyril left of the Taylor instrument, such a study was no doubt irrelevant. For Cyril, in the annals of the Taylor/Johnston rivalry and replacement wars, the Bournville contract must have been satisfying. Bournville was Europe's first modern carillon. It may not have escaped Cyril that its 1906 date was the very year he discovered, at age 22, Canon Simpson and harmonic tuning after the peal of six bells he had made for the Elstree School was found wanting, with threats to turn the order over to Taylor! [See Chapter II]. When Cyril was done with Taylor's 42-bell instrument at Bournville, he had recast all but four Taylor bells, and added six of his own including a new bass of 3¼ tons. The conversion is not unfamiliar in his history, or in fact that of any bellfounder. In Cyril's past, it accords with the large number of English change-ringing sets he restored, putting his stamp on old peals, maddening the bell conservationists, and showing what he might do today were he alive. I'm sure he would be at the forefront of change and renewal, not just as an entrepreneur and businessman, but in the interests of musical improvement. The Bournville instrument—at 48 bells, 44 of them cast in Croydon—became essentially his. In a much delayed retribution, during the 1990s Taylor was allowed to decimate Cyril Johnston's historically important 51-bell 1924 carillon at St. Stephen's Church—a Ralph Adams Cram structure—in Cohasset Massachusetts, leaving 15 G&J basses, installing 42 Taylors on top.

It was Cyril's friendship with Clifford Ball, carillonneur at Bournville from 1924–1965, that made the Bournville contract possible. Ball may have wanted a bigger instrument, and was no doubt justifiably convinced that after 23 years uplifts were due; but he would also have wanted to help the bellfounder, knowing he was not in great shape financially. This would be painfully apparent from an American inter-office Rockefeller memo in June 1933 limning a dispute over a final bill received from Cyril for work on Riverside; and a letter Cyril wrote to JDR Jr. in 1934 requesting a loan. But also, the Cyril Johnston Trust Estate documents show loans and mortgages and sales of stock in G&J, the latter ultimately enabling others to wrest control of his company away from him [See Chapter XVII]. In the 1933 Memo, a claim of Cyril's for £2,341 conflicted with an interpretation by Rockefeller's officers that Cyril was overpaid £1,866. They concluded that if the Church sued, there would be additional expense, unpleasant publicity, and small chance of collecting in any event. JDR's officers decided to call the matter closed, with the understanding that Cyril would retune the Riverside trebles at his own expense. And they told Junior what they were doing on his behalf: ". . . as an indication of your good will, and an expression of your interest in Carillon Art and [Cyril Johnston's] unprecedented achievement in expanding the compass and improving both the tuning and quality of carillon bells, thus bringing greater artistic beauty and enjoyment of bell music to the world," you are sending him a draft for $2500."8 The following year, on July 16th, 1934, Cyril wrote to Rockefeller directly:

"I hesitate to appeal to you but . . . a crisis has arisen in my business and I am in imminent danger of losing all that I have worked for and valued beyond money. The long period of general depression has incurred losses in the last 18 months beyond my firm's and personal resources, one factor being the lack of carillon orders, the demand for which had been growing especially in the U.S.A. Before [the present period] set in we had carried out on more than one occasion considerable extensions to the premises and plant to enable us to cope with contracts placed with us for big carillons . . . Without some financial assistance I am unable to carry on . . . Is there any hope of your being willing to help me over this difficult period? A loan of 10,000 pounds repayable in a period and on terms approved by yourself would save the business. I do hope you will forgive my writing to you. Many of our employees have served the firm for periods ranging from 20 to 40 years and I feel a serious responsibility towards them and their families, whilst my mother and my family are entirely dependent on my earnings."9

If Cyril hoped Rockefeller might note the passage where he implies that the wealthy capitalist could take some responsibility for his plight—"considerable extensions . . . to cope with contracts placed with us for big carillons"—it would be to no avail. Again Rockefeller was advised by his officers, with one of them writing to Cyril, "Mr. Rockefeller wishes me to say he is exceedingly sorry not to see his way clear to make the loan you desire. It is his fixed policy not to make business loans, and he feels you would understand the situation in which he would find himself, were he to make an exception even in this instance to the practice which he has followed for so many years."[10] The next year, in May 1935, Cyril wrote to the donor again, this time restoratively, nicely overlooking Rockefeller's earlier refusal to help him, saying "new capital" had become available to him [See Chapter XVII], with "business improved at a rate we had not experienced for two or three years." He said he was sailing to New York to settle one carillon order and look into other prospects. He was ready, he seemed to be saying, to tackle unfinished business at Riverside. Not until May, 1939, however, would Cyril resume taking up the matter of re-tuning the sixty-one Riverside trebles, meeting for discussions at the church in New York with Mayer, whose backing he firmly had, and with George Heidt and Kamiel Lefévere. Writing to JDR Jr., Mayer said he would not like to see the project hurried, but wait a year, even two, while the bellfounder experimented a little more with other carillons he may be building. But if Cyril was going to do the job at all, they had not a moment to lose, as war was almost upon them. On September 3rd, Britain and France declared war on Germany. By November Cyril was writing to Mayer more about conditions of war than plans for bells, saying life was "very strenuous" in the UK. While he had strong government backing to keep up his normal trade overseas (bells had recently been shipped to Holland and Canada, and he was casting a carillon for St. Paul, Minnesota), his home trade was vanishing, and he was now busy with several war contracts, expanding the foundry to cope with them. He had to face sudden considerable expenditure in Shelters and other Air Raid Precautions to protect his employees and foundry; his children (Arthur and Rosemary) had been evacuated but were home again, and he had a "first rate dug-out" in his garden.

After a gap of seven years, on the post-war date of December 23, 1946, Cyril met Lefévere and Mayer at the church again to confer on the upper 61 bells. But now, a job that would have cost $21,150 in 1939 would be more than doubled at $50,000. The affair was stalled, and Cyril was undergoing cures for his arthritis in Switzerland. In 1947 while on his last visit to America, he was hospitalized (in Boston) with a thrombosis. By the end of '48 it was reported that he had lost control of his firm, and was out of it. In the meantime Kamiel Lefévere, carillonneur at the church since 1931, had become interested in the Dutch firm, van Bergen. After testing many of their bells when in Holland, he spoke of their "beautiful tone." With Cyril inoperative, Mayer only nominally in the picture, and Lefévere looking to the Continent (his place of origin after all), the die had been cast for the great van Bergen scandal.

The van Bergen foundry in Heiligerlee, Holland, goes back to 1795, when Andries Hero van Bergen (1768–1847), the oldest known ancestor of the van Bergen bellfounding family, started up in the town of Midwolda. After Andries died, there was an interim when mainly tower clocks were produced. In 1862, Andries' grandson Andries Hero II, restarted the bell side in Heiligerlee. It was a descendant, another Andries, who became the man of the hour for Lefévere and thus Riverside, in 1955.

According to Harry, his father Harmannus knew Lefévere and became friends with him at the World's Fair in 1939, where Lefévere was playing the carillon at the Belgian Exhibition. Harmannus had installed a van Bergen carillon in the Dutch Pavilion and another in the Dutch Garden at the Fair that he would later sell, giving him the idea of opening up a market for bells in America. Lefévere, warming to Harmannus speaking Flemish, his native tongue, with him, was leaning toward Europe. The trouble with the van Bergen import to Riverside in 1955 was that by then the firm's best carillon-making days were over, and their best in the 20th century had never been as good as the English. With van Bergen (along with other Lowland founders, but also Paccard in France) missing out on the tuning renaissance taking place in England at the end of the 1800s, their bellscape for a period of time belonged humiliatingly to the English. Between 1911 and 1934 the Dutch suffered a delivery of 21 carillons by the colonizing English firms John Taylor and Gillett & Johnston. After that, the Dutch founders gradually reclaimed their craft. While the Netherlands in 1916 had a total of 60 carillons, by the end of the 1990s there were about 200. (Compare this to the 180 carillons at present writing in all of North America).[11] In 1932 van Bergen had produced its first properly tuned carillon. Then the quality they had mustered went into decline following WWII, and they faltered behind the increasingly good work of their Dutch competitors Eijsbouts and Petit & Fritsen. In 1980 the van Bergen foundry closed down, the premises converted to a museum showcasing their historical bells.[12]

It has been said that the 56 G&J bells were taken down from the Riverside tower in the still of night, to avoid any clustering of curious onlookers—making the event sound like a clandestine operation. They were then "quietly" crated, transported to a Black Diamond freighter, and borne across the Atlantic to the Netherlands. Jim Lawson, arriving at the church in 1960 to replace Lefévere as carillonneur, and noting that "something was wrong with these bells [the van Bergens]," called in experts of whom one echoed the nocturnal allusion, "This was done in the dead of night and nobody knew about it." Lawson went so far as to assert that Lefévere, known to be very friendly with Harmannus van Bergen, may have been a paid consultant on the job. Peter Hurd, unable to imagine that the G&Js had been anything other than "perfect," and decreeing the van Bergens "awful," has a similar verdict: "Definitely there must've been a shady transaction between Lefévere and van Bergen, with money under the table." Lawson's successor Joseph Davis (1989–1998) has minced no words in pronouncing on the van Bergens. Their trebles were "too thin, poorly tuned, lacking in sonorousness and not complementary with the G&Js." The dire musical consequence of the van Bergen replacement has been an infectious rumor, not unsubstantiated by those who have played or guest-played the admixed instrument. The whereabouts of the dethroned G&Js, though perhaps a figment of curiosity to carillon professionals, has not otherwise engaged them. I seem to have been alone in this interest.

Since the 1950s I have been driving by the Riverside Church, up or downtown on the West Side Highway along the Hudson

River. Beginning 1981 for a period of years I drove by it every weekend with Ingrid when heading north out of the city to help out my daughter with her two small children. In case I had not taken note before, Ingrid now made sure I did, adopting the habit as we passed the soaring Gothic tower going either north or south of saying: "There's your church." Then once I started writing this book, I took extra note, looking up and eastward every time we approached it, sometimes preempting Ingrid's view of my over-lordship, saying, "Yeah, there's my church." I never drove by the 10 lb. F Sharp bell owned by Harry van Bergen because it was taken down before I had a car. My interest in Harry's F Sharp broadened to take in the fate of its 55 companions. Were they really all melted down? Cyril Johnston left a lot of bronze around bearing testimonial inscriptions. I like knowing where all his bells are. Information can be manna, providing a sense of ownership, especially when it's difficult to get. Harry has been an obliging hindrance in my quest for both the F Sharp, and knowledge of its fellows. On the latter, he has equivocated from the beginning, confirming in one interview the official story that they were all melted down and recast; in another that he thinks they have or may have survived, and gone elsewhere. "Elsewhere" has consis-tently been the city of Belo Horizonte in Brazil. Harry has had Belo Horizonte in his brain for a long time, but no other accom-panying information. On the F Sharp, he played the bullish sales-man, not unaware that his potential buyer had at least a vague historic claim to his property. Our bond as children of bell-founders made us friendly antagonists. It's a special bond. How many such children can there be in the world?

In our sales talk, I could afford to play the laid back cus-tomer. Many carillon musicians and GCNA associates might be happy to have the little bell, but for five thousand dollars? In cor-respondence with Harry, I never answered to his stated cost, only reiterated my interest in the bell, and in seeing photos of it showing its inscriptions. He never sent any (the bell was dark he said, and it was hard to see the inscriptions), but did much better, bringing it to New York with him when he and his wife flew north to spend Thanksgiving with their son in Queens. I had invited him and wife Peggy to lunch. All on his own, in a letter before he came, Harry had brought his price down to $4000 ("to be paid $2500 cash upon delivery and the balance paid $100 per month"), evidently considering it a done deal since he added, "I will personally deliver the bell to you." That was very nice of him, but my objective was to get the bell for nothing. To that end, over our five-hour lunch I initiated a writer's barter scheme. I would write a history of his family and firm in exchange for the bell. At long length the bell itself was produced. Harry had brought it in a black bowling-ball bag. He said it had set off alarms and questions in South Carolina at the airport metal check. I investigated its inscriptions first thing. Around its top band it reads: *GILLETT & JOHNSTON CROYDON ENGLAND 1930*. Under a space between "Gillett" and "1930" is incised Cyril's monogram, "CFJ," set in a circle. From Alan Buswell's tuning book database, I find the bell's casting date: February 27, 1930. Then, since my barter talk with Harry though polite was going nowhere, I had perforce to make an offer, and I announced, "I can't possibly offer you more than a thousand dollars for the bell." Harry countered, "If I gave you a thousand dollars, would that be enough for you to do a van Bergen book?" My answer, "Good point, no it would not," produced no more conversation. And Harry and Peggy departed in a wave of affability, leaving the bell behind without my knowing it. The next day Harry called to say he accepted my offer. With great reluctance, I sent him a check. I hated giving him a penny, and the story did not end there exactly.

A longtime artist friend of mine, famed sculptor of soaring works in steel Mark di Suvero, was at that very moment inviting me to a 70th birthday lunch for his dealer Dick Bellamy, at his studio on the East River in Long Island City. Mark loves bells, and has included them on occasion in his work. He has known my birth history for as long we've known each other. While he was inviting me to his party on the phone, I told him my van Bergen tale, and said I would bring the bell over to show it to him. At his lunch, Mark examined it even more carefully than I had, and with an intensity bordering on excitement. Then he disappeared, and upon returning covertly pressed a check for a thousand dollars into my hand. At 10 lbs. the bell weighs the same as an inch-thick piece of steel Mark once gave me with my forename in my own handwriting punched out of it. Did he think my seller Harry van Bergen should have given me the bell? If so, he joined others who had that thought. Jim Lawson on the other hand, a veteran carillonneur at Riverside (Jim died in 2003, aged 82), envisioned the bell placed in a museum, the makings of which exist in the Riverside tower. I can't imagine what Frederick Mayer was thinking about in 1947 when he wrote to Rockefeller saying that if they scrapped the upper 61 Riverside bells, and installed them as part of a 4-octave carillon at the Cloisters, the tiny discarded top octave *"would make valuable souvenirs, as dinner bells, for your growing family, if I may so suggest."*[13] My 10 lb. hunk of F Sharp bronze, as tiny as they got, only possible to lift, by myself anyway, by gripping it around its skirt rim with both hands, would make an interesting dinner bell.

As for the museum idea, a 10 lb. A note, companion to my F Sharp, found recently in the tower, could as easily emblematize the original instrument. So two of the 56 are accounted for. Are some of the others in Belo Horizonte? Harry's murmurings on this city were confirmed when a GCNA website showed that 36 van Bergens were installed in Belo Horizonte and saying "Installation was completed in unknown year with bells made for a Cathedral by van Bergen." *Unknown year!* And in a "Cathedral" *of unknown name!*[14] Questions of how van Bergen dealt with the 56 G&J bells they removed in 1955 are overshadowed by the Riverside instrument as it now exists.

With seven of the larger bells cast by Whitechapel bearing the inscription, "WHITECHAPEL, LONDON 1999, AFTER GILLETT & JOHNSTON, CROYDON," an homage to "the most important work of the late Mr. Cyril F. Johnston" as Bonaventura Eijsbouts once put it, exists in some commemorative way. These inscriptions bear witness to the original G&J profiles of the bells removed in 1955 by van Bergen. Yet the untouched 16 basses by G&J, among the 72 dedicated in 1931, remain an indelible testament to Cyril Johnston's pioneering work in America.[15]

Chapter XIV

£500 WITH INTEREST

It's psychologically true that he [my father] was dead,
so I've never really wanted to know the facts
—Pat Barker

It is in the "name of the father" that we must recognize the support of
the Symbolic function which, from the dawn of history, has identified
his person with the figure of the law
—Jacques Lacan

In April 1988 the coloration of my life as the de facto daughter of Cyril Johnston changed when I met Helena Kennedy for tea at the Waldorf in London. Helena, a criminal law barrister who defended battered women and the likes of one of the Guildford Four, was well known in England. Originally from a working class laborite Scottish family, in 1991 she became a QC (Queen's Council), and is now actually a Lord, a peer for life, appointed along with 17 others in a shake-up of the Upper House by Tony Blair when he became Prime Minister. A lawyer friend of mine in New York, who knew Helena through Leonard Boudin, father of

Kathy Boudin with whom Helena was close, had suggested I consult her. The thought was that she might know some way around or through my status under the law to help me gain access to my family. The last time I saw my half-brother Arthur had been in 1986, two years after the Centenary service for Cyril's birth in Croydon—the moment when it became clear that Arthur formed an impenetrable block with his mother [See Chapter VIII]. Once he saw the two volumes I had published of a projected trilogy, with the third presumably in the works and meant to introduce his father to the world, he had pleaded with me to have consideration for the women he was protecting, his mother and sister. If it had been only him, he said, it would be different. His mother had "led a very sheltered life." Twice he enumerated her years of widowhood, 34, and marriage, 20—"a long involvement." And confided that his sister had recently had surgery. I told Arthur I would not want to upset these ladies. By 1986, when last I saw him, I was no longer, to his evident relief, working actively on the book. It is tempting for me to think I had acted altruistically on behalf of his interests, and after all for a good cause. I may well have been guided by Arthur's pleas. But if so, the feeling entered I should say unconsciously into a skein of developments leading me away from the book of contention and toward other writing ventures. So why was I going to see Helena Kennedy in 1988? Well the book was only on hold, not forgotten or shelved forever, and I had business in London that could easily include an exciting meeting with a radical barrister. More to the point, my lawyer friend in New York had led me to believe that in the passage of several 20th century English Family Reform Acts there was hope for my future legality. So there were two issues, not unrelated— legal status and family access—and all for the book, once it got started up again.

Like another Glaswegian, the revolutionary psychiatrist Ronald D. Laing, Helena never altered her Scottish brogue to accommodate England, adopted as home by each of them. That April 1988 I would see them both. I had known Ronnie since the early seventies. He and Helena trolled in very different circles and, rather amazingly since one was already important to me and the other was fast to become so, they would be domiciled successively with their respective families in the same big house on Eton Sq. in Hampstead, a place I knew well from visits with Ronnie. When I saw him that April at the Swiss Cottage Hotel, he was virtually a homeless man, albeit a privileged one, on the lam with his former secretary Marguerita and their new baby, trying to figure out where to settle down. His (second) wife, still at Eton Sq. with the three children he had had with her, later sold the house to Helena and her surgeon husband.

Meeting Helena was not quite so exhilarating, or nerve-shattering, as meeting my half-brother a decade earlier. But I put great store by this my first encounter with English law. The law has never appealed to me and I have rarely sought recourse to it. By adversarial means, lawyers cost people money and pain. I have avoided it plaguishly. When it came however to my birth circumstance, beyond biology a purely legal affair, as is every birth, I was about to entertain a fatal weakness. Having often joked that I was at war with England, who or what could possibly be my enemy if not the law? My birth certificate, a copy of which I obtained at Somerset House the moment I arrived in England in 1968—my first trip back since my mother left with me aged two—tells the whole story. One can see why my mother left it behind. Jill is registered under her maiden name as "Jill Crowe," with a dash in the box space under "Father." In Italy this entry might have read "Non Noto," a slightly fuller description than a dash. Unlike my mother, I treasure my birth certificate. It bears the imprint and harbinger of my entire future. As Jacques Lacan, that difficult French psychoanalyst and thinker, has said, "Every personal experience is determined by the individual's relation to the law which binds them." My relation to the law, following the critical fact of birth and long into adulthood, was personally one of ignorance. There was a cover-up, as initiated by the abandoned birth certificate, and succeeded by altered identities in a distant country, along with the perpetration of lies. When I was 20 and the truth began to emerge, my ignorance continued unabated since its agency, my mother, was unable to explain why exactly she had had to lie. I had no context, nor any other examples; our situation seemed unique, exclusively personal, and profoundly bad. One terrible thing was a longtime developing estrangement that blighted our relationship. By a stroke of luck, as the world changed in the nineteen-sixties when I was in my thirties and revolution consumed us, ushering in the so-called second wave of feminism, challenges to the system under which we lived revealed the system itself like a long lost template. Now I had context. A legal substructure supporting our state, preeminently the institution of marriage, made my mother's predicament not only clear, but part of a very large archaic picture. I could never have approached the law in England without that education.

Helena came across right away as my deliverer. Warm, intimate, charming, empathic, attractive, smart, she had all sorts of intriguing ideas for how I could take a stand in England, and gain access to my family, notwithstanding my half-brother's opposition. The law would be behind me, but my legal status was probably unalterable. If this was an obvious oxymoron, at the time I disregarded it, entranced by practically everything my new exalted advisor had to say. She asked me right off what my priorities were. Armed with the inflated words of my New York lawyer friend that I could "spearhead a movement for reform," I said I wanted to change the law, meaning the Family Law Reform Act of 1969 which granted new rights to the illegitimate but was not retroactive. In her beguiling brogue and lilt, Helena said such a reform was out of the question. And since her reasons, while altogether damning to my interests sounded like literature to me— new thoughts in colorful prose with a dramatic conclusion—I quite forgot what I had announced I wanted to do. She said there simply had to be a cutoff point (1969), because "what's left of the British Empire would crumble if all the scullery maids' children," those "products of all the king's men's mistresses or one-nighters, were to crawl out of the woodwork and lay claim to inheritances." "Think of the thousands of cases . . . " she confided collusively. "Imagine what terrible pain it would cause. It would

totally undermine the whole economic system." Wow!—I saw a
breathtaking picture, the havoc I could create by leading a successful reform, perhaps the very downfall of Britain. No, she
wrapped up her brief, the law could not be changed, but I could,
she said, be a "special case."

My "special case," she explained, would pivot upon something called a Declaration of Paternity, where my "proof"—as I
had described the instructive clause in my father's will to his
wife—would come in handy. A "live issue" had to be concocted
first—a probate, or any interest my family might have in suing
me, like over my book project. Helena saw us getting a "publicized declaration" to a higher court, leading to a meeting with
family in the "inner chambers" of a Lord she knew, a "liberal
peer." Another enchanting sounding scenario had me flushing out
my family by simply blitzing the media with my story—articles I
would write on roots, an appearance on her own ITV talk show,
that sort of thing. And should any of this happen, what, as I was
able to deliberate in some deep mental recess buried under my
bewitchment, would the family think if not that I wanted their
money? The law would loom here. And money had never been in
my sights. Somehow I had understood the law better than I
thought. Eventually I would understand it very well.

Reforms are really plays of smoke and mirrors. In our system
of patrilineal descent, protected and enabled by the institution of
marriage, there is simply no way to alter the status of children
born outside the system without terminating it. There is value of
course in reforms. A law passed in 1624 by the English King
James I "to prevent the murthuring of bastard children" (addressing the widespread practice of infanticide as a solution to the
illegally begotten) would have given large numbers of children the
right just to live. The feminist movements of the past two centuries were perforce almost completely reform-driven, designed to
improve the lot of women living under a system not their own. In
the wake of reform, with the system still intact (and snugly reinforced by backlash), the invention of self as practiced by, say,
artists, seems, as it always has, a liberating possibility, the most

nonpolitical, if one can say any life is nonpolitical, of separatist agendas.

I tend to see origins, encompassing ancestral input, as blueprints for mandatory futures. My birth certificate has an important dash in it. My inheritance was unknown; I would have to make it up myself. And unerringly, after the age of 20, it evolved in the direction of a book. The English novelist and Booker Prize winner Pat Barker describes the same "dash" in a piece of autobiographical fiction she wrote titled *The Man Who Wasn't There*, published the year I met Helena, in 1988. Colin, her 12-year old protagonist, unfolds his crumpled birth certificate, which shows his own name and sex, his mother's name and occupation, and then: *Name and surname of father:——; Rank and profession of father:——.* Since Barker not only never knew her father but knew nothing about him either, and she never believed anything her mother told her about him, chiefly that he died as an RAF pilot in WWII (Barker was born, like "Colin," in 1943), fiction became an obvious medium for her to create and claim him, and by association or by transcendence, herself. Since I knew my father's identity and profession, by which he left bells galore and a huge paper trail around the world, I had the means of recreating him non-fictionally. The public record is large and accessible; the private domain, guarded by family, could seem to cry out for a fiction writer. It was the family documents and memories I hoped Helena's machinations could deliver, once the family became frightened by my tales in the media, then were inveigled to meet with me in her Lord friend's inner chambers.

Precisely the adversarial scenario, never mind its sheer nuttiness, I knew deep down was not the way to go. If meeting Arthur was a good example, I had shown myself to be the best mediator of my own situation. Anyway, deprived of family access, plenty can be discovered by aligning dates from various sources to establish credible narratives. Outstanding in the public record are the factual riches to be found in the birth, marriage and death certificates (applied for in the UK once you find the names and code numbers in big weighty books, green for birth, red for marriage, black for death), and the wills. I have a large stash of them reaching back into the 1700s. Ship's Passenger Lists have been invaluable. Lists of all sorts involving bells make up a special file. A reference library of bell books has hardly been a bad thing to have. An enormous clipping file from a service hired by Gillett & Johnston and kept in the Croydon Library was laboriously copied. The carillon archives, at schools, universities, churches, or other reserves like the Rockefeller Archive Center in Pocantico, New York, the Anton Brees Library at the Bok Tower in Florida, or the Eijsbouts Foundry Archives in Asten Holland, became the "bourdon" of my files. The gold is in the contracts and correspondence, invariably showing origins, supported by clippings, photographs, brochures, concert programs and stray literature. Rarely has one of these archives been sent to me on request. I have had to get there, and find it myself, or obtain unusual assistance to unearth it.

Once in Madison Wisconsin in 1984 to attend the GCNA Congress there, it was easy to obtain what could be had in the University library. Once at the Mercersburg Academy in Pennsylvania in 1993 to attend a Mid-Atlantic Carillonneurs Conference and to speak casually about Cyril Johnston, I would have thought that while there it would be easy to get their archive too. But the school library yielded little, and the carillonneur who had invited me to speak found it uninteresting to help me locate it. The same thing happened in June 2000 while I was at the Academy again, this time to deliver a formal slide-lecture on the bellfounder. A year later, incidentally one month before 9/11, I came across the Mercersburg material I had wanted in an unexpected place. It turned up in Ottawa while I was vetting the vast Percival Price collection, 100 plus boxes of papers, at Canada's National Library. Included are letters written in 1925 between Price and William Irvine, headmaster at Mercersburg from 1893 and a rare bell visionary. Irvine was seeking Price's advice on a carillon planned for the $700,000 chapel and tower he was having designed for Mercersburg by Ralph Adams Cram to be dedicated in 1926—how many bells to have, their costs, and which bellfounder to employ. Price asks Irvine to allow him to make inquiries to Gillett & Johnston, saying he knew "of no firm which will produce better work, nor do it more reasonably," and raising the stakes for G&J by pointing out that they were making the Rockefeller carillon for New York City (Park Avenue) and an equally large one for the Parliament Buildings at Ottawa. These were both instruments Price would be hired to play in residence. But Irvine must already have known he wanted Gillett & Johnston. In another Price collection letter written by Irvine to William Gorham Rice, Irvine describes a trip he made to England with his wife in 1923 that included a visit in July to Croydon, where they were guests of Cyril and his mother. This coincidentally was one month before the Rockefeller visit to the G&J foundry with three of his sons, there to be entertained by the same couple. Irvine went on to tell W. G. Rice that he later spent a weekend with Cyril Johnston in Devonshire listening to bells.

A web of connections involving Price, Rice, Rockefeller, Mayer, Lefévere, now Irvine (who heard Lefévere play the G&J instrument in Cohasset in 1925), Charles Reiman chair of the Princeton carillon committee (Irvine, a Princeton graduate, learned from him of the G&J contract for Princeton) provides some idea of the network that was by the mid-twenties in place supporting Cyril Johnston as the bellfounder du jour, and of how he garnered the lion's share of North American contracts during that decade.[1]

The Mercersburg 43-bell carillon, costing $40,000, belongs to a group known for their spectacular surroundings. Upon seeing the Blue Ridge Mts. 25 miles to the east, and the Tuscahoras four miles to the west, with the luscious Cumberland Valley rolling between, Cyril was quoted as saying, "never before have I placed a carillon in a location more favorable to bringing out the beautiful quality and charm of the music"[2] The Mercersburg carillon is unique in that the bell metal at pouring was rich with valuable or historic coins and other costly metal scraps gathered by William Irvine beginning in 1920, when he already knew he wanted bells for his chapel (though at first, like Rockefeller for Park Avenue, he imagined a chime). Irvine would not be happy to know that portions of his precious, arduously collected fragments are no longer embedded in the Mercersburg carillon, gone with a dozen bells that were taken down through renovation. The headmaster's astounding numismatic amassment—223 pieces of copper for the bourdon alone—included coins from many countries around the world, some minted before Christ; a piece of gun-money of James II, minted in 1689; medals from two of Lord Nelson's flagships; pieces of copper shells from famous battlefields; copper from Pierpont Morgan's yacht the *Columbia,* from a number of American battleships and the Presidential yacht the USS *Mayflower.* A shaving of copper from the Liberty Bell after it first cracked in 1835 while tolling for the funeral of Chief Justice John Marshall was considered the most valuable piece in this assemblage offered up at casting in 1926 for deliquescence.[3]

Even more satisfying to obtain than the Mercersburg data— if the charm of difficulty is a factor—was the carillon archive at St. Paul's School in Concord, New Hampshire. Here I would eventually enjoy special assistance. It became well worth the delay from 1985 when first I approached the school with Ingrid, to be told by a hostile librarian that no carillon archive existed there, and she had no time anyway to serve the public. The Rector himself had been discouraging; he might look into the records, but it would take some time. Fourteen years later, David Sinkler, a St. Paul's alumnus whom I knew through his wife Rebecca, an editor of mine, said he wanted to help. He made the inquiries and contacts and set up an appointment. On October 7, 1999, with David and his wife as impressive chaperones, we marched upon the library knowing there was a treasure trove of papers there. Copies of the material were delivered not by the librarian himself, but by a predecessor, an old man once a Cuban national, sitting way in a corner deep in the bowels, pleasantly curious about the project for which he had uncovered the papers. With folder securely in hand, I proceeded in a group of six now including the librarian and the chapel organist a hundred yards or so over to the venerable old Henry Vaughan Chapel, once enlarged by R.A. Cram, to see the carillon. I had had my doubts in 1985 about climbing the tower. Now the tiny wooden pointed *Alice in Wonderland* door in the chapel's interior, opening I knew on a barely lit stone spiral staircase of 64 steps, looked just as dubious. This time however I understood I had to do it.

Cyril Johnston was up there metaphorically. I would be viewed surely as the proper guide to the works, concerning which those prized papers had been so gallantly secured. The chapel organist led the way. I followed her with grave misgivings, ducking into the door opening exaggeratedly, impersonating a giant advancing on a dollhouse. Ingrid was behind me, then Rebecca, David, and the librarian, another David. By step seven or so I was already panting, and with each pant sputtering pathetically "I don't think I can do this." As if the airlessness and darkness and dizzying spirality are not enough, the cement walls of this vertical tunnel close in on your shoulders, massaging them in a crushing sort of way. There was clearly no going back. In plunging downwards I would have to damage and disorient four people behind me. Ingrid kept telling me to breathe. I was counting the steps and studying my shoes. Once there, the relief was diluted quickly by wondering how I was going to get back down. Yet I felt triumphant, and went right over to claim the carillon clavier, a reassuring antique of 23 oaken baton keys, its small brass plate inscribed "Gillett & Johnston 1933," to play *God Save the Queen*. I developed this habit long ago upon arriving intact at a belfry, should any presiding carillonneur indulge me. It's not a virtuoso performance exactly. I pick out the notes in the key of C, one at a time like a child at a piano or as if the instrument were a chime. Amateurishly I enjoy wondering—not unlike I suppose all the regular or professional tower inmates who sit at these keyboards—if anyone out there in the neighborhood is listening. Once the six of us surveyed the 23 bells, their inscriptions, and the clock mechanism a floor above the playing room, I braced myself for the 64-step descent. I asked if we had any food. Rebecca produced three chiclets, and came down directly behind me conducting a diversionary conversation, discussing my shoes or shoes generally. Since I went first, I knew I could pitch forward in a hurry and kill only myself.

Later I would read in an archival letter dated 1932 that Cyril Johnston had been at the school and "clambered all over the Chapel tower," thus learning that he had climbed St. Paul's neo-medieval spiral staircase 65 years before me. A broad-shouldered man, I imagine he had had to hunch over and attenuate himself to clear the walls. He was there on December 7th, four months after the birth of his son Arthur.

In May 1995, seven years after my galvanic, dead-ended encounter with Helena Kennedy, and what would turn out to be my last meeting with R.D. Laing in England, my book was still on hold, and I found out that Cyril's widow had died—on December 10, 1994. She was 93. For reasons that are not now very clear to me, I troubled myself over the law once again. One word, though, sticks out: "Probate." Back in 1988 Helena Kennedy had said "probate" was something that could be a "live issue" in arriving at a Declaration of Paternity, and reaching détente for access to family. In 1995 such an entity existed in Mary Johnston's will, once it cleared the courts. Here was the instrument of legal pressure that had been missing earlier. It seems I had forgotten that once the artifice of the law involving a natural enemy (the traditional position taken by legal family members toward a "relative" born ex-paternitas) was invoked, feelings simply assumed would now be activated—a result inimical to my interests. Luckily nothing came of my new misconceived foray, but not before I had spent all summer faxing and telephoning across the big pond with a seemingly inexhaustible supply of solicitors and barristers, including Helena. And spent a sum of money for nothing, exceeding the amount by £50 that Cyril Johnston had once asked his wife in his will to send to my mother.

A death can arouse strong feelings in survivors, causing them to think and do extraordinary things. I had never even met Mary Johnston, but she was a powerful figure in my nexus of family realities and imaginings. I was a de facto survivor of sorts. I believe I wanted something to happen to externalize my complex emotions over her long-dead husband, or perhaps more accurately over the bizarre circumstances by which I once learned of his existence. Something striking did happen: as a result of obtaining and reading Mary Johnston's will, it became apparent that her son Arthur had probably predeceased her. He was missing from her list of inheritors. And indeed, as subsequently discovered, he had died in May 1993, a year and a half before his mother. So here were the deaths of two of the three people closest to Cyril Johnston, both raising up the specter by proxy of my original ignorance and the shock of my mother's disclosures concerning Cyril's own death in 1950. Cannonading England and its legal experts by fax and phone the summer of 1995, it would appear in retrospect that I had been up to nothing better than ventilating.

Mark Stephens of Stephens Innocent, the law firm recommended by Helena to represent my slim to fanciful case, made things interesting on several accounts. One day, calling me by cell phone from his car in London, he told me, *"The stigma of illegitimacy doesn't exist any more."* I understood his reference—i.e. the post-feminist loosening of marital customs and mores in the West—but asked him how he would feel about telephoning a 60 year old woman (Arthur's sister Rosemary) and being the one to inform her that she had a half-sister, assuming she was still unaware of my existence. Evidently he got my drift, or took the point seriously, because later on he became the one barrister to try to liberate me from his profession, and save me money, advising me to seek counsel from a social worker who united family members lost to each other—admittedly a less glamorous expedient than meeting with family in some Lord's inner chambers. But I was game. On September 18, 1995 I flew to London and met the next day with Ariel Bruce, the social worker recommended by Mark Stephens. The day after that I went to Stephens's firm, Stephens Innocent, and presented them with a check for £550 for having pored over their big law books and determined, as I already knew, that I had no case involving my father's estate. This was not a total loss. It became a title and a story, chief currency of writers. And financially actually I came out somewhat ahead.

A publication had sent me to England on this occasion, offering me a thousand dollars for both travel expenses and article that I would write about my adventures with the law.[4] Subtract £550 from a thousand dollars, and the difference can be computed more or less. Then the money was alchemized in my article by title—*500 Pounds with Interest*—referencing the amount that Cyril's widow sent to my mother in 1950.

As for Ariel Bruce, my enthusiasm in meeting her was dissipated through time and distance and a self-saving unwillingness I had to handing over control of my family fortunes to anyone else. I had been forewarned by one of her first questions: How would you feel about being rejected? Not good at all was my unspoken response. She had been describing her tactic of writing letters on behalf of clients to intended family targets; she favored approaching the younger generation, like in my case the daughters of my half siblings, who each had one. Now that Arthur was gone, I might try to get to his sister Rosemary through her daughter. Ariel was sophisticated on the systemic sources and ramifications of family dismemberment, and on the entrenched cultural methods— cover-ups and creation of secrets, often in the wake of the transference of property known as adoption—for dealing with extramarital births. "People like your mother," she said, "were victims of the sexual mores of a bygone generation." Another remark, that my mother "led a life of subterfuge to protect Cyril's decision" would have appealed to Ronnie Laing, who rather interestingly had traditional attitudes that ran counter to his own life as a father. Ronnie died of a massive coronary in 1989, aged 62, one year after I saw him in London at the Swiss Cottage Hotel. He was playing tennis on the Riviera in Saint-Tropez, girlfriend Marguerita and their baby nearby on the sidelines.

In Ronnie's opinion, Cyril was the villain of my piece, an established stance in the West toward fathers in births of my kind, and a position I have been fond of entertaining and questioning [See Chapters VII, VIII, and XVII]. There seems no doubt that it lay behind the fears Arthur and his mother had over any publication of a work on their father and husband in my assumed surname. Not that they themselves would have thought, necessarily, that Cyril had done anything wrong. After all, for one important thing, he had not been married when he had the affair with my mother. But a child did emerge. And in not claiming the child, his culpability was socially written. High on the mission list of his survivors was the ordinance to protect his reputation, i.e. to leave the world none the wiser. Jean-Paul Sartre, writing on Jean Genet, the precocious French orphan and convict turned author, said, "What is important is not what people make of us but what we ourselves make of what they have made of us."

Endearingly, Ronnie once made fun of Cyril's outfit in my flagship photo of him standing between King George V and Queen Mary, pointing out that next to the King his cuffs were not right; they didn't extend below his coat sleeves, and his spats and vest were wrong somehow. Ronnie was kind of dancing around and gesticulating wildly in front of the huge framed picture, enjoying his exercise in trying to discredit my father (though not by way of exalting the King; this antisocial rebel and Scottish expat was no royalist)—possibly imagining he was having a convincing effect. He was in my apartment with baby and girlfriend Marguerita, whose unmarried state was of some concern to me. She was herself unconcerned, excusing Ronnie as having just been through a messy divorce. When he died a year or so later, she was left unprotected. Ronnie had had eight legitimate children, with two different wives, and besides Marguerita's out-of-wedlock child he had had one other. Marguerita's inheritance was a son with Ronnie's name, which she assumed of course on her own recognizance.

The moral may be clear. Any judgment as I see it is not. Inside every story lie extenuating circumstances, unknown to people at large, even to family members.

Chapter XV

THE DUTCH CONNECTION

If God loves us why did he turn us into bellfounders
—Alan Hughes

*Bellfounding was entering a new era which was to see the integration of
the old craft with present-day techniques and it is not surprising
that Eijsbouts was playing an innovative part in this*
—André Lehr

*Since the dawn of the twentieth century, bell and cannon have ceased
to be the sole rivals of the mighty thunderbolt*
—Alain Corbin

Visiting the Dutch bellfoundry of Royal Eijsbouts in Asten, Holland with Ingrid, March 25, 2004, I enjoyed the attentions of two men who care a great deal about Cyril Johnston's bells. Eijsbouts, one of only six bellfounding firms left in Europe, has roots like Gillett & Johnston in building tower-clocks, then adding bells and carillons decades later. The two firms were closely connected during the 1920s and 30s, when Eijsbouts had yet to begin making carillons. Of Cyril Johnston's 53 created world-wide, 10 were cast for Holland, all through the agency of Eijsbouts, who was also the installer. Imported between 1925 and 1931, the very years of Cyril's great bellfounding triumphs in North America, a bridge now spanned the old world and the new, where the recovered secrets of tuning, once owned and monopolized by Lowlanders, were on glorious display.

The John Taylor Co. of course shared this conjugational honor with Gillett & Johnston. In Holland in fact Taylor had led the way. By 1925, the year Eijsbouts obtained G&J's first Dutch carillon orders, Taylor had already swept the country with five instruments, beginning at the early date of 1911. Represented by another Dutch tower-clock maker Floris Addicks, Taylor delivered its eleventh in 1934, the pre-war cut-off date for the English run at this very Netherlandic concert product.[1] The reason for the unexpected deathblow to English makers was that the Dutch government began subsidizing its own bellfounders, van Bergen and Petit & Fritsen, enabling them to build their first carillons tuned on modern principles. After WWII van Bergen, as we know from New York's Riverside Church fiasco in 1955 [See Chapter XIII], lost its touch.

Our hosts at the Eijsbouts foundry March 25, 2004, were Joost Eijsbouts, aged 43, president/director and great grandson of founder Bonaventura (b. 1847), and Joep van Brussel, vice-president also in charge of sales. The current premises of Eijsbouts foundry have existed in the Dutch southeast town of Asten since 1905, two hundred yards from its original 1872 site, where Bonaventura Eijsbouts, a watch repairer, set up shop to build tower-clocks. Entering Asten by car, the road sign announcing the town is adorned with a large colorful drawing of a bell. So you know this is a place identified with its bells, and famous for its foundry. There is even a bell museum in the town, the National Beiaardmuseum founded in 1980. I had met Joep, a very tall handsome Dutchman, at the 2003 GCNA Congress in Berea, Kentucky, where he gave me a beautiful photo-rich booklet advertising the foundry. It had long been apparent to me that I had to get there.

Cyril had personal connections with the Eijsbouts family as well as sixteen years of doing business with them. In emails, Joep promised interviews, a tour of their premises, lunch, and a casting. At a last moment, with plane reservations from New York made and paid for, he said there was something wrong with their ovens and he doubted a casting would take place. I wrote back protesting that I would be "gravely disappointed" at such an outcome, and he replied that he would "do [his] utmost" to arrange it.

He arranged it in spades. The molten metal for a 4½-ton bell, a size not cast every day, was due to be poured sometime after our lunch. Following a tour of the foundry we were having this lunch *à quatre* at a posh place called Café Restaurant 't Eeuwig Leven (Eternal Life), close to the foundry. Joep awaited a call from his foreman to warn him that their 10-ton capacity oven had heated to the prescribed 1100 degrees centigrade, when we should return for the casting. After our tour, the appetizer at Eternal Life was bracing. A Dutch delicacy perhaps—consommé soup in a tall-stemmed glass with mushrooms floating in it, a jigger of dark purple wine set on your plate to toss in for a kick—it took my mind right off the challenge of heavy tools and machinery in a sooty environment, a place of unique disorder to the uninitiated. Eijsbouts is the third bellfoundry I have toured, after Whitechapel in London and Taylor's in Loughborough. My eyes run selectively toward the bells themselves, a shape I love and possess along with many of the thousands who work in this business one way or another. In these anachronously ancient fire-breathing bronze-forging settings, the bells hang or lie about on the foundry floor dirt in family groups in all stages of development, from the early moulds to the final highly burnished gold-shine product, bearing proud inscriptions, ready for shipment. Some old bells dismounted from their towers hang or sit in rows awaiting restorations, if not smelting or liquefaction. I search out the ovens too; I know what they do. At Eternal Life, Joep got his call from the foundry saying they were on countdown for the 4½-ton birthing. We had been discussing world politics and my story. Joep, knowing the latter in outline from a couple of my presentations at Guild

Congresses in America, now hearing added details, showed he had a handle on my project when he concluded wittily, *"If you want someone to write a book about you, have an illegitimate child by a foreign woman you meet on a boat."* On Cyril's bells, Joep and Joost have reverential attitudes.

Walking back to the foundry, Joep said he loves the "color" of English bells, and that Eijsbouts bases its methods specifically on the G&J bell sound. "We are not able to copy the bells 100% but I think we come really close to the sound that is quite similar to G&J." Joost in interview said that at the end of the 1940s his Uncle Tuur (a nickname to be found in the next-to-last syllable of Bonaventura), then Eijsbouts' president, and getting ready to cast carillons for the first time, wanted Cyril to act as consultant for the firm, and "sell" them his formula. Nothing came of it, but in August 1949, less than a year before his death, Cyril, infirm and arthritic, was in Asten to help celebrate Eijsbouts' first carillon, an inaugural instrument guaranteed to attract attention. A Traveling Carillon, 23 bells hung on a steel frame and mounted on a lorry, it functioned imaginatively as an advertisement, driven on wheels around the country. André Lehr (deceased 2007), the eminent bell historian from Utrecht, 19 at that time and recently hired to work at Eijsbouts, remembers Cyril at the unveiling, his hands shaking, saying, "He was an old man." We were visiting André, then 74, and his wife at their house in Asten following the day at the foundry and Eternal Life spent with Joep and Joost.

A coincidence of Cyril's impending death and the Dutch firm's entry into the carillon market could seem like a hand-off. On April 3rd, 1950, Tuur Eijsbouts attended Cyril's funeral in Croydon, and in 1955 he would be one of the parties protesting the removal by van Bergen of 56 G&J bells from New York City's Riverside Church, hailing the instrument as "the most important work of the late Mr. Cyril Johnston" [See Chapter XIII]. The connection between the Johnston and Eijsbouts families continued through Cyril's widow, who maintained a friendship with Tuur's sister, Joost's Aunt Mies (b. 1916). She had lived in the Johnston household in Croydon in the mid-1930s. Hoping to improve her

English, she had acted as an au pair, assisting in the care of Cyril's son Arthur, born in 1932.

The business relationship between Eijsbouts and G&J throughout the 1920s and 1930s was not always so cozy, with the English language a drawback for the Dutch, and the 1930s a frustrating time for Cyril. He expected naturally to continue casting carillons for Holland into that pre-war era, then found himself blocked by forces he didn't understand. With the official subsidy of Dutch bellfounders, both Eijsbouts and Addicks (on behalf of Taylor) were increasingly constrained to follow their government's lead and act in the civic interest by favoring their Dutch compatriots. It was in 1936 over a potential carillon contract for the catchily named town of Bergen Op Zoom, situated on the North Sea fjord of Ooster Schelde, that Cyril became aware of the new government policy. St. Geertruidstoren in Bergen Op Zoom wanted 35 bells—3 chromatic octaves with a G bourdon of 635 kilos, ready for a historical feast day in 1937. Johan Eijsbouts (b.1878), father of Tuur and Cyril's main correspondent, met with the town burgomaster to impress him with the great number of carillons they had delivered with Croydon bells. Then wrote to G&J, "They gave us the impression our chances are good but they already have a provisional tender from Omer Michaux in Louvain [Belgium], and considering their low prices it could be difficult for us."

The Belgian interest in this case was promoted by Jef Denyn, then 73 years old, the great bellmaster of St. Rombouts Cathedral at Malines. Denyn performed as consultant on a number of carillon projects in Holland, as well as Belgium during the 1920s and 30s. Authorities from Bergen Op Zoom had visited Denyn in Malines, when the tender from Michaux would have followed. Michaux was representing Marcel Michiels of Doornik, the only bell-caster of consequence in Belgium then. Omer Michaux had become Michiels' agent after an unsuccessful run at bellfounding himself. According to André Lehr, Denyn had been entangled for some time in business interests with Belgian founders, an involvement that could help account for the fact that the two English founders, so dominant in that period, were virtually shut

out of the Belgian carillon market.[2] The single exception was
G&J's 48-bell instrument for Louvain University Library installed
in 1929, the gift of sixteen American engineering associations in
memory of colleagues who had died in the Great War. Denyn also
became implicated (posthumously) in a bell scandal bigger by far
than the Riverside/van Bergen deal, even than that other 1950s
delictum—the covert seizure by Schulmerich Electronics in
Pennsylvania of a G&J carillon from the Ward-Belmont School in
Tennessee [See Chapter XII].

During that very year of 1936 when Bergen Op Zoom was in
the offing, the two Belgians Omer Michaux and Marcel Michiels
were conniving to peddle a carillon of the most dubious origins to
an American university. In their fantastic and improbable plot—to
sell 18 counterfeit Pieter Hemony bells (dated 1674) to Alfred
University in New York State as part of a 42-bell carillon—they
would pull in Jef Denyn to authenticate their fake goods. Just how
complicit or aware Denyn was remains inconclusive. Known as a
gentle soul with impeccable character credentials—so revered
throughout the carillon world that anything he did or said was
considered *ne plus ultra*—he would come to seem a most unlikely
party to a crime of forgery, which was discovered and proved out
long after his death in 1941. If he was indeed involved, the excuse
for him would have been that he was old and perhaps addled.

There was nothing shady about Denyn's involvement in the
contract for Bergen Op Zoom. Like his Dutch counterparts, he
had an interest in helping his Belgian compatriots in those years
of financial adversity. He was certainly not going to endorse
Gillett & Johnston for the job. Naively, Cyril journeyed to
Malines to talk to the old man, imagining that their history
together—they had known each other well since 1922, the year of
the first carillon installations in North America, and of the opening of Denyn's School at St. Rombout's, with Denyn demonstrating new G&J carillons at the Croydon foundry, and entertaining
Cyril and his sister Nora in Malines—would serve him. Cyril, had
he lived, would have been shocked and incredulous over the
Alfred University story, especially any part played in it by Jef

Denyn, who was to him the great man second only to Canon
Simpson in the carillon renaissance he once rode in on.

November 7, 1936, Johan Eijsbouts wrote to G&J saying the
fate of the Bergen Op Zoom contract was now in the hands of
Dr. J. Casparie, President of the Dutch Society of Carillons, thus
an influential figure in Dutch carillon politics. "As you know,"
wrote Eijsbouts, he "was an admirer of your bells, and we always
have his protection." Dr. Casparie (1873–1948) was a neurologist
and psychiatrist who had taken an interest in astronomy and
music, in particular the carillon. Cyril had enjoyed his friendship
and backing since 1924 in connection with G&J's first and most
impressive Dutch contract—for Sint Janskathedral (St. John's) at
s'-Hertogenbosch: 45 bells with a 5-ton bourdon installed in
1925. However, in 1936 Dr. Casparie was in a difficult position,
as Cyril would discover once he saw him at Den Bosch—the short
name for s'-Hertogenbosch. November 7th, Eijsbouts had urged
Cyril to come to Holland as soon as possible, saying, "We have
not a moment to lose."[3] Two days earlier, November 5th, Cyril's
daughter Rosemary, his third and last child counting myself, had
been born. He was eager to travel but was "laid up with influen-
za" as he cabled Johan. On the 14th he embarked on the
overnight boat from England's East Anglia port of Harwich, arriving in Hoek van Holland, the international seaport close to The
Hague, Dutch seat of government. He then proceeded by train to
Bergen Op Zoom to see the burgomaster. In the afternoon at Den
Bosch, where he had a "long interview" with Dr. Casparie, whom
he described as "personally just as friendly disposed to us as he
always has been," he learned that he was up against "the
Authorities of The Hague," and would likely lose his bid to van
Bergen. Before returning home, he met socially with Dr. Casparie's
daughter Corrie and her husband Otto in The Hague. "We had a
merry meeting once more," he wrote to the doctor when he got
home, while in the same letter, still assuming Bergen Op Zoom
could be his, he outlined moves he typically played to win a contract.[4] He would send lists of his carillons worldwide to date, and
he proposed that Dutch Carillon Committee members including

the doctor and a representative from Bergen Op Zoom come to England to hear and test his latest carillon, in Bournville, Birmingham—his 1935 replacement of a 1906 Taylor carillon [See Chapter XIII]. Cyril would transport the party by train or car to Bournville and bear the costs. Half a year later, he received word from Eijsbouts that indeed van Bergen got the contract.

The Croydon bellfounder's entry to the Lowland carillon field in 1924 was marked by an apocryphal story showing his chutzpah in coming from behind. As he knew, the John Taylor Co. was well established in Holland, a fact that Eijsbouts would be fond of reminding him whenever squeezed by the price wars. Visiting a tower in the Belgian town of Turnhout and observing a cracked bell in its Van den Gheyn carillon of 1775, Cyril offered to replace it at his own expense, showing that the quality of his bells was equal to the Van den Gheyns. Andreas Josef Van den Gheyn (1737–1793) was no doubt a fair choice for this test of excellence. A cracked bell by Pieter or François Hemony would obviously not have been. While Cyril was capable of matching the Hemony sound (in fact his sonorous basses have been likened admiringly to the large Hemony bells), the Hemony name was too great to with-stand comparison from a foreign interloper, even surely by any native upstart. A.J. Van den Gheyn, descended from the famous Louvain family of musicians and bellfounders of that surname, made outstanding bells, second only to the Hemonys in his prodi-gious output and tonal superiority. It was after his time that the secrets of tuning consummate carillons were lost. Cyril's offer to replace the cracked Van den Gheyn was accepted, and his bell is said to be distinguishable from the others only by an acute ear in the belfry. Percival Price who tells this Turnhout story in one of his books,[5] appears to imply that Cyril's first Lowland orders—for St. John's in 's-Hertogenbosch and Saint Joseph's Church in Tilburg—came as a result of his Belgian experiment, but in 1924 Cyril had notched a more significant item in his resumé.

That year, with just four carillons to his credit—the fourth dedicated in September at St. Stephen's Church in Cohasset Massachusetts—he was under contract with J. D. Rockefeller, Jr.

to cast the 53-bell carillon for his Park Avenue Baptist Church in New York City, a size exceeding any Dutch or Belgian instrument ever mounted. As Eijsbouts opened negotiations at the beginning of 1924 to represent G&J in Holland, he registered his awe over the Park Avenue order. "We read in the newspapers here that you delivered a great carillon to America, a total weight of about 50,000 kilograms."[6] Eijsbouts had been the go-between for Taylor for two instruments (1913 and '14), but Addicks was Taylor's main man, and with the newcomer G&J, Eijsbouts could better compete in the Dutch market. It would be the only market in Cyril Johnston's career, for peals, chimes, carillons or single bells, where he had to go through an agent. And I wonder how he liked it. In his own letters, he (or his lieutenants) stayed the course in the standard ultra-cool business argot, while his intermediary was constantly challenging, captious, and reproachful. This may be a familiar style for agents, pulled two ways over prices and deliveries, with the ones they represent, the supplicants, more or less at their mercy and required to sound at least above it all. But Eijsbouts revealed an extreme end of the anxieties and frustrations of agents. G&J prices were always convulsing them. In September, 1924, trying to tie up three contracts, for 's-Hertogenbosch, Tilburg and a new one, Hilvarenbeek, Eijsbouts wrote, "We wish not to conceal that your quotations have frightened us exceedingly." And on a general note, rather insolently, certainly impoliticly, "It is not so easy to convince everyone that your bells are so much better [than Taylor's]."[7] Their correspondence doesn't always read congenially, but in addition to normal pressures, among them Eijsbout's dependence on these carillon contracts for a chunk of the income (they constructed the frameworks and keyboards and in fact did everything but the bells), in dealing with the English, they were aggrieved by a language problem.

The common currency of English on the Continent, a gradual development after World War II, of course didn't exist then. Gillett & Johnston appeared to have no trouble understanding whatever Eijsbouts was saying, although the Dutch English, compromised by endless typos, misspellings, punctuational oddities, grammatical and syntactic distortions, tended to bring forth a dada compound, a study in linguistic disadvantage. One typical piece of phraseology, "We don't conceive nothing of this prices . . . " points up the one-sidedness of their exchanges. Eijsbouts was not in denial over the difficulty. In September that year they begged G&J to correspond with them in French, saying French would not be perfect for them but much easier than English. "If you prefer however your own language [and G&J did!] we will do so and you will excuse us for our faulty notion of the English." Somewhat later, even more exasperated, worrying that they "translate [G&J] letters wrongly," they ask the clearly impossible, for G&J to write to them in Dutch![8]—Despite the language divide and competition from the Taylor/Addicks duo, Eijsbouts never failed through the twenties and up till 1931, to land all the carillon orders they went after for their English bell providers. And after 1931 they obtained a number of orders for single bells, sometimes two at a time, or four.

The new s'-Hertogenbosch or Den Bosch instrument of 45 bells, dedicated June, 1925, set the pace. St. John's, a magnificent Gothic Rococo cathedral, built between the 1300s and 1500s and dating in early Romanesque versions from the early 1200s, unsurprisingly had a rich bell history. (The cathedral once accommodated paintings by Hieronymous Bosch, a native of the city, born actually Jeroen van Aken, c. 1450–1516, the city's best-known inhabitant). Its first recorded carillon of 14 small bells, 1505 by Willem and Jasper Moer, would have been a primitive carillon by modern standards, with manual and automatic capacities but no keyboard as we know it. Later in the 1500s a son of Jaspar Moer installed 19 bells, either replacing the earlier 14, or some of them. A fire in 1584 left only 13 hanging. In the mid-1600s a mixed carillon of 26 old and new bells existed. It was the 1872 carillon of 49 bells cast by Andreas van Aerschodt the Belgian founder from Louvain that Cyril Johnston essentially replaced. Van Aerschodt (1814–1888) has had the misfortune of being associated with the bad reputation of carillon tuning in the 19th century. Lehr calls his Den Bosch instrument a "very false carillon,"[9] and has written that of van Aerschodt's carillons virtually none remain. They were, "very handsomely cast bells, but the overtones . . . sound utterly confused."[10] Three van Aershodt bells were left in the new 1925 Den Bosch carillon, but retuned by Gillett & Johnston. And these three are still there as part of yet a newly reconfigured instrument in a great 2004 restoration.

Besides the three van Aerschodts, the new 45 G&Js kept company with a 1641 bell by Jacob Noteman, and two bells by the Hemonys—one by François dated 1663 made for Den Bosch, the other by both brothers dated 1644 but originally hanging in a tower at Zutphen, destroyed by fire in 1920, then brought into this new G&J 1925 carillon.[11] The two Hemony bells were sent to the G&J foundry in Croydon, but by no means for retuning. The authorities at Den Bosch, "of the opinion that these bells are absolutely pure of tone," wanted them left alone.[12] When founders are under contract for new carillons, old bells marked for inclusion are often sent to them simply to be measured and tested, helping to determine profiles overall. In 1955 Eijsbouts recast a broken G&J bell and enlarged the carillon by three small bells. With the 2004 restoration—38 G&Js left, six originals replaced by Eijsbouts—one can see the gradual seizure and encroachment by bellfounders, something both endemic and epidemic in the carillon business, creating a potpourri of bells by different makers in any aging tower, indeed in a vast daisy chain of aging towers across the world. Questions of musical improvement vs. commercial advantage are often topical, then fade into the horizons of history. There is now in Holland a Monument Protection Law, passed in the early 1990s, to preserve every bell over 50 years old, including carillons and keyboards and the structures that house them. For Cyril Johnston, he should, I think, be pleased to know that for the time being at least his 38 remaining bells at Den Bosch still co-exist with the two Hemonys. It is his only carillon in the Lowlands, or the world, where his bell voice mingles with that of his illustrious 17th century predecessors.

He lived long enough to know that a number of his Dutch carillons vanished during World War II. Only four in fact out of the original ten, and including Den Bosch, still have his bells in them. Taylor's instruments fared little better, with five extant but no longer intact. They fell in the German requisition, which decimated the pride of the Netherlands and Belgium—their incomparable historical carillons, numbering close to 300 at that time. An act of war akin to the most intimate kind of property damage or theft, bells were wantonly removed and sent to the ovens for conversion to munitions, or stacked up in yards and warehouses, so many abandoned parts of bodies. Bell plunder is known from the early 15th century, most notoriously for transformation to cannons. The erection of steeples in the Lowlands reflected the heraldry of place, proclaiming town status and ascendancy. And the bells were their crowning manner of speaking. A tower without its bells has been called a "headless body." Prior to 1940, the worst desecration of "sacred bronze" in the Lowlands occurred during the French Reign of Terror, 1795–1801. France was itself victimized in 1941 when Hermann Goering ordered the removal of its church bells— "the most important and last reserve of copper and tin." In Belgium a 1941 general census of bells was ordered by the Nazis in advance of confiscation, and fiercely protested by ecclesiastical authorities. A slogan circulated in the Flemish countryside: *He who shoots with bells/Does not win the war.* In 1944 by one count 4,568 bells, weighing a total of 1,721,040 pounds, were deemed missing.[13] Over 50% of the bells in both countries were looted. Bells in every era of hostilities have been routinely, preemptively, taken down by the townspeople, to be hidden or buried until they were safe. Joost Eijsbouts told me there was a "gentleman's agreement" with the Germans to leave their Hemonys alone (several hundred of them survived the war), while old 20th century bells like Taylor's and G&J's, were not allocated as important.[14] Of the approximately 383 bells cast for Holland by Cyril Johnston either singly or for carillons, about 126 are left.

For Eijsbouts, it became clear that once the war was over there would be a tremendous demand for bells. The peace became the firm's opportunity—a decisive moment in their graduation to bellfounding. By now, 55 years after they started, they have cast a staggering number of bells, simply tens of thousands, and of their carillons, 30 or more in the U.S. alone, in excess of the number Cyril Johnston left in North America at the time of his death. During André Lehr's tenure at the firm, 1949–1990, he pioneered the use of computers as a tool in designing new bells and in testing old ones. The computer is used also as an aid in tuning, but only adjunctively to the old fashioned benefits of the human ear. "The critical ear," says Eijsbouts in its publicity, "will always have the last word in the tuning process."

After lunch at *Eternal Life* we were standing around in the Royal Eijsbouts works awaiting the promised casting, bellfounding's marquee event. The 10-ton capacity oven, built into a brick wall, was roaring like a dragon, getting ready to advance on us breathing fire and smoke. Eight or ten men liveried in bulky silver asbestos suits with matching headgear and gloves, masked or goggled, spacemen, were moving around the center of attraction— the partly hidden steel-encased "sculpture" of moulds that took weeks to prepare for this moment. Inside the structure is the void that forms the exact model of the future bell. Several of the silver spacemen were maneuvering the huge cauldron or "casting ladle" which was positioned to hang from high overhead steel beams, and travel by chain and tackle, first to take the flaming hot molten metal from the oven, then to pour it into the moulds. Here the excitement was intense, the air beginning to reek of sulphur. Joep was explaining the process to a group of visitors. Joost and Ingrid and I were closer to the event, and Joost was trying to hold me back. He grabbed my camera, mounted the five steps to the steel platform where the pouring was happening, and shot a close-up for me. He was quite stirred up himself, saying with a wild sort of look in his eye that a casting never stops being exciting. I thought he meant the mesmerizing incandescence of the molten alloy, once described by King George V as a color "unmatched"; but perhaps what Joost had in mind was the possibility of a miscasting, which he described as being "enough to keep us modest."

Still, less than 1.0 percent of castings, he told us, are rejected. Then he quoted Alan Hughes of Whitechapel as saying, "If God loves us why did he turn us into bellfounders?" A miscasting will be costly, but is that the only reason God might be questioned over bellfounding? What would Cyril Johnston say? I know he loved his business, and he could hardly have had my appalled perspective on moving huge amounts of bronze and steel around. Or on dealing with people for whom his product was terrifically expensive and who had little idea how it is made. On the latter maybe he did. The architect Philip Johnson at age 90something once told an interviewer, "Don't be an architect," and when asked why, said, "Because it's too hard to please the client." But do the makers take pleasure in their results? Does the pleasure of others please them? Do they ever hear about it?

Leaving Asten the day after the casting we headed for Antwerp, a drive southwest of an hour and a half, to hear a carillon concert at Antwerp's pride, the Onze-Lieve-Vrouwekathedraal, built between 1351 and 1521, the same span of time as St. John's at Den Bosch. At noon Geert d'Hollander, Onze-Lieve's carillonneur, who appears frequently on the concert circuit in America, was due to play. He has the municipal post once held by Anton Brees's father Gustav, the post Brees would have inherited had he not decamped to the U.S., playing first for Rockefeller in New York, and ending up as resident carillonneur at the Bok Tower in Florida. Geert ascends 500 interior stone spiral steps to get to the belfry. The 49 bells he plays are primarily a Hemony instrument: 36 by the brothers, 1655; one by Hoerken, 1469; 12 by Eijsbouts, 1972. It was a chilly 45 degrees in Antwerp, not exactly the weather for basking outside a café listening to a concert. I was hunched in winter jacket over an expresso at an outdoor table of the café called "In de Schaduw van de Kathedral." The cobbled plaza is surrounded by small shops and Onze-Lieve, which soars impressively to 400 feet above it. We were the only concert-goers. People en route to places never looked up or seemed aware that a concert was going on. I have often seen this before, for instance at the Crystal Cathedral in Garden Grove California where people leaving Sunday services walk in droves past the most gorgeous reflective steel campanile

216

(designed by Philip Johnson and housing a 1989 carillon of 52 Eijsbouts bells), apparently quite unaware of the music originating 160 feet above them, timed to greet their exodus. If the carillon, as has been said, is a poor man's concert instrument, by default it also generates the classiest outdoor muzak. It was in Belgium in 1981 that I first heard a carillon concert in the manner approximating indoor performances—sitting on the grass in a row of chairs holding a program sheet. In other instances, I have heard concerts as the sole audience member. In Louvain in 2001, after Luc Rombouts valiantly but futilely tried to escort me to the Louvain University Library belfry, he played its 1929 48-bell G&J instrument while I sat alone in a designated listening area, a small amphitheater, below the tower.

Cyril's bells have often been described as "clear." He achieved rich overtones and distinct fundamental notes—the ambiguous equation for a superb carillon sound. When a virtuoso musician with a sensitive touch like Luc Rombouts plays such a carillon, making its range of capabilities transparently intelligible, you are likely to be carried away. That day in 2001 was one of my memorable experiences listening to the "poor man's instrument." Geert D'Hollander is a fine musician as well, though the stratosphere of Onze-Lieve at Antwerp the day I was there, captured and dissipated too many of the Hemony sounds I was straining to hear.

In 1944 Cyril Johnston gave a lecture with 75 slides that included a number of Dutch and Belgian towers cum bells, dwelling possessively on those with Hemonys. He had climbed the 458 steps of Utrecht's famous Dom Tower, where the greater number of bells, like those at Antwerp's Onze-Lieve, are Hemonys. He thought "Herr Wagenaar the carillonneur [J.A.H. Wagenaar, the third of that name, had been resident since 1906] . . . the finest player I had heard in Holland."[15]

The present municipal carillonneur at Utrecht, Liesbeth Janssen, who happens to be Geert D'Hollander's wife, has been a popular guest at towers in America, where I have heard her three times—once at Mercersburg Academy Pennsylvania on the 1926 G&J, when this carillon was still in a pristine state. A slight woman of no more than 30 at that time, her playing is simply sublime. I wonder if Cyril was ready for the preternaturally beautiful on one of his own instruments.

Chapter XVI

LUNCHES AT BEAULIEU

When I tell people my father was a bellfounder,
they never know what that is
—Lady Rosemary Price

Maybe the approach was wrong. Taking a train, say, instead of a boat. It was April 4, 2000. A 10:30 A.M. train at Waterloo Station in London would bear me to Brockenhurst, a town in Hampshire quite close to Southampton, the port city where Cyril Johnston often embarked for North America, sometimes with bells or a whole carillon. And where my mother shipped out for New York with me twice, the second time for good on the SS *George Washington*. My plan, along with the train, seemed all right, if one-sided in conception. On that day, for the first time I would meet my half-sister Rosemary, who had been led to think I was "Joan Castile, " recalling the precise method of meeting her brother Arthur in 1978. Once I got to her house I would reveal my true identity. Not right away of course. There would be amenities, including lunch, and she would produce material relating to her father, fulfilling the terms of our appointment—to help Ms. Castile in preparing to write a book about him, a contract signed in New York by Jill one month earlier. After twenty-two years, "Joan" was making a comeback, like an actor whose role is dusted off for a revival or a rerun. The other actors can vary somewhat (Arthur here becomes Rosemary, whose husband will play a supporting role) but the principal's purpose is the same, to search out her father's relatives, the people she thinks can best help her with more personal aspects of her book. As stand-ins for England, they could be seen as a gateway to repatriation, a thought belied by Jill's original paper of identity, filed at Somerset House—the birth certificate. In the certificate's blank space (adorned with a dash) under "father," a soothsayer posing as a clerk might have inked in, "Will eventually write a book by way of explanation."

Under protection of "Joan" I stepped off the train onto the platform at Brockenhurst April 4, 2000. I had other protection. Ingrid also dismounted from the train, but from another car, in order not to be seen in my company, and to await my return. Toward my left I saw a tall elderly gentleman looking sideways at me, which together with his impassivity and the lack of anyone else on the platform appearing to wait for somebody I took to mean he thought I was the woman he was there to pick up. I walked over and introduced myself and momentarily we were in his car. I had called from London to confirm my appointment, made under various covers by Ingrid from New York. If this encounter on a train platform was the first action in a drama, there had been opening-day jitters in London the night before, at the house of an editor/publisher friend, Nikos Stangos. The upcoming meeting at Beaulieu (pron. Byu-lee by the English), where my half-sister and her husband live (an eight-mile drive from Brockenhurst), became an uproarious subject. Nikos and Ingrid had me locked up in the couple's basement once I revealed myself. I didn't find the scenario so preposterous, and was convulsed with a fear-driven hilarity.

Sir David Price, Rosemary's husband and my pick-up man, is a retired Parliamentarian, having spent 40 years as a Conservative

MP serving Eastleigh in Hampshire, 1952–92. From an edition of *Who's Who* I knew this and other things about him, for instance that he was born in 1924, that he attended Eton, and Trinity College at Cambridge, and his "Recreations" included swimming, wine, cooking and gardening. He seemed a reasonably fitting representative of a country that had pointedly not given me a father (when withheld always a glorious type of figure) and who might therefore be appropriate to know. More important than what I had learned from *Who's Who* about Sir David was prior knowledge I had concerning his wife Rosemary, who became Lady Price in 1980 when he was knighted. Her brother Arthur had told me when first we met in 1978 that she was confined to a wheelchair. He had elaborated a bit, saying that in her 20s she had had an accident, falling from a window when she was pregnant, miscarrying and becoming paraplegic. I knew also that she and Sir David had a daughter called Arabella. As he drove me toward their house in Beaulieu, not realizing of course that I knew anything, he informed me that his wife was confined to a wheelchair due to an accident. He had been politely pointing out features of his landscape—we were in the New Forest, wooded land centuries ago, now largely treeless but abounding in yellow gorse and grazing ponies. Beaulieu itself, a picturesque village marked by a single boutique-lined street and dating back to the 13th century, grew up around an Abbey founded in 1204 by Cistercian Monks on land given to them by King John. Following the dissolution of the Monasteries by Henry VIII, the Abbey was transformed, and became a Palace House, home to the Montagu family and their descendants since 1538. Moonhill Lane, a quarter-mile away, is a secluded residential area of very nice houses and gardens partially hidden behind gates and groves. The Price place off this unpaved lane is a modest one-story stone ranch dwelling suited to Rosemary's requirements. When Sir David opened the door, she was right there, smiling broadly and enthusiastically, ready not to waste a moment in showing me material about her father.

With no amenities whatever beyond shaking hands she wheeled herself into their living room toward a side table where albums and articles lay in a neat stack. The gesture was entirely reminiscent of her brother Arthur's in 1978 when we met for lunch at the Ebury Street Steak House in London and with no formalities at all, he launched a monologue on his father's business. In both instances I had a very similar reaction to the "material"— Arthur's speech, and Rosemary's pile of albums and papers. I was not that interested. In a breathlessly suspended state between identities, waiting my moment to spring the news that I was not the person they thought I was, I could hardly focus on anything resembling what I had said I was looking for. Here in Beaulieu however something quite different and unforeseen happened. Where in Arthur's case I had simply interrupted his speech within ten minutes in order to begin laying Joan Castile to rest, at the end of roughly the same amount of time with Rosemary I concluded this was not possible, not then anyway. There was no exposition to interrupt for one thing. I was being plied almost wordlessly to look at her collected contents, and with barely a hint of conversation, I found no opening.

The perfect opening would have been a question such as Sir David had asked me on the car ride to their house, "How did you become interested in the bells?" To which I had replied, "It's a long story, I believe I should tell your wife." Now his wife seemed unapproachable, and he was nowhere around. In the vacuum, which I flooded with imaginings over her feelings with regard to her father, I became seized with apprehension about disturbing her. I feared the impact my disclosure could have. If my own safety was what I really feared for, I found the ideal correlate in my perception of Rosemary's fragility. In crumbs of conversation, in an atmosphere full of intimations, in the sense that I had invaded her father's citadel, that her father was for her a godlike unknowable untouchable luminary (she had been only 13 when he died), I decided to go on being Joan Castile. The custodianship of the memory of Cyril Johnston resided right here. An "archive" of great coziness and upper middle class comfort wreathed with family pictures not least of which is a framed portrait of Cyril and his wife, Rosemary's mother, when newly married, looking like movie stars, glowing in photo-manipulated auras, gazing off romantically in half-profile into a promising future. What was I going to find here? A lost sister? I didn't think so. Any more than Arthur ever appeared to be a lost brother. A trunk full of treasures with personal correspondence and such documents along with photographs? It seemed most unlikely, though I was sure it existed. An objective view of our bellfounder father? I much doubted it, especially after asking Rosemary a leading question: "What was your father like?" And she paused a while, staring at her lap for help, at length murmuring, "He was very kind." I was sure that was all I would ever get. She asked me a leading question too: Did I intend to tape record her? After all I was there as a journalist. And of course I had not given it a moment's consideration. I was an imposter with a conscience, more honestly with a self-saving instinct. I could be held accountable later for a violation of privacy under false pretenses. I could also appear unprepared for my announced assignment.

Lunch overlooking their front garden, in a lovely alcove with bay windows, clearly an addition built out from their long low rectangular house, presented a further opportunity for sitting on my American hands. A fair imitator, by now I had absorbed my half-sister's virtual muteness, and felt I could survive the day by muzzling myself in an exemplary fashion. At table anyway we were in Sir David's domain. He had either made or arranged for the lunch; he sat at the head; any conversation would be on his terms. The New Forest was a topic, continuing where he left off in the car. It was not just treeless but "full of oaks and beeches" as well. On behalf of my presence, Rosemary issued a single hesitant protest, trying to remind her husband of why I was in their house. Two things of note did happen. As I was addressing Sir David, searching for Rosemary's name and faltering over "Lady Price," Rosemary chimed in firmly, "Rosemary." The second provided a great opening that was by now foreclosed. Rosemary was saying, "When I tell people my father was a bellfounder, they never know what that is." Without thinking, I commented, "I have had the same experience." In this context, I meant of course in the process of my research work, and since no eyebrows were raised (except my own) and there was no pause before moving on to oaks and beeches or the like, I suppose it was taken that way, if indeed the remark had been heard or registered.

After lunch Sir David disappeared again, and I was left alone once more with Rosemary in their living room. I was sitting on one of their two facing couches; she was facing me in her wheelchair across a coffee table. I had selected some papers from her pile of material that Sir David had said he would copy and send to me. He had been enlisted only after she had seemed inclined to just let me take whatever papers I wanted with me, later to be mailed back to her, and I had asked her if she was comfortable with that. On second thought, which she communicated nonverbally, she was not. Now I was treated to certain powers of clairvoyance she seemed to have and that may have been linked to her taciturnity. I had forgotten myself and in a very unEnglish lapse was asking her what had happened to her, if only by the vaguest gesture and utterance. And she said simply, "I fell," not looking at me, and reaching for something on the coffee table, closing a scarcely mentioned case. As I waited near their door for Sir David to drive me back to the train station, looming over her in my black suit, hands in pockets, gazing into some middle distance, I became aware of her eyes on me. Did she perhaps divine a connection to her father? I have height, and the suit was more or less right; otherwise I look nothing like him. (Nor does she). More plausibly, she was wondering if I seemed a proper candidate to write about her father. And/or, if *I* thought my visit had been worthwhile.

At the train station I would learn from Ingrid that it had decidedly been a bust. Ingrid could not believe I had not told them who I was. She was simply incredulous. It was hard to explain. It took up the whole train ride back to London. It went on through the rest of the trip.

Five months later, September 23, 2000, I made the boat approach, boarding a beautiful British cruise ship at pier 88 in New York harbor—a "Superliner" called the *Oriana*. In seven days time I was due to land in Southampton. The following day I had an appointment in Beaulieu, seven miles away, for another lunch. The cast of characters remained the same. Ingrid had put me on the boat in New York, and would meet me in Southampton in a rental car. Joan Castile was still playing me. It had been an uphill challenge making another appointment for her, causing me to think she had not created the most favorable impression. Much later, once I started calling Joan's visit in April a reconnaissance mission, and she was not refused for a return lunch, I would view her as having served me well. Now I had assigned her the most difficult job of all, to give herself up. I spent time on the boat creating a speech for this purpose. I had time also to wonder whether "Joan" and I would make it to this new appointment at all. A storm of unusual ferocity overtook us, creating a rogue wave that attacked the ship, bashing in cabin windows, injuring passengers, flooding lounges and corridors, causing emergency conditions and a *Titanic*-like panic. It wasn't hard for me to see the fates at work. One thousand four hundred and fifty seven of the voyagers on board were British pleasure-seeking tourists. I was headed for one of life's major engagements, now threatened by a tempest at sea. Suppose for a moment that my story of tangled identities and paternal disrepute had been publicized over the ship's speaker system. I could have been cast overboard like Jonah, a sacrifice to the larger good—a role incidentally enthrallingly updated in the 2004 *Master and Commander* film starring Russell Crowe. It's a paranoid fantasy that isn't beyond me. But no, I was quite safe, if not from the rogue wave, within a quasi-official role I had maneuvered for myself on the boat.

The *Oriana*, a 69,000-ton cruise ship, belongs to the P&O or Peninsular & Oriental Steamship Navigation Co., the line cofounded in 1837 by Cyril Johnston's Shetlander great-uncle Arthur Anderson [See Chapter III]. I had talked the ownership into trading a write-up of the voyage for my passage, making sure to include Anderson in my resumé. We can, in the middle of our stories, sometimes find ourselves in a meaningful transit where vital interests converge. It would be my first transatlantic journey by ship since I was two. I was hoping to glean some idea of what it was like for my subject, the bellfounder, when he made all these crossings. One of them was nasty enough to make him record it. March 27, 1931 he wrote to F.C. Mayer, "The *Aquitania* has just given us the roughest passage she has had for years: snow, gales, then fog . . . so again one of us saved the Cunard Line the expense of meals!"[1] In 2000, it seemed appropriate to me to travel like him, on business, in this obsolete maddeningly idle fashion aboard a gilded floating prison, to re-encounter his English daughter. I love the art of making travel-barter deals—a mainstay of my life in journalism and research. And of course the P&O line was a big draw. In her memoir Nora Johnston wrote about sailing in 1933 from London to Port Said in Egypt (en route to Jerusalem) aboard a P&O ship, the *Viceroy of India,* proudly claiming Arthur Anderson as an ancestor [See Chapter XI].[2] A centerpiece on the *Oriana* is a saloon in his name, Anderson's—described in P&O literature as a bar designed to evoke the atmosphere of an "intimate gentleman's club." Never lingering for a drink, I took some pleasure in it as a mini-museum, with its bronze bust of the Shetlander in a deep niche, portraits of himself and his co-founder Brodie Willcox, and oil or watercolor renderings of their early wooden sail and paddle steamers such as the *Don Juan* and the *Hindostan.* It perversely amused me also that of the 1,526 passengers aboard, I was surely the only one who ever heard of the bar's namesake. When the storm blew over and damages were repaired or under control and the ship's management issued free drinks throughout the extra day and night it was going to take us to get to Southampton, Anderson's and the rest of the bars were sardined with merrymakers celebrating our survival. The chief purser, my contact for the trip (he arranged interviews for me with ship's personnel such as the captain, the chef, and the Cruise or Entertainment Director) gave me copies of articles in UK newspapers he had received by fax, about our misadventure at sea. So I knew I would arrive in Beaulieu with advance notice. Sir David and his wife had known how "Joan Castile" was getting there.

This time I drove into Moonhill Lane in the rental car Ingrid had hired at Heathrow airport and then met me with it at the

Bells ready for shipment in Southampton, UK, for the Walter N. Maguire Memorial Carillon of the First Presbyterian Church, Stamford, Connecticut, 1946
Behind bell, second from right, Cyril F. Johnston

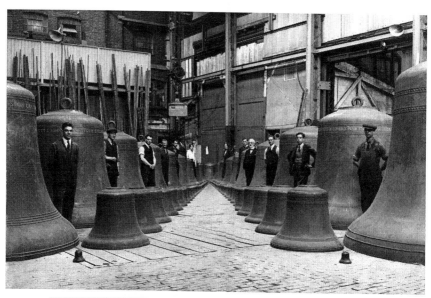

*Top: The Laura Spelman Rockefeller Memorial Carillon for the University of Chicago on display in
the Gillett & Johnston Bellfoundry
Bottom: The bourdon being hoisted onto ship*

Top: The bourdon for carillon at University of the Chicago Chapel being lowered into hold of ship
Bottom: the University of Chicago carillon bells on train transport

Bell being hoisted into belfry of the University of Chicago Chapel, 1932

The bourdon for the carillon of the University of Chicago Chapel in the Gillett & Johnston Bellfoundry

Top, left to right: Cyril F. Johnston, H. Gordon Selfridge;, Princess Wlasensky, the Lord Bishop of Norwork (Dr. Pollock), Mrs. C. F. Johnston, Princess Wlasensky's daughter, Mrs. Pollock
Bottom: Bow Bells cast by G&J in 1927, financed by H. Gordon Selfridge

Top: *The Freedom Bell for the City Hall, Berlin, Germany, on flatbed truck in Croydon*
Bottom: *The Freedom Bell on docks ready for transport, 1951*

The Freedom Bell being hoisted onto ship

The Freedom Bell being hoisted into City Hall in Berlin, Germany, 1951

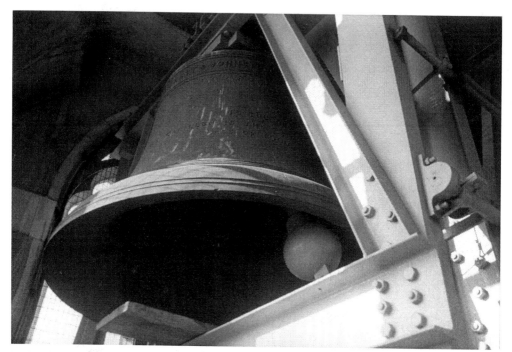

Top: Carillon bell in the Cleveland Tower, Princeton University, Princeton, USA
Bottom: Jill Johnston voyaging from New York to Southampton on P&O ship the Oriana,
September 2000 for appointment to meet half-sister Lady Rosemary Price and her husband Sir David Price

Top: Half-sister, Rosemary Price, née Johnston, with her husband, David Price in their garden in Beaulieu, Hampshire, England

Left: Rosemary and David Price

Bottom: Jill Johnston and Rosemary Price at latter's home in Beaulieu

The 20-ton bourdon as it hangs in the Riverside Church, New York

boat. I was armed with my boat-prepared speech for unloading
Joan. A composed delivery, I have learned, is not a bad fortifier
against fear. Sir David opened the door, now smiling invitingly, a
new aspect, excusing his wife as looking at closing Olympic
moments on TV. Making my first move toward becoming Jill, I
buttonholed him while we stood drinking elderflower water (I had
declined alcohol), asking him, "Will you sit down with us?" With
his ongoing smile, it seemed obvious he would, once his wife
appeared. While we waited for her, he asked me politely about my
ill-fated *Oriana* voyage. Here I struggled over an American delivery, full of incomplete sentences or indecisive ways of finishing
them, and my desire to sound more rhetorical, i.e., British. As Sir
David was rescuing me from my conflict by telling a ship story of
his own, Rosemary appeared. Now I was "on."

A leading question of course in my denouement was whether
Sir David and his wife had any prior knowledge of the existence
of Jill Johnston. Our places "on stage" in their living room
seemed set rather perfectly. Sir David and I sat across from each
other on their facing couches. Rosemary, after receiving my greet-
ing, had wheeled herself to the edge of the couch where her
husband was sitting, facing toward their mantel, thus in profile to
him and myself. Addressing her with no introductory delay, omitting even a preludial line I had composed—"I don't know if you
have any thoughts about why I'm doing this work on the carillon
and Cyril Johnston . . . "—I ventured, "When I visited you last
April and your husband drove me here from the train station, he
asked me how I became interested in the bells . . . " Rosemary was
staring at her lap. Only a line or two further, she stopped me. The
very mention of her brother Arthur, once I said I had known him,
produced recognition. She had heard about me from Arthur in
1984, during the time of the centenary of Cyril's birth in Croydon.
The surprise was on me! Now, like Arthur before her, she turned
interviewer and asked me, "How, when, did you know about
Cyril"? The question seemed preordained.

She had had sixteen years to wonder about this. On my side,
I had capsulized my story so many times for people; it was like a

favorite poem I had memorized and would recite by heart on demand or at my own whim. Over time, the manner of telling it changed. There was a divide. Early on, in the years after Cyril died, I must have conveyed something sad and immutable because I remember people shaking their heads slowly side to side, looking disapprovingly grim, or pitying, over my mother's lie—the way she handled the situation, and the estrangement it caused between us. Then later, by, say, the late nineteen sixties, having found my story in the mythology of the heroes, albeit males exclusively, my portrayal had another gloss, making drastic origins sound more like the beginning of an odyssey.[3] Whether I was understood or not, what seemed to matter was what I had come to think about it myself. And my new position was that this was a story with a future, and I could entertain dreams. One such dream, meeting English relatives, was enacting itself for the second time, here in Beaulieu in the millennial year 2000. For Rosemary, I chose my most minimal and matter-of-fact delivery. I knew of Cyril by the age of comprehension—perhaps four, or five. My mother always said he was dead, that he succumbed to pneumonia in my infancy. I knew his name, nationality and profession. When I was 20, my age the year he actually died, I learned from my mother of his death. There was a long pause. Rosemary's hands were folded in her lap, and she had still not glanced up or toward me. I had a strange impression of her as Whistler's Mother. Now she murmured in undertone, "That must have been difficult for you."

Difficult! My marbles bounced around in my brain for a bit. She said it again. Of course—it had been monumentally difficult. But I wasn't inclined to say so. If I did, it would register as a complaint, obscuring all my transmutations and innovative expedients. On the other hand, I couldn't deny the obvious, that I was conceived immaculately and born into exile from human society. I had to come up with a sensible irresolute difficulty. So I told them about my mother's ban on knowing English family members. By contrast with Rosemary, Sir David was leaning across our divide of couches, on the edge of his, regarding me with a parliamentary intensity. After disposing of the "difficult," I moved on quickly, saying brightly, "But I always thought it was great to have a father like that." By which I meant a father of stirring accomplishment in a thrilling and virtually unknown profession. No sign of approval or acknowledgement was forthcoming here. I had in effect said that I had a father after all—a claim throwing me into a no-man's-land, where battle lines were drawn centuries ago. Resting on an untenable premise—that Cyril Johnston had done nothing wrong where my birth was concerned—my claim overlooked conventional reality, that this type of paternity is considered base or ignoble, even (loosely) criminal. So bad in fact that a man's produce under the circumstance would be deprived of his name or any knowledge of him, often of life itself. The next thing I said returned me to a consideration of sympathy, though this was hardly my motive. And the response wasn't easy to read.

"My mother," I was saying, "upon having me and returning to America with me, had to have a story." Sir David and Rosemary warmed to this. They displayed modern liberal attitudes, different from Rosemary's mother, and my mother herself, who defied codes she believed in to have me. But as we know, liberal attitudes, born into generality in the 20th century, can co-exist easily with traditional assumptions, which become simply hedged about by understanding and benevolence—all provided there is no challenge to elemental beliefs in the natural or cultural order of things. Anger for instance, the most prevalent emotion of any underclass in a revolution, would appear unacceptably confrontational. One implementation of indulgence, of toleration, even of help or improvements in status, is curiosity. And on October 1, 2000, after having passed a preliminary test of character (I seemed surely far from angry or bitter), I found myself reveling involuntarily in a most hospitable environment of curiosity. Ultimately I would have to separate their interest in me from at least Rosemary's dim view of my claim to Cyril Johnston, i.e. in any official sense. And they would have to separate my interest in them or in being their friend, from my designs on their help in completing my book.

Lunches at Beaulieu became four-hour marathons, occurring at least twice a year. At lunch #2, when I became Jill, Sir David became David after Rosemary corrected me as I was using his title. I learned that David had suspected I was Jill when I visited them the first time as Joan. And that he didn't relay his suspicion to his wife because it wouldn't have been "polite." We passed beyond curiosity to real exchanges. Over the lunches, I would learn many things, much as I did in meetings with Arthur. Yet with Arthur I never had the thought, as I did now with Rosemary, that here was the one other person in the world besides myself with a tireless outsized interest in the same man. When I told her she seemed more attracted to the bells than Arthur, she hastened to put in that her brother knew much more than she did about Cyril and his business. But I saw that she clearly was the one who had the emotional bond, thus fixation on the shape of a bell, or any bell cast by her father. Her brother, Rosemary said, failed to follow Cyril into the business because he wasn't musical. But "nonmusical" seemed to me a way of saying he was on a course dictated by his mother, who while a brilliantly supportive wife to Cyril, and tremendously admiring of his work, would want a career for their son more along her own lines of interest in Conservative politics, hoping at the same time to save him from the unremunerative and punishing rigors of bellfounding. One lunch afternoon Rosemary produced a black and white photo of herself aged 12, Arthur at 16 and Cyril 63, in the year 1948, showing a traditional nuclear family alignment. Cyril is trying to smile but looks rather grim. He leans on a cane and is within a year or so of death. Rosemary huddles against him, possessive, protective, sympathetic, her hand wrapped firmly around his arm at the elbow. Arthur stands to his father's right, apart and aloof, appreciatively disposed toward the one shooting the snapshot, his mother. The foursome, Rosemary told me, was attending a Conservative conference in Brighton.

What would Rosemary have done with an older sister in her picture? As I have long felt blessed to be an only child, I cannot picture it at all. But by at least lunch #4, I began to notice a pattern that I suppose even one utterly inexperienced in the dilemmas of siblings could identify as rivalrous. When speaking of the men in her family, Rosemary's intonations were possessive. "My father," "My grandfather," "My great great uncle," with the slightest but unmistakable emphasis on the "my." As well no doubt she was entitled to do. I didn't grow up with any of these people, or in their milieu and culture. (Nor of course with her, making her, as many people might see it, a rather questionable relation, apart from the serious issue of legitimacy). At an early lunch, Rosemary looked blankly—a sign of denial I would begin to recognize—when I asserted that my mother liked to say that my son Richard resembled Cyril. Her muted paternal emphases were perhaps not enough to seem convincingly competitive. But one day I used the phrase "My father" myself, this in context of my book. I was poised to give her a chapter to read by which I intended to inform her that I had not left my own story of origins out of this work about her father. So by way of warning, I said, "Sometimes I call Cyril 'my father.'" At which Rosemary whipped her head around, *as if in alarm,* to look at her husband, sitting on the couch behind her. As she recomposed herself, looking back at me again, I continued, "Well I have to call him something, so it's either 'Cyril,' 'Cyril Johnston,' 'the bellfounder' or 'my father.'"

It was lunch #8, November 1, 2003. An acme had been reached. I was at last using a tape recorder. As with Arthur I had tried to convince Rosemary that my mother was not marriageable material, that she was very independent and in fact had never married at all and that Rosemary's mother had been the proper wife for Cyril, implying that all therefore had turned out for the best, that I had normalized my own position, with my fatherlessness proving a most fortuitous stroke. I had entertained Rosemary and David with the long story of how Cyril fled England in 1928 when my mother was pregnant and he was in the middle of difficult recastings of the Riverside bourdon [See Chapter VII]. Rosemary, crossing the great divide of our upbringings and histories, once again seemed charmed that we both write lefthanded while we do everything else with the right, conveying an impression that she thinks such an oddity must be a shared genetic imprint. I had delighted Rosemary with the gift of Nora Johnston's memoir, which she had not known existed, and had sent them some writings of my own. I had taken to kissing the couple goodbye upon leaving, and hello when I arrived. I had been encouraged to contact their daughter Arabella when I happened to be in London, where Arabella lived. The three of us had taken pictures of each other, inside and outdoors. David had sent me one he took of Rosemary and myself that I had framed and hung on my wall.

At the previous lunch (#7) I had learned from Rosemary that she was or was planning to write about Cyril herself. She had been prompted to tell me this while I was relating a recent discovery, found in the interview I have with her mother that Arthur was searching for someone to write a book about their father [See Chapter XIV]. Through her most studied nonverbal communication, modestly regarding her lap, Rosemary indicated that she was the one. Or that the responsibility now rested with her, since her mother and Arthur were gone.[4] Here was a cue for me to ask her what she was up to in this respect. Instead I had a major hiccup, having become accustomed to dividing Cyril neatly into the father Rosemary knew personally and grew up with, and the father I never knew but could claim in a book. After unwisely blurting out, "That makes us competitors," I smothered my dismay, abiding by "the right thing," encouraging Rosemary to do it, whatever it might be, noting, "Your father died when you were so young." In my thank-you letter when I got home I went overboard, saying it had always seemed helpful to me to "meditate," through writing, upon "a loved one so long lost." Later I even offered to send her material she might need about her father, saying she should feel free to ask me for anything.

Now at lunch #8 I became perhaps the beneficiary of my (apparent) refusal to struggle over possessorship of the father. Rosemary surprised me, growing warm and intimate. She gave me a moving account of Cyril's death. When I mused over whether Cyril had been in love with my mother or not, she huffed most agreeably, "Of *course* he was in love with your mother." She con-fided that Arthur was the typical older brother who gave her a hard time but eventually became fatherly toward her, much the way Cyril had been to Nora. She came achingly close to telling me of her accident, and finally she stunned me by announcing, "I think you're a wonderful writer" followed by, "I think it's terrific that you're doing this [the book about Cyril]." Much as I would want to cling to such ideal-sounding expressions of support, com-ing especially from a prized source of legitimacy, more phases were in our future. I had after all left with her on this occasion the chapter I had written showing that her father was under claim as such by her "wonderful writer."

This Anglo-American matchup continued to unfold, along-side the book, with its theme of reconciling Cyril Johnston's paternal conundrum resulting from his premarital affair, with his amazing career.

Chapter XVII

UNTIL HER MAJESTY'S PLEASURE
BE KNOWN

When I die I want it said of me, he dignified and ennobled commerce
—H. Gordon Selfridge

*I think C.F.J. may well have a wry smile to see how much interest and
enthusiasm there is for his eponymous legacy half a century on from that
inauspicious day that saw an end to bellfounding in Croydon*
—Andrew D. Higson (Bellmaster, John Taylor Bellfounders Ltd.)

*The queen's majesty is the head of the law and must of necessity
maintain the law; for by the law her majesty is made justly our queen
and by it she is most chiefly maintained*
—Proceedings in Parliament, 1576

*Can there be a creative secrecy,
a secret communication between the living and the dead?*
—Albert Camus

Cyril Johnston was involved in many Anglo-American
matchups, not least the one he had with my mother. In business, John D. Rockefeller, Jr. may have been his most important

American pairing, with F.C. Mayer as JDR's advisor coming in a close second. But with H. Gordon Selfridge, the self-made American from a small town in Wisconsin who established London's famous luxury department store in his name in 1909, Cyril had a special affinity, and the two men collaborated on a very singular project. They had ways of doing things in common, and they would both endure losses of place in their own business-es due to pecuniary misjudgments (an understatement in the case of Selfridge), finally going down you might say with the empire. Their endings coincided with the onset of Britain's divestment of its global colonial holdings. Selfridge, born in 1856, died in virtu-al poverty in 1947, the year India gained its independence (by 1980, 48 other territories under British rule would become self-determining). During 1947, while Cyril Johnston was in the United States, his last visit to the U.S., he would be hospitalized in Boston with a thrombosis, and major G&J stockholders in Croydon would conspire to oust him from his company. Back in 1930, five years before Cyril made the financial moves fore-shad-owing the possibility of his losing control, he became friends with Gordon Selfridge over a pending contract for a restoration of twelve bells for which Selfridge proposed to become the donor. The relationship had begun when in 1931 Cyril installed a clock bell and four quarter-bells for Selfridge at his Oxford Street store.

In the bellscape of Britain, the twelve to be restored was no ordinary deal. The controversy over Simpson tuning vs. the conservation of old bells still raged. The twelve at issue were the historic Bow Bells at St. Mary-le-Bow Church in London's Cheapside, the most famous ring in the land. They had Whitechapel's proud imprint on them since 1738. Albert Hughes, of the family that has run Whitechapel since 1884, and Cyril's fierce competitor in the English peal market, intended to keep it that way.[1] St. Mary-le-Bow, destroyed in the Great Fire of 1666 and rebuilt by Christopher Wren, was so called for the "bows" or arches that supported its steeple. Anyone born "within the sound of Bow Bells" has been said to be a true Londoner, or at least a Cockney.

Bow Vestry, the Restoration Committee, asked for competitive bids from the three foundries, Whitechapel, G&J, Taylor, the latter declining to put one in. Bow needed fifteen thousand pounds, much more money than they could raise themselves. At a 1931 Committee meeting, a letter from Cyril Johnston was read along with a letter he had enclosed from an "anonymous American" offering to pay for the entire restoration of the bells on condition that the work be done by Gillett & Johnston.[2] After heated debates and vigorous objections by Hughes and others, with most hating to accept money from an American especially in those anti-American times, when England's once lost colony was being blamed for the 1930s recession, trade barriers and unemployment woes, the Restoration Committee felt it couldn't turn down the offer. On March 20, 1932, a Consistory Court hearing at St. Paul's Cathedral took place, Cyril squaring off with the Chancellor F.H.L. Errington, his old antagonist from the late 20s involving a ring for St. James in Clerkenwell, London. But it was the 1927 battle over the restoration of ten bells at Coventry that would be replayed most closely in the case of Bow Bells.

Alas, at Coventry Albert Hughes had been the victimized bellfounder when he lost *that* war to Cyril Johnston—to recast what had been considered one of the finest rings in England, by Whitechapel dating from 1774 [See Chapter IX]. The conservative bell community was even more outraged by the Bow Bells contest than the Coventry saga. Now the issue was not so much Hughes's resistance to the tuning revolution—a counterproductive stance he had been slowly overcoming—as the stark need for money, and the association of an American merchant with an Englishman whose business practices were generally either suspect or despised. Moreover the Bow Vestry and the Restoration Committee remained at loggerheads, the former being traditionally in favor of Hughes.

Gordon Selfridge's offer under the table (his identity was not revealed until the end of a very heated meeting when it seemed certain the gift would not be rejected) made the Consistory Court hearing at St. Paul's a moot proceeding. The opportunity however to depict the Selfridge/Johnston alliance as bad form was not wasted, and Cyril was maligned by the Chancellor as a man who "opened his mouth [to let] the plum drop in"—from Selfridge. The case was adjourned by Errington for a week. Albert Hughes, fulminating over what an "underhanded and crooked business" the duo represented, did his best behind the scenes to stop the transaction.

The G&J peal was dedicated July 7, 1933 by the Archbishop of Canterbury as a national event, with 300 ringers from around the country in attendance. With Selfridge's name inscribed on the newly recast tenor bell—the destruction of the old tenor or "Great Bell" of Bow was the most devastating thing for Hughes—it has been noted, without intent to flatter, "In one sense at least, this American had returned to Albion."[3] Albion, a rhetorical word for Great Britain, can refer, if qualified by "perfidious," to her alleged treacherous policy towards foreigners.[4]

Selfridge had "returned to Albion" in a number of spectacular ways. His store was the grandest England had ever seen, classically designed, bigger, with 230 departments, and more innovative than John Wanamaker's in Philadelphia. He bought a castle called Highcliffe in Hampshire and a stable of racehorses. One of his two daughters upon marriage became a Princess, the other a Viscountess. He always appeared publicly with patrician distinction, wearing a smart cut-tail coat with striped trousers and silk top hat. He loved his adopted country, and in 1937 became a British subject. Both Selfridge and Cyril Johnston had adoring mothers who were ambitious for them. And they were both latecomer specialists. In 1906 Selfridge, once a poor Wisconsin boy, now 50 years old, emigrated to Britain, having accumulated a fortune as a partner at Marshall Field in Chicago. The two men understood the power of publicity, the unEnglish pursuit of advertising—for Selfridge a factor in overcoming foreign origins that were already humble and in Cyril's case his long established bellfounding competitors, as well as the obscurity of his profession. A lavish tea given by the store magnate in 1933 celebrating the Bow Bell dedication chimed nicely with Cyril's own extravaganzas in Croydon. The support and interest he had from Selfridge resonated with the American money that made his reputation as a builder of carillons to the west across the Atlantic. It was respective vulnerabilities they had over money that contributed to their downfalls before death.

By 1933 when Selfridge was 77 years old, with his wife and mother gone and his children long grown, he was leading a prodigal lifestyle, spending extravagantly at casino gambling, on ladies of leisure or the theater, on generosities such as Bow Bells, using up his annual £100,000 income, borrowing increasingly from banks. With borrowings finally from his own company, in 1939 when he was 83 his shareholders forced him to retire with a pension, which he also gambled and wasted away. Cyril Johnston never had Selfridge's kind of money, or wanted it so far as I can determine. He was quite content within the bounds of bellcasting and his family. His troubles were with the way the world was going, and the consequent drain on his business, with its periodic expansions, and its trappings of travel and speculative entertainments. Bellfounding to begin with is an exhaustively expensive craft, needing tremendous investments in materials—steel and metals, tools and machinery, ovens and demonstration instruments, premises and shops—just to get going. Cyril's wife Mary cited money as one of three strikes against her marrying him. (The other two being that she was Roman Catholic and that she wasn't in love with him). She said her family was "not poverty stricken by any means" but she didn't have the money she thought necessary to help a husband in such a difficult profession, mentioning for example all his employees, averaging 120 or so at any time.[5] She made up for her lack of dowry with her enthusiasm for what he did, and her wifely participation in the many social aspects of his business; also she "appreciated," she said, "all his good qualities." But on at least one occasion she was able to help him more concretely, setting him up for an order—the first satisfaction in any business.

This can be deduced circumstantially. Mary Johnston met her husband-to-be at a country estate in Chobham, Surrey, called

Westcroft Park, perhaps as early as 1923, when Cyril installed 18 bells in a small campanile there. The owner of the estate Henry Oberline Serpell, a wealthy biscuit manufacturer from Plymouth, and an uncle of Mary Johnston's, became a witness at her wedding to Cyril in 1930. The campanile is a lovely structure of mock Tudor brick and timber. In 1932 Cyril cast a 28-bell carillon for it, the original 18 evidently melted down. When H. O. Serpell died in 1943, aged 90, his widow broke up the carillon and sold off the bells or gave them away. I suppose this distressed Cyril (who bought back a few of them), but more upsetting by far, from the view of his trophy carillons or rings—the prestigious ones that added to his renown—would have been the loss of his Bow Bells on May 11, 1941 when German bombs destroyed much of St. Mary-le-Bow. At last, with Cyril dead and the war over, in 1951 Whitechapel reclaimed their history with Bow, and cast the church's new ring. Thus ended the Anglo-American matchup of H. Gordon Selfridge and the Croydon bellfounder.

Of all such relationships, my own with Cyril Johnston, in of course his posthumous state, has to be the most futuristic and improbably promising, heading into a mystical area full of unanswerable questions. It did lead solubly to this text, according "my bellfounder" an afterlife with a chance of delivering him beyond his insular bell world. Bells populate the world to an extraordinary extent, why shouldn't their histories and the lives of those who make them be available to people at large? My role in this consignment seems fraught with dreams. Realistically, I have long felt saved from being Cyril's English therefore legal daughter, from being raised as part of his environment which would have included knowing him. A darker side, revealed in some nighttime dreams, adds another, not unexpected, dimension to my social pragmatism or embrace of history. I have had some interesting dreams about Cyril. In one, dreamt in 1993, he had very dark hair, which he had, and blue eyes, which he did not; moreover he seemed too short and too young. So I was thinking in the dream how very embarrassing—after all this research and Cyril isn't really my father, wherewith I went up to him and said he should produce proof of paternity!—reversing the normal burden on the child.

In a more recent dream, he was youngish and looked unlike himself in my photos. But he was tall and lean and within the dream decisively my father. A third unidentifiable party was expediting a meeting between us. Cyril seemed vaguely interested. I was in a strong passive mode. We were in America. Next, I dreamt the Queen was nearby inside a structure where a party was taking place, perhaps for her. Or it was for Cyril since his bells were hanging up high (outside), attached somehow to the structure. I was alone now. Presumably Cyril had gone in. I had to get in myself. A woman guarding the entrance was skeptical to worse, but when I said I was writing a (or *the*) Big Book, she allowed me in—"at her majesty's pleasure." Once inside, I found the Queen, put my hand intimately on her arm (as if I knew her well), and asked her if she would like to meet the bellfounder. She said oh yes—so I steered her over to Cyril and introduced them. Cyril sort of swooned while bowing deeply, holding her hand. Coming up, his head lolled to one side in an attenuated El Greco expression. I was watching, entranced, enthralled by his choreography.

Multiple associations or interpretations aside, notably I had achieved entrance to a sanctum sanctorum, a holy place where the father and his Queen were enshrined. As a mere author, I facilitated their meeting. I knew them both, and could get them together. The guardian to the entrance had let me in "at Her Majesty's pleasure"—a phrase deeply embedded in English law. It can be found in "Proceedings of Parliament" in the late 1500s, during Elizabeth I's reign. One entry of 1559 has the Queen's treasurer making a declaration "of her majesty's pleasure" that they should choose a speaker. Another in 1571 had the Speaker mentioning an order for licences [*sic*] "by her majesty's pleasure." Every wish of her majesty, or of her minions concerning matters of state, was at her pleasure. As Parliament grew in power, rendering the sovereign ultimately a figurehead (beginning with the 1688 revolution), the phrase has remained in use as a formality, a vestige, signifying origins of power now fully arrogated by government. The phrase belongs to "The Royal Prerogative." Parliament acts in the name of the Crown ("at her or his majesty's pleasure") to invoke the Royal Prerogative.[6] If for instance Parliament were to make a Declaration of Paternity on my behalf [See Chapter XIV] it would be done "at her majesty's pleasure." Waiting for such an event could be defined by an associated Royal Prerogative phrase, UNTIL HER MAJESTY'S PLEASURE BE KNOWN. "Until . . . " is linked mainly with matters of crime, either felonious or committed while insane. A Mental Health Act of 1800 provided that defendants acquitted of a charge of murder, treason or felony on grounds of insanity at the time of the offense were to be detained in strict custody "Until Her Majesty's Pleasure Shall be Known." A book review in 1998 of Simon Winchester's *The Professor and the Madman* reads, "The lunatic in question . . . an American surgeon, Dr. W.C. Minor, went mad during . . . his service in the American Civil War, committed a murder in London, and was confined to Broadmoor 'Until her Majesty's Pleasure Be Known.'" The reviewer added, "A rather nice legal phrasing for 'indefinitely, but probably a very long time.'" Indeed, Minor, who contributed to the making of the *Oxford English Dictionary* (the subject of Winchester's book) from his cell, using a library he was allowed to have there, was never released.

The Royal Prerogative deals with Foreign and Domestic Affairs, each with its assigned number of categories. Under Foreign Affairs for example is "the power to make declarations of war and peace." Under Domestic, on the list is the "the granting of honours." By *his* majesty's pleasure (George VI), in June 1948 Cyril Johnston was granted an O.B.E., or Officer of the Order of the British Empire, "for his services in the art of bellfounding and tuning." He heard about it while undergoing treatment for arthritis in Switzerland. Two months later Cyril resigned, after bitter disagreements with his board, from the directorship of Gillett & Johnston, becoming a man without a job. The honor, though not so grand as a C.B.E., or a knighthood, must have cheered him up a bit. Not that he rested on it. He became very busy trying to raise money for a new foundry, for which he had architectural plans drawn up, or planning a consultancy to an established firm, with Eijsbouts in Holland tops on that list. His resignation from G&J marked the end of the firm, which staggered on after his death in 1950 until 1957 when bankruptcy was declared.

Of the two men who took over in 1948, one of them, Michael Howard, figured prominently in financial choices Cyril had made in 1935, setting himself up for the possibility of losing control later on. One year earlier it will be remembered [See Chapter XIII], Cyril wrote to Rockefeller requesting a loan—saying a crisis had arisen in his business and he was "in imminent danger of losing all I have worked for and valued beyond money." Rockefeller had turned him down, and in 1935 Cyril tried to cover his tracks and perhaps "cock a snook" as the English expression goes, writing to the American millionaire that "new capital" had become available to him, improving his business considerably.

His new capital consisted of cash investments in G&J by two parties, totaling £7000—one Frank Brown, a London certified accountant and Gilbert Howard a London solicitor—in return for a large number of shares, giving the two men certain rights and some power over the company. Brown was now a Director. Cyril, no longer the majority shareholder, was hired by his company as Managing Director at an annual salary of £1,200. A prior debt of Cyril's to Lloyd's Bank from numerous loans amounting to £21,000 was indemnified by the pledge of G&J holdings as collateral. Cyril had also put up his house as collateral against loans, and had sold his life insurance. Oh, he was going to the wall. With Gilbert Howard, the larger investor by far, Cyril struck up a kind of devil's pact over Howard's son Michael. In effect, Howard was buying his son Michael a vocation, a place in Cyril's business. In return for the 4,500 shares he purchased, Howard made Cyril agree to fully instruct Michael in all branches of the business for a term of three years. If Michael for any reason terminated his employment, Cyril was obliged to buy back those 4,500 shares with accruing dividends to the date of sale. If Michael fulfilled his 3-year tenure, and was then fired, again Cyril was obliged to buy back the 4,500 shares. As security, Howard required Cyril to give him a second mortgage in his father's estate (against which Cyril had also been making loans—an estate that of course belonged to his mother, who would die in 1941). Cyril's only demand in the agreement was that Michael not divulge any knowledge or information (i.e. trade secrets) he acquired while working for G&J, in particular in learning how to tune the bells.[7] Michael never left, and as inheritor to his father Gilbert who died in 1937, by 1948 evidently felt powerful enough and sufficiently expert at tuning to take over from the ailing Cyril Johnston. According to Cyril's son Arthur, Howard was the villain of the 1948 appropriation. Arthur called him a "snake"—for supporting the stockholders against his father, and wanting to be Managing Director himself.[8]

Howard's designs on Cyril seem stunningly confirmed by a lecture he delivered on "Bell Founding" to the Institute of Musical Instrument Technology in November 1948—three months after Cyril's resignation. While demonstrating a broad knowledge of the history and technology of the craft, Howard made no obeisance to his employer and mentor, not even mentioning his name. "My own firm, Gillett & Johnston of Croydon . . . " is how he identified the enterprise Cyril had turned into a world-class concern.[9]

It was a sad time for Cyril and his family. A close family always suffers when its head is undergoing a dire loss. And Cyril was not well, although what plagued him—his rheumatoid arthritis—was not what would kill him. Like his father before him he keeled over from a coronary, and at the same age of 65. If smoking had anything to do with it, Cyril "smoked like a chimney" as Mary Johnston put it. Cyril's father had been playing golf in Croydon. Cyril was in London, having been driven by his chauffeur to Victoria Station to meet his wife, returning from Austria where she had been attending an ill sister. Rosemary and Arthur were away at school. Nora, Cyril's sister, had been staying with him in Croydon. There was a Swiss girl also, helping to keep house. It was March 30, 1950. His wife Mary said it was a cold day. After he met her at the Station they went to a favorite club of his, the RAC, where they had coffee and he usually had a biscuit.

She said, "Aren't you going to have a biscuit?" And he said, "No, I have indigestion." Getting back in the car they were driven to a store where Mary wanted to pick something up. Now, as Mary recounted, he uttered his last words. She asked, "Do they want anything at home?" And he replied, "I think they want . . . "—with which his head fell down on his chest. Mary said, "I believe he died right then." And they drove off to Westminster Hospital where he was pronounced, "Dead On Arrival."

In Rosemary's mournful account of his death, upon mentioning Westminster Hospital she started to bring up her accident: "Strangely, that was where I spent my time after my . . . "—then checked herself. Rosemary told me Cyril was brought home and laid out in his large dressing room, which had doubled as his study. She had been sick with flu at school, and when she was called home was unable to attend the funeral. Her absence was momentous in its way, not just for herself, but for a gathering that could hardly have been aware of the gravitas of Cyril's youngest mourner, the one who lost the most, alone at home with a Swiss housekeeper. In all our lunches and meetings, Rosemary never alluded to her father as "Cyril." He was always "my father." She told me she called him "Daddy." Her mother was "Mummy"—until she died at 93. I remember my mother being a "Mummy" when I was a child. I don't recall what I called her later, though toward the end of her life it was "Olive." To my children I have always been "Jill." As for "Daddy," it sounds peculiar to me no matter who says it about whom. Cyril as "Daddy" is especially odd. Yet I like thinking, and here I may misunderstand myself, that he had a daughter known by him in that way. She was the one with great feelings for him, his champion in the realm of the heart. I may also misread Rosemary, but I believe she never quite laid him to rest, and that her absence at his funeral when she was 13, however necessary due to illness, was a sign of such a future.

Cyril, curious as it may seem, left his family in pretty good shape when he died. He bequeathed over £20,000 in cash. At death, his Trustee Henry Hilbery pursued a considerable investment of Cyril's from the 1920s when the clock side of his firm had split off—with clocks still made in the foundry—under F. W. Elliott Ltd. The shares, of which Cyril owned a good chunk, never paid dividends because the company seemingly never operated at a profit. With Hilbery determining that F.W. Elliott Ltd. had a net asset of £36,614, he established a figure of about £1,500 per annum in dividends for Mary Johnston, who became the beneficiary of another substantial bequest when her deceased husband's sister Nora Johnston died in 1952 (also aged 65, like Cyril and their father). Tucked away in the siblings' family history was a very special figure, their mother's unmarried sister Eugenie Harriet Brouneau, who lived close to her sister Amelie and in-laws in Croydon for many years. Mary Johnston called her "the famous little aunt." Michael Howard, whom I interviewed in 1974 when I knew little about him, described Eugenie as "a lot of fun." If she was fun she was also well off. Upon dying in 1936, Eugenie left significant gilt-edged stock investments, actually everything she owned in equal shares to Cyril and Nora—a total cash worth of about £25,448. Nora's inheritance from her maternal aunt was tied up in a trust, securing her an income for life, and this estate is what Mary Johnston received when Nora died. The year of Aunt Eugenie's death, a bell cast by Cyril—one of 12 for St. John's Parish Church in Croydon in '36—was given in her name by the two siblings. When Rosemary was born that year, she received Eugenie as one of her middle names.

Cyril Johnston's legacy to bellfounding seems less clear than he might like. While he may be as famous and admired as the Hemonys in campanological circles—one of the two English creators who spearheaded the second golden age in tuning—his dubiously regarded methods of going after contracts and celebrating his victories have not been forgotten, in England at least. It's the historians who carry on like this. The change-ringers, the musicians, have less complicated attitudes, simply rating the G&J bell tonal quality highly, and feeling it's a pleasure to ring on them. A bell historians' chatgroup website that originated in Britain shows due respect and attention to Cyril's bells while often casting him personally in a Machiavellian light. Facts may be distorted to this end. An entry about a 1951 UK job for 12 bells has Cyril Johnston doing his vaunted bad things, like unfairly under-bidding his competition and increasing his price for extras after work had begun, but Cyril is misidentified here since by the end of 1948 he was no longer in his firm. Unheralded as an employer, he had a solid reputation as a just and caring one.

Across the great waters to the West, Cyril's bellfounding rep-utation is a lot more unalloyed. He helped, after all, to pioneer the carillon on the North American continent, and American car-illonneurs are proud of owning their instrument's new home. In the Netherlands, Cyril's third market of consequence after Britain and America, he is unequivocally appreciated. The English resent-ment of Cyril's deemed defection abroad, becoming famous for casting bells not of their type, plays into their position on him. In the end, he just didn't fit the profile of a lowly or anonymous manufacturer. He didn't keep his place—a hallowed code in Britain. It's tempting to think that his country wasn't ready for him. His bellfounder competitors were good but private figures by comparison. Cyril stepped out like an actor, an actor with a stentorian voice. He was a large personality, full of hubris and ambition, with tremendous belief in himself and pride in his work. This was his nature. Without it, he might not have over-come the handicaps he inherited.

Fittingly, Cyril's signature carillon in America, for New York's Riverside Church, dedicated in 1931, became his last pro-fessional point of reference. Discussions that began in the 30s over retuning or recasting the instrument's 61 trebles [See Chapter XIII], resumed when the war was over and persisted right through 1949, during the year after his resignation from G&J, half a year before he died. Frederick Mayer championed the bellfounder to the end. Rockefeller, ever his advisor's follower, kept right up with the discourse, and when Cyril was in the States on his last visit in 1947 even thoughtfully sent him to one of his doctors for consul-tation. If Cyril had been healthy and stayed on as G&J's Managing Director, a contract might have been reached. During 1947 JDR balked over the price, which had doubled after the war.

In December, 1948, he backed up and inquired of George Heidt his business manager, "What has happened about the carillon?" He remembered a possibility of Cyril acting in conjunction with an American bellfounder (by whom he meant one of the two fraternal Meneely foundries in Troy and Watervliet, New York; they would both shut down in 1952). Heidt replied that there had been no new developments, while informing JDR, "Mr. Johnston is a very sick man." In March, 1949, Mayer jumped in, writing to Rockefeller, Jr., advising against any involvement with G&J as it existed without its founder. "Frankly, I do not believe that anyone but Mr. Johnston could accurately tune, or retune, the Riverside Carillon to our satisfaction, especially the trebles." After this date, no more was heard.

Now another ending is at hand—finishing this book. Updating the last two lines in my Introduction, which summarize my twin subjects—"Such a long shot for history [Cyril Johnston's career as bellfounder] would obviously involve a trade-off; I have never imagined telling this story without an account of how I became the one to do it"—I see a genotype at the heart of the book. Call it the crossover syndrome. You see it everywhere in art and writing: the synaptical joining of disparate parts, or of parts that have been made to belong together but need transitions and invented passages to make them whole. You see it in the life of anyone who approaches life itself as a creative process. I wonder what we build on in this if not the hand we were dealt at birth. A twice-dead father and the thing he made that brought me here were ace cards in mine. A secret and a mother unable to accept the consequences of her choice in having me were like wild cards. There were cultural understandings or assumptions, the driving forces behind every birth. Who are we in the social order? What designs are there for us to discover? In my crossover world, I had to deal with parents who never formed a family with me as their child, suggesting a metaphoric one—this book. Behind them were their countries of origin, America and Britain, making docking the two countries, the two continents, imperative in understanding my "family plan."

The bells loom as a medium, their function as it happens in the world at large. They presented a special challenge in themselves: bringing them out of their towers and their guilds, freeing them from the exclusive domains where they are kept, in aspiring to make them broadly interesting. As a medium, bells have served my book in ways I could never have predicted. I see them ringing throughout, silently, symbolically, holding stories together—a thematic thread or chain, preserving continuity, providing unlikely commentaries.

In the spirit of Cyril Johnston's celebrations, I would like to swing some real bells, better, swing *on* them, preferably mighty ones, make a fearsome racket.

EPILOGUE

VOX DOMINI

A t 10:30 A.M. every Sunday morning at Riverside Church in New York, five of the biggest sixteen Gillett & Johnston bells left hanging, the major bass chord, are released from their steel frames and set to swinging for three minutes. The 20-ton Bourdon, note C, with its two colossal flanking companions, notes F and G, and two more above them, an A and another C (an octave higher) alone among the 74 that comprise the entire carillon, are capable of swinging. You will not see or hear anything like this in the world. To hear and to see them is the thing. Heard on the street 400 feet below, the sound is powerful and arresting. Viewed up close in the tower, they come at you and swing away from you like giants having a heavenly rumpus—the gods of bells in a deafening obstreperous command performance. The first time I heard them I was halfway up the iron staircase leading to a platform where the enclosed clavier room is located. One of the titans had got loose, riveting my eyeballs, freely swinging upwards, wildly, vertiginously, opening its mouth right in front of me, its huge tongue at perhaps an arc of 120 degrees tolling uproariously against its bronze membrane. Quickly I saw it wasn't alone. Several others, including the Bourdon, were swinging in concert, however all at different stages in their arcs. I was looking at a mega-weight of 82,251 pounds in thunderous motion. The clapper of the Bourdon alone weighs two tons. The cacophony was stupefying—consuming and dematerializing.

It's been said that seeing the Bourdon swing can make you believe in God. I don't know about God, but I had a religious experience that day. Church bells, I had always known, once liberated by rope or clavier were supposed to represent God's voice. Inscriptions to that effect, such as *Vox Domini* on an 1175 bell in Limoges, France, abound. The Bourdon hanging in the 1939 G&J Grace Cathedral carillon in San Francisco is inscribed on one side with the name of the donor (once a poor English immigrant who made good in the U.S.)[1] on its reverse side with the quotation from John, "I am the Way, the Truth and the Life." In our secular postmodern world, the carillon as concert instrument seems a logical development from its religious origins. Yet it sits in gothically high places, often with propitiatory inscriptions, inevitable reminder of godly aspirations. Then too, it has its divine role as an art form.

The swinging constellation at Riverside set me back, way back, to something primordially, inchoately wondrous.

NOTES

Chapter II: Elstree

1. André Lehr. *The Art of the Carillon in the Low Countries.* Tielt, Belgium: Lannoo Printers and Publishers, 1991, p. 94; p. 100.

2. Gillett and Johnston (clockmakers and bellfounders) traced their origins to the clockmaking business of William Gillett in Hadlow, Kent. In 1837, Gillett moved his business to Clerkenwell, London; and in 1844 to the site in Whitehorse Road, Thornton Heath, which it was to occupy until 1957. In 1854, Gillett was joined in the business by Charles Bland (d. 1886), the firm subsequently being known as Gillett & Bland. In 1877, Arthur A. Johnston (1851–1916) bought a partnership, and the firm became known as Gillett Bland & Co., and then, from 1884, as Gillett & Johnston. A.A. Johnston extended the firm's business into bell-founding. *See,* AR1 Gillett & Johnston Records, 1877–1983 at Croydon Public Library.

3. A tale that has passed into bell founding folklore is that shortly after the Great War, Cyril Johnston persuaded the Trinity House corporation (which managed Britain's buoy bells) to arrange a trial whereby two buoy bells were moored a mile apart, one being a standard buoy bell cast by Warner's and the other an experimental Gillett & Johnston bell tuned to the True Harmonic principle. Observers on a launch moved away from the bells until only one could be heard and of course it was the Gillett and Johnston bell. Presumably as a result of this trial, Trinity House produced a specification and drawings for the 'improved' buoy bell. *See,* "Trinity House Bells" by David Kelly, *The Ringing World,* October 24, 2003. This story was first told in a letter from Messrs Gillett

and Johnston to William Gorham Rice, who published it in his 1925 edition of his book: *Carillon Music and Singing Towers of the Old World and the New*, p. 295.

Chapter III: The Royal Exchange

1. *Building News,* December 24, 1920. *See,* Cuttings AR/2/1, 1919–1925, p. 108, Gillett & Johnston Records, Croydon Central Library, Local Studies and Archives, Croydon, England, hereinafter referred to as G&J Records.

2. There were 70 male employees occupied in making clocks and bells when the war broke out. A few days after, the firm undertook a contract for 5000 ammunition boxes. In 1915, a few girls were employed, and in July the making of fuses began. . . . By April of 1917, 30,000 fuses a week were being made, by October 40,000. When the millionth fuse was completed, it was set aside as a memento. The staff had grown to 234 men and 916 women. *See,* "Under the Clock Tower: How a Peaceful Industry Became a Mighty War Machine," the *Croydon Advertiser,* November 23, 1918.

3. *Building News,* December 24, 1920.

4. Interview with Mrs. Mary E. Johnston, London, England, April 1987. *See,* Jill Johnston Literary Archives, Carillon Research, Family Box 1, folder # 22, hereinafter referred to as JJLA-CR.

5. It is interesting to note that as a Bellfounder Arthur A. Johnston cast six bells in 1889 (when his son Cyril was five years old) for a church in Greenock, Scotland, his father's ancestral home. The church was the Greenock Free Middle Church. In 1911, the bells were augmented to eight, and in 1913 all the bells were replaced. Cyril Johnston was evidently responsible for the 1911 and 1913 contracts. *See,* email from George Dawson to bellhistorians@yahoogroups.com, December 12 2006; Dawson's source, Alan Buswell.

6. Besides being Chairman of the P. & O., Anderson was a director of several other companies: The Marine and General Life Assurance Society; the Crystal Palace Company, and The Union Steam Ship Company (p38). Anderson also started the Shetland Island's first newspaper, named the *Shetland Journal.* And he was an ardent politician, identifying himself with the Radical wing of the Liberals. Between 1847 and 1852 Anderson represented the Shetland and Orkney Islands as a Member of Parliament, passionately defending their interests. *See, Arthur Anderson: A Founder of the P. and O. Company,* by John Nicolson, T. & J. Manson, Lerwick, 1932.

7. October 29, 1922, letter from F.C. Mayer to J.D. Rockefeller, Jr.
See, Rockefeller Archive Center, Sleepy Hollow, N. Y., hereinafter referred to as RAC.

8. May 24, 1927 letter from F. C. Mayer to JDR Jr., "... The actual casting is being done in a large bronze foundry [The Manganese Bronze Company] in London, a corner of which Mr. Johnston has leased." See, RAC

9. Mark Regan, "The bells of London's Royal Exchange." *The Ringing World,* December 19/26, 1997, pp. 1268-70 and 1289-91.

10. *Ibid*

11. By 1905, Gillett & Johnston had its first tuning machine. According to Nigel Taylor of Whitechapel, an "intermediate" size machine was bought by Cyril in 1909. Then around 1925, according to both Nigel Taylor and George Elphick, Cyril acquired a large machine from John Warner and Sons when their bellfoundry closed. Elphick says this big machine "was reputed to have been bought for tuning the second Big Ben, which they had hoped to cast. *See, The Craft of the Bellfounder,* by George Elphick, Phillimore 1988, p. 102.

12. Keith H. Fleming, "The bells of Wimborne Minster, Dorset." *The Ringing World,* June 13 1986, p. 516-517.

13. August 23, 2002, email from Keith H. Fleming, bell ringer at Wimborne Minster, to author.

14. Mark Regan, "The bells of London's Royal Exchange." *The Ringing World,* December 19/26, 1997, pp. 1268-70 and 1289-91.

15. August 23, 2002, email from Keith H. Fleming, bell ringer at Wimborne Minster, to author.

Chapter IV: The Millionaires' Church

1. September 28, 1923, letter from F.C. Mayer to J.D. Rockefeller, Jr. *See* RAC.

2. *Ibid*

3. January 15, 1924, letter from F.C. Mayer to J.D. Rockefeller, Jr. *See* RAC.

4. September 27, 1921, letter from Archer Gibson to Buchanan Houston. *See* RAC.

5. A Rockefeller in-house memo, October 14 1921, by Buchanan Houston. *See* RAC.

6. January 31, 1922, letter by F.C. Mayer to J.D. Rockefeller, Jr. *See* RAC.

7. April 18, 1922, letter by F.C. Mayer to J.D Rockefeller, Jr. *See* RAC.

8. April 24, 1922, letter by F.C. Mayer to J.D. Rockefeller, Jr. *See* RAC.
9. June 11, 1922, letter from F.C. Mayer to J.D. Rockefeller, Jr. *See* RAC.
10. July 8, 1922, letter from F.C. Mayer to J.D. Rockefeller, Jr. *See* RAC.
11. July 26, 1922, letter from Chester B. Massey to J.D. Rockefeller, Jr. *See* RAC.
12. June 8, 1922, letter from J.D. Rockefeller, Jr. to F.C. Mayer. *See* RAC.
13. June 25, 1922, letter from F.C. Mayer to E.D. Taylor. *See* RAC.
14. July 5, 1922, letter from F.C. Mayer to J.D. Rockefelle, Jr. *See* RAC.
15. August 8, 1922, letter from F. C. Mayer to J.D. Rockefeller, Jr. *See* RAC.
16. *Ibid.*
17. October 2, 1925, letter from J.D. Rockefeller, Jr. to Anton Brees. *See* RAC.
18. July 28, 1923, letter from J.D. Rockefeller, Jr. to F.C. Mayer. *See* RAC.
19. October 29, 1922, letter from F.C. Mayer to J.D. Rockefeller, Jr. *See* RAC.
20. September 6, 1923, letter from F.C. Mayer to J. D. Rockefeller, Jr. *See* RAC.
21. September 10, 1923, letter from F.C. Mayer to J.D. Rockefeller, Jr. *See* RAC.

Chapter V: Onward to Riverside

1. June 9, 2004, Email to author from Victor Jordan, Associate Archivist at the Riverside Church Archives: "The 16th Century Flemish Stained Glass windows were donated by the Marston family and moved to the Narthex [of Riverside Church] from the Park Avenue Baptist Church 1929–30 at the same time as the Carillon bells."
2. February 16, 1922, letter from F.C. Mayer to J.D. Rockefeller, Jr. *See* RAC.
3. Harry Emerson Fosdick, *The Living of These Days*. New York and London: Harper ChapelBook, 1967, p. 177-178.
4. *Ibid.*
5. August 21, 1923, letter from J.D. Rockefeller, Jr. to F.C. Mayer. *See* RAC.
6. *The New York Times,* "New York Has a Carillon" January 25 1926
7. April 9, 1924, letter from F.C. Mayer to J.D. Rockefeller, Jr. *See* RAC.
8. International Pitch is the proposed universally accepted standard of tuning all instruments to an A of 440 cycles per second (Hertz); *See also,* http://www.btinternet.com/~keltek/sapage1.html

http://www.time.com/time/magazine/article/0,9171,931255,00.html
http://www.schillerinstitute.org/music/rev_tuning_hist.html
http://www.uk-piano.org/history/pitch.html

9. Author's interview, via phone, of Anton Brees, Jr. September, 2003. *See*, JJLA-Carillon Research.

10. February 17, 1925, letter from J.D. Rockefeller, Jr. to Cyril F. Johnston. *See*, RAC.

11. July 2, 1925 letter from J.D. Rockefeller Jr. to F.C. Mayer. *See*, RAC.

Chapter VI The King's Bell

1. February 24, 1923 letter from F.C. Mayer to J.D. Rockefeller Jr. *See*, RAC.

2. Nora Johnston. *A Memoir*. New York, N.Y.: Print Means Inc. 2002, p. 17.

3. "Croydon Times Souvenir of the Visit of Their Majesties The King & Queen to Croydon." Special Supplement of the *Croydon Times*, Saturday May 12 1925. *See*, Gillett & Johnston Records, Croydon Central Library, Local Studies and Archives, Croydon, England, hereinafter referred to as G&J Records.

4. *Ibid.*

5. The Vicar of St. Mary's Church, Leicester, David Cawley, wrote to author that the name Gillett & Johnston would have been known within the Royal Household for professional reasons—Arthur Johnston received the Royal Warrant ("By Appointment") for supplying clocks in 1882, when he put up a new clock at St. James's Palace in London. On it, he put a plaque, "V. R. By Order of Her Majesty Queen Victoria, the old clock was replaced by a modern Turret clock, made and erected by Gillett & Johnston, Croydon, 1882." He had also supplied the clocks at Windsor Castle and at Queen Victoria's private Residence, at Osborne House, Isle of Wight. *See*, JJLA-Carillon Research.

6. June, 1986, author's interview with Douglas Hughes, Manager of Whitechapel Foundry, London, England. *See*, JJLA-Carillon Research.

7. Summer, 1984, author's interview with Mrs. Don Hunter, Redlands California. *See*, JJLA-Carillon Research.

8. Interview with Mrs. Mary E. Johnston, London, England, April 1987. *See*, JJLA-Carillon Research, Family Box 1, folder # 22.

9. September 19, 2005, email from Vicar David Cawley to author quoting 1982 letter from Mrs. Mary E. Johnston about Cyril's looks. *See*, JJLA-Carillon Research.

10. Conversations between author and the late carillonneur of Riverside Church, James R. Lawson, during 1988. *See,* JJLA-Carillon Research.
11. Medical Board Report on a Disabled Officer, May 3, 1918 regarding Second Lieutenant C.F. Johnston, Special Reserve, Grenadier Guards. *See,* National Archives, Kew, Richmond, Surrey, 70859, ref.: WO339/72079.
12. "Royal Visit to Croydon." *The London Times,* Wednesday May 13, 1925.

Chapter VII: Heavy Metal—The Mother of all Bourdons
1. February 25, 1930, letter from F.C. Mayer to J.D. Rockefeller, Jr. *See* RAC.
2. March 2, 1928, letter from J.D. Rockefeller, Jr. to Cyril F. Johnston. *See* RAC.
3. December 16, 1927, letter from J.D. Rockefeller, Jr. to Cyril F. Johnston. *See* RAC.
4. *The London Times,* April 4, 1927. *See,* G&J Records.
5. February 18, 2007 email from Carl Zimmerman to author: "The Wellington carillon was enlarged from 49 to 65 bells by Taylor in 1986, replacing some trebles and extending the treble range. In 1995, Eijsbouts cast 4 great bells to extend the bass range to a new total of 69 bells. The largest of these is 12¼ tons. Although Eijsbouts cast the bells, they were under subcontract to Whitechapel, and they used G&J profiles, G&J decorations, and G&J bronze mixing ratios. Whitechapel then supplied 5 small bells of similar character in 1996, so that the instrument now totals 74 bells." *See,* JJLA-CR, Correspondence with Carillonneurs.
6. June 1, 1928, letter from Cyril F. Johnston to J. D. Rockefeller, Jr. *See,* Riverside Church Archives, Riverside Church, New York, NY, hereinafter referred to as RCA.
7. *Ibid.*
8. June 20, 1928 letter from Frederick Mayer to Cyril Johnston: "Let me say in closing that we all realize that you are doing pioneer work in casting this large bell, and that you are having many difficult and new problems to solve. For this reason, we have been willing to aid you in every reasonable way, seeking to get these two rejected bells made satisfactory." *See,* RAC.
9. July 1, 1930, letter from Frederick C. Mayer to John D. Rockefeller, Jr. *See,* RAC.
10. June 25, 2003, email from Carl Scott Zimmerman to author. *See,* JJLA-Carillon Research, Correspondence with Carillonneurs.

11. November 20, 1928, letter from Frederick C. Mayer to Cyril F. Johnston. *See, RAC*.

Chapter VIII: Nineteen Eighty-Four

1. September 20, 1987, Jim Lawson called the author and gave her the following account, from a lunch he had had with Mrs. Mary E. Johnston and her son, Arthur Johnston, at her home in London: When Arthur went out of the room for some reason, Mrs. Johnston asked Jim if he "knew a woman in New York who calls herself Johnston" and Jim said, "You mean Jill? – Yes I do, and she's a friend of mine." Then Mrs. Johnston told Jim that "Cyril [Johnston] had been deceived [by Jill's mother] but he did support this woman . . . that a scandal had to be kept quiet at that time." She added that she had never replied to any correspondence from her [Jill]. Jim said he knew Jill, he admired her work, that "she has contributed enormously, and is a very gifted writer." And she said no more. *See, JJLA-CR*

2. "The Heroes Reconsidered." *See* www.jilljohnston.com Archived Columns, Volume 1, Columns #10 and 11, and Volume 2 #1.

3. April 23, 2003, email from Richard P. Strauss to author. *See, JJLA-CR* (carillonneur correspondence).

4. In a January, 1925, lecture with slides given by Cyril Johnston, he said, ". . . you must call a bell 'she' –and yet, perhaps this is not extraordinary, there are other kinds of 'Belles,' all called she; but the real reason for this definite determination of gender is said to be attributed to the fact that bells have clappers, which are sometimes called tongues." *See, JJLA-CR* (FAM1-27).

Chapter IX: Coventry

1. In 1947, a carillon of 36 bells was given to the First Presbyterian Church of Stamford, Connecticut, by the Nestlé Corporation, then headquartered in Stamford. The instrument was built by Gillett & Johnston, with a C# bourdon of 4,319 pounds. In 1968, the carillon was expanded under the direction of Arthur Bigelow to 56 bells, cast by the French Bellfounder, Paccard. [See Chapter XII on Bigelow's expansion of the Princeton G&J carillon, also cast by Paccard]. Of the original 36 G&J bells, 22 were incorporated into the new Paccard instrument. Of the 14 remaining G&J bells, 2 were stolen, and in 1977, 12 were given to the New Skete Community, a Russian Orthodox monastery in Cambridge, New York. *See, JJLA-CR*

2. "Ottawa's Magnificent Carillon." *Evening Telegram* June 8, 1927, Toronto, Canada. *See,* AR 1/2/2 Cuttings 2, 1927–1930, p. 35. *See,* G&J Records.

3. John Eisel "The CCCBR and SPAB—A Warning from History" Part 3, pp.1290-01. *The Ringing World,* December 21/28, 2001.

4. "The Ickleton Case," *The Ringing World,* June 24, 1927.

5. "Ickleton Bells." *The Ringing World,* September 30, 1927.

6. "Consistory Court. Restoration of Church Bells. Faculty after Illegal Removal." *The Times,* February 4, 1929. *See,* G&J Records AR 1/2/2 p. 76A.

7. *The Ringing World,* May 3, 1929, p. 281.

8. "St. James' Clerkenwell." *The Ringing World,* May 10, 1929.

9. Letter July 7, 1925, from E. A. Young to W. Brovoett, Esq. *See,* "Coventry Bells and how they were lost (1926)," and JJLA-CR.

10. Letter (59) January 18, 1926, from E. A. Young to H. Drake. *See,* "Coventry Bells and how they were lost" (1926), and JJLA-CR.

11. Letter (14) July 8, 1925, from Cyril F. Johnston to E. A. Young. *See,* "Coventry Bells and how they were lost (1926)," and JJLA-CR.

12. "Ringing Controversies: The Battle over Coventry Bells" by William Butler. See, *The Ringing World,* September 4, 1987, p. 798.

13. October 29, 1922, letter from Frederick C. Mayer to John D. Rockefeller Jr. *See,* RAC.

14. Frank Percival Price. *The Carillon.* London: Oxford University Press, 1932, p.36.

15. Letter (#39) November 30, 1925, from E. A. Young to (a circular letter). *See,* "Coventry Bells and how they were lost" (1926), and JJLA-CR.

16. December 2006, email from David Cawley to author: "In the last 30 years or so the number of new change ringing peals—especially in the eastern states—has significantly increased. They have been cast largely by Whitechapel. . . . a new Taylor ring of 12 (the first in the U.S.) is anticipated for NY City. This is for Trinity Church in lower Manhattan." *See,* JJLA-CR.

Chapter X: Rodman Wanamaker's Big Ben

1. "Church Bells." *See, Croydon Times,* February 28, 1928, and Mark Regan, "The bells of London's Royal Exchange." *See, The Ringing World,* December 19/26, 1997, pp. 1268-70 and 1289-91.

2. *The London Times* 1925 anonymous letter re Big Ben.

3. Interview with Mrs. Mary E. Johnston, London, England, April 1987. *See,* JJLA-Carillon Research, Family Box 1, folder # 22.

4. According to David Cawley, in 1856 Warners were the Royal Bellfounders by Appointment to Queen Victoria, having recently cast the clock bells for Balmoral. *See,* JJLA-CR (D. Cawley correspondence)

5. John Darwin. *The Triumphs of Big Ben.* London: Robert Hale Ltd. 1986, p. 80.

6. *Ibid* p. 95.

7. Ray Biswanger. *Music in the Marketplace.* Bryn Mawr, PA: Friends of the Wanamaker Organ, Inc. 1999, p. 156.

8. April 30, 1926, cable signed by Rodman Wanamaker to Arthur Newson. *See,* Wanamaker Collection at the Historical Society, Philadelphia, PA.

9 May 12, 1926, letter from Arthur Newson to Rodman Wanamaker. *See,* Wanamaker Collection at the Historical Society, Philadelphia, PA.

10. May 15, 1926, letter from Arthur Newson to Rodman Wanamaker. *See,* Wanamaker Collection at the Historical Society, Philadelphia, PA.

11. The world's largest single swinging bell, outside Russia and Japan, is in Newport, Kentucky, USA. It is called the "World Peace Bell," and weighs 33 metric tons. *See,* http://www.gcna.org/data/NAOtherGreatBells.html

12. Ray Biswanger. *Music in the Marketplace.* Bryn Mawr, PA: Friends of the Wanamaker Organ, Inc. 1999, p. 167.

13. *Ibid* p. 167.

Chapter XI: Jerusalem the Golden

1. Nora Johnston. *A Memoir.* New York, NY: Print Means Inc. 2002, p. 79.

2. *Ibid* p. 80.

3. *Ibid* p. 75.

4. October 13, 1924, letter from Cyril F. Johnston to Jef Denyn. *See,* reprint of letter from Mrs. Mary Johnston to Margo Halsted in *Carillon News,* No. 41, Spring 1989.

5. *See,* Nora Johnston. *A Memoir.* p. 4.

6. July 7, 1932, letter from F. W. Ramsey to Gillett & Johnston Foundry, Croydon, England. *See,* YMCA International Work in Palestine/Israel Records, Jerusalem YMCA, Kautz Family YMCA Archives, University of Minnesota Libraries, Minneapolis, Minnesota, hereinafter referred to as YMCA Archives.

7. March 25, 1933, letter from Nora Johnston to F. W. Ramsey. *See,* YMCA Archives.

8. April 23, 1933, letter from Nora Johnston to Waldo H. Heinrichs, General Secretary. *See,* YMCA Archives.
9. May 6, 1933, letter from Waldo H. Heinrichs, to Cyril F. Johnston. *See,* YMCA Archive.
10. *Ibid*
11. May 10, 1933, letter from Waldo H. Heinrichs, to the captain of SS *Italia. See,* YMCA Archive.
12. May 10, 1933, letter from Amelia F. G. Jarvis to Cyril F. Johnston. *See,* YMCA Archive
13. Letter May 17, 1933, from Waldo H. Heinrichs to Mr. F. W. Ramsey. *See,* YMCA Archive.
14. Letter May 24, 1933, from Cyril F. Johnston to Waldo H. Heinrichs. *See,* YMCA Archive.
15. Letter June 1, 1933 from Waldo H. Heinrichs to Cyril F. Johnston. *See,* YMCA Archive.
16. November 17, 1927, letter from R. F. A. Housman, GM of Gillett & Johnston, to George Wintringer, recommending Ruth Conniston to play the Cleveland Tower Carillon. *See,* Graduate College Carillon in Mudd Library, Princeton, NJ.
17. Nora Johnston. *A Memoir.* New York, NY: Print Means Inc. 2002, p. 29.
18. *Ibid* p. 65.
19. *Ibid* p. 64.
20. *Naval and Military Records,* May 30, 1928. *See,* G&J Records, AR 1/2/4 cuttings, p.85.
21. Nora Johnston. *A Memoir.* New York, NY: Print Means Inc. 2002, p. 73-74.
22. *Ibid* p. 91.

Chapter XII: The Bell(e)s of St. Mary's

1. Nora Johnston. *A Memoir.* Print Means Inc.: New York, NY 2002.
2. November 13, 1951, letter from G. J. Schulmerich, President, to John L. Cottrell, Treasurer. *See,* Belmont University Library, Special Collection, hereinafter referred to as BUL-SC.
3. Beverly Buchanan, "The Carillon of Belmont." *See, Bulletin of Guild of Carillonneurs of North America,* Volume XLV, 1996, (pp. 18-48), p. 27.
4. June 5, 1952, letter from Clarence Duncan, Director of Public Relations, to Percival Price. *See,* BUL-SC.
5. July 12, 1954, letter from Denny Breneton to Martin Gilman, MA. *See,* BUL-SC.

6. June 30, 1927, letter from Henry B. Thompson to George C. Wintringer. *See*, Seeley G. Mudd Manuscript Library (Graduate College Carillon), 65 Olden Street, Princeton, NJ, hereinafter referred to as SGMML.

7. May 1, 1928, letter from William Gorham Rice to Dr. Charles D. Hart. *See*, SGMML.

8. September 23, 1925, letter from Charles D. Hart to Professor V. Lansing Collins, Princeton University. *See*,SGMML.

9. September 18, 2007, email from Carl Zimmerman to author: "In summer of 1966, the Princeton instrument consisted of 58 bells—25 G&J basses and 33 Paccard mids and trebles which had been cast earlier that year, and which Bigelow had just installed along with a new 74-note playing keyboard built by himself and his students. On hand, but not yet installed, were another 12 Paccard trebles which had been cast along with the 33, and were intended to make an instrument of 70 bells. But Bigelow died before he got around to installing the last treble octave. The three smallest unistalled bells "dissappeared" before someone (I don't know who) got around to installing the waiting bells in 1968, so the final installed count was 67 bells. The 1993 renovation added one bass bell (cast by P&F to G&J profile, I believe), and removed the smallest treble to the University archives. Thus the number of bells remained unchanged, but the transposition to the keyboard was changed." *See*, JJLA-CR.

10. "Report on the Graduate College Bells" by Arthur Bigelow. *See*, SGMML

11. Margo Halsted wrote: "Besides his association with Paccard, Bigelow was employed for ten years, beginning in 1946, by Schulmerich Carillons! . . . Arthur Bigelow always said he was only a consultant for Schulmerich . . . [he] played the dedication recitals for many Schulmerich electronic bell instruments and also taught students to play them . . . the stigma of his work with Schulmerich stayed with him, and tainted his relation with members of the GCNA, even for many years after he severed relations with Schulmerich." In the same article, she notes that when Bigelow began a business relationship with Paccard, again "he called himself a freelance consultant." She quotes from a letter to the President of Princeton, Robert F. Goheen, from an anonymous source, September 4, 1963: "Several years ago [Arthur Bigelow's] consulting activities were brought to my attention. There were his alleged activities as a bell salesman, and he convinced me [once] that he was acting only as a consultant. I am particularly annoyed he has continued to use Princeton U. stationery in his consulting activities. I had asked him to refrain from using U. letterheads in connection with any of this work . . . It may be that we are

now being forced to consider asking Arthur Bigelow either to discontinue his consulting activities entirely or to resign from the U. faculty." Halsted also notes that Bigelow pioneered designing treble bells of larger scale, helping to balance the carillon instrument, and that "as a scholar he is generally recognized as the leading consultant on bells and carillons in the U.S." *See,* Margo Halsted, GCNA Bulletin XLIV, 1995, pp. 44–54.

12. "Report on the Graduate College Bells" by Arthur Bigelow. *See,* SGMML.
13. *The New York Times,* October 22, 1996 (Metro Section).
14. Letter from Ruth Russel Loftus (1908). *See, Quadrangles,* Volume VII, Number 4, November 1977.

Chapter XIII: Riverside Redux

1. December 6, 2003, email from Richard Watson to author. *See,* JJLA-CR.
2. October 22, 1955, letter from Bonaventura Eijsbouts to John D. Rockefeller Jr. *See,* RAC.
3. September 5, 1955, letter from A.M. Craig to F. C. Mayer. *See,* RAC.
4. September 29, 1955, letter from George Heidt to John D. Rockefeller, Jr. *See,* RAC.
5. December 4, 1932, letter from F. Mayer to John D. Rockefeller Jr. See, RAC.
6. Author's journal, Spring 2003.
7. Alan Buswell's data base of "The Tuning Books of Gillett & Johnston (Bellfounders)" *See,* A. A. J. Buswell, 12 Park Road, Denmead, Hants, PO7 6NE, England.
8. June 22, 1933, memo to John D. Rockefeller, Jr. *See,* RAC.
9. July 16th 1934, letter from Cyril F. Johnston to John D. Rockefeller, Jr. *See,* RAC.
10. August 8, 1934, letter from R. Gumbel to Cyril F. Johnston. *See,* RAC.
11. September 14, 2007, email from Carl Zimmerman to GCNA members and associates, "With the latest update, the GCNA Website now lists more than a thousand tower bell instruments in North America: 181 baton-keyboard carillons, 123 carillons with non-traditional mechanisms, 700 chime-sized instruments (including 50 rings).
12. André Lehr. *The Art of the Carillon in the Low Countries.* Tielt, Belgium: Lannoo Printers and Publishers, 1991, p. 250.
13. January 15, 1947, letter from Frederick C. Mayer to John D. Rockefeller, Jr. *See,* RAC.
14. Some of the G&J bells removed from Riverside Church by van Bergen may be hanging in Nossa Senhora Do Carmo in Belo Horizonte, Brazil.

15. February 21, 2007 email from Nigel Taylor to author:
    Inscription details of new Whitechapel bells for Riverside Church:
    F1 to B1: WHITECHAPEL, LONDON 1999, AFTER GILLETT &
    JOHNSTON, CROYDON (7 bells)
    C2 to F2: WHITECHAPEL, LONDON, 1999 (6 bells)
    F# to C4: WHITECHAPEL, 1999 (19 bells)
    The top 26 bells are sand castings and are uninscribed.
    The new bells replace 58 bells cast by van Bergen in 1956.
    The 16 original G&J bells of course remain as installed.
    [These are the biggest, anchored by the 20-ton bourdon]. *See,* JJLA-CR.

Chapter XIV: 500 Pounds With Interest

1. Letters quoted in these paragraphs between William Gorham Rice,
   William Irvine, Percival Price, Cyril Johnston are located in the National
   Library of Canada in Ottawa, in the Percival Price Collection.
2. Bryan Barker, Program of Carillon Recitals, 1932, p. 6-7; p. 11.
   See, Carillon Archive in Lenfest Hall, Mercersburg, Mercersburg, PA.
3. "Dedication." *Time,* Volume VIII, Number 16, October 18, 1926,
   p. 7. *See,* Carillon Archive in Lenfest Hall, Mercersburg,
   Mercersburg, PA.
4. *On the Issues,* Spring 1996.

Chapter XV: The Dutch Connection

1. According to Carl Zimmerman, Taylor made 14, André Lehr says 11.
2. André Lehr. *The Art of the Carillon in the Low Countries.* Tielt,
   Belgium: Lannoo Printers and Publishers, 1991, p. 253
3. November 7, 1936, letter from Johan Eijsbouts to Cyril F. Johnston.
   See, Eijsbouts Archives.
4. November 17, 1936, letter from Cyril F. Johnston to Dr. J. Caspari;
   November 16, 1936 letter from Cyril F. Johnston to Messr. Eijsbouts.
   See, Eijsbouts Archives.
5. Frank Percival Price. *The Carillon.* London: Oxford University Press,
   1932, p. 66.
6. December 27, 1923, letter from Johan Eijsbouts to Cyril F. Johnston.
   See, Eijsbouts Archives.
7. September 27, 1924, letter from Johan Eijsbouts to Cyril F. Johnston.
   See, Eijsbouts Archives.
8. October 27, 1924, letter from Johan Eijsbouts to Cyril F. Johnston.
   See, Eijsbouts Archives.

9. April 30, 2004, email from André Lehr to author. *See,* JJLA-CR.

10. André Lehr. *The Art of the Carillon in the Low Countries.* Tielt, Belgium: Lannoo Printers and Publishers, 1991, p. 209.

11. May 10, 2004, email from André Lehr to author. *See,* JJLA-CR (Box 11).

12. October 7, 1924, letter from Johan Eijsbouts to Cyril F. Johnston. *See,* Eijsbouts Archives.

13. Nora Johnston. *A Memoir.* Print Means Inc.: New York, NY 2002. p.115 ff.

14. March 24, 2004, email from Carl Zimmerman to author: "477 bells and 16 carillons." *See,* JJLA-CR.

15. "Lecture on Bellfounding" (with 75 slides) by Cyril F. Johnston, 1944. *See,* JJLA-CR.

Chapter XVI: Lunches at Beaulieu

1. March 27, 1931, letter from Cyril F. Johnston to F. C. Mayer. *See,* RAC.

2. Nora Johnston. *A Memoir.* Print Means Inc.: New York, NY 2002, p. 77.

3. "The Heroes Reconsidered." *See,* www.jilljohnston.com Archived Columns, Volume 1, Columns #10 and 11, and Volume 2 #1.

4. February 19, 2006, email from David Cawley to author in which he quotes a letter he received from Mollie Johnston: "The story is, Cyril Johnston during his life was asked, many times, to write his life." *See,* JJLA-CR.

Chapter XVII: Until Her Majesty's Pleasure Be Known

1. Mark Regan, " Gordon Selfridge and the 1933 restorations of Bow Bells." *See, The Ringing World,* December 20/27, 1996, pp. 1289-95. (*See also,* Christopher Pickford "Whitechapel Foundry Booklet." August 26, 1984 (Edition, April, 28, 2002).

2. *Ibid* p. 1291.

3. *Ibid* p. 1292.

4. *See, Oxford English Dictionary.*

5. Interview with Mrs. Mary E. Johnston, London, England, April 1987. *See,* JJLA-CR.

6. *See,* brianrisman@thelawjournal.co.uk.

7. Cyril F. Johnston Estate Papers. *See,* JJLA-RC, Box 10.

8. September 28, 1982, entry author's journal. *See,* JJLA.

9. Howard, Michael: Bell *Founding.* (A lecture given by H. M. Howard M.A., Director of Gillett & Johnston Ltd., on November 20th, 1948 to

The Institute of Musical Instrument Technology).
See, JJLA-CR.

Epilogue
1. The donor was Dr. Nathaniel T. Coulson.
   See, Rosa Baldwin. *The Bells Shall Ring,* and
   http://www.gracecathedral.org/enrichment/crypt/cry_19980701.shtml

Appendix 1
Cyril F. Johnston
Personal Facts

May 9, 1884	Birth of Cyril Frederick Johnston, Croydon, England
August 3, 1886	Birth of Cyril Johnston's sister, Nora Violet Johnston, Croydon, England
1898–1902	Attended Whitgift School, Croydon, England
1903	Entered the Gillett and Johnston Bell Foundry, Croydon, England
March 9, 1914	Entered military service, the Grenadier Guards; the Royal Fusiliers
October 26, 1916	Father, Arthur A. Johnston died, Cyril Johnston took over directorship of Gillett & Johnston Bellfoundry
May 17, 1929	Daughter, Jill Johnston, born
Nov. 29, 1930	Married Mary Evelyn O'Leary
August 6, 1932	Son, Arthur Francis Evelyn Johnston, born
November 5, 1936	Daughter, Rosemary Eugenie Evelyn Johnston, born
1948	Cyril F. Johnston awarded the OBE
March 30, 1950	Cyril Frederick Johnston died

DESCENDANTS OF JAMES JOHNSTON

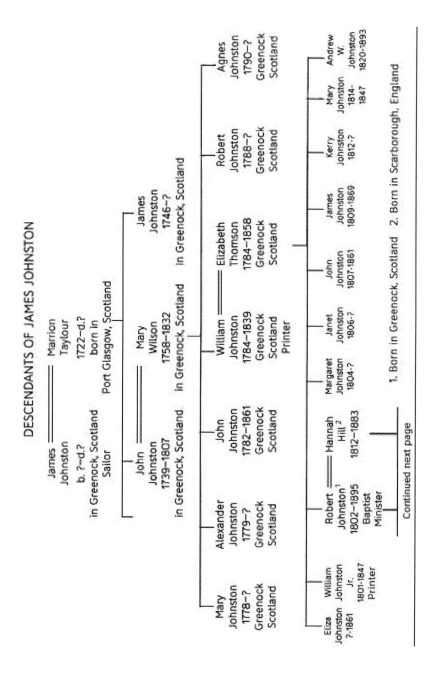

James Johnston
b. ?–d.?
in Greenock, Scotland
Sailor

Marrion Taylour
1722–d.?
born in
Port Glasgow, Scotland

John Johnston
1739–1807
in Greenock, Scotland

Mary Wilson
1758–1832
in Greenock, Scotland

James Johnston
1746–?
in Greenock, Scotland

Mary Johnston
1778–?
Greenock
Scotland

Alexander Johnston
1779–?
Greenock
Scotland

John Johnston
1782–1861
Greenock
Scotland

William Johnston
1784–1839
Greenock
Scotland
Printer

Elizabeth Thomson
1784–1858
Greenock
Scotland

Robert Johnston
1786–?
Greenock
Scotland

Agnes Johnston
1790–?
Greenock
Scotland

William Johnston Jr.
1801–1847
Printer

Eliza Johnston
?–1861

Robert Johnston[1]
1802–1895
Baptist
Minister

Hannah Hill[2]
1812–1883

Margaret Johnston
1804–?

Janet Johnston
1806–?

John Johnston
1807–1861

James Johnston
1809–1869

Kerry Johnston
1812–?

Mary Johnston
1814–1847

Andrew W. Johnston
1820–1893

Continued next page

1. Born in Greenock, Scotland   2. Born in Scarborough, England

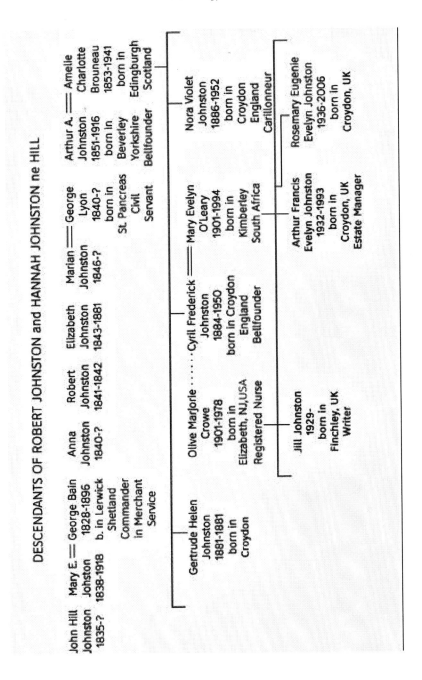

DESCENDANTS OF ROBERT JOHNSTON and HANNAH JOHNSTON ne HILL

Appendix 2
Carillons Worldwide
by Gillett & Johnston during
Cyril Frederick Johnston's directorship

1920
A chime or a carillon cast and installed in G&J foundry tower (unknown number of bells and how they were played)

1922
Cast and installed **1st** G&J carillon of 23 bells for Metropolitan Methodist Church (The Massey-Drury Memorial Carillon), Toronto, Ontario, Canada

1923
Cast and installed **2nd** G&J carillon of 23 bells for Grace Episcopal Church, Plainfield, New Jersey, USA; donor Albert Pittis

1924
Cast and installed **3rd** G&J carillon of 23 bells for St. Stephen's Episcopal Church (The Bancroft Memorial Carillon), Cohasset, Massachusetts, USA, gifted by Mrs. Hugh Bancroft; 1925 G&J added 20 bells, 1928 G&J added 8 bells

1924–25
Cast and installed **4th** G&J carillon of 23 bells for Norfolk County War Memorial, Simcoe, Ontario, Canada

1925–26
Cast and installed **5th** G&J carillon of 23 bells for St. George's Church (The Cutten Memorial Carillon), Guelph, Ontario, Canada

1925
Cast **6th** G&J carillon providing 36 of 38 bells for St. Georgius Church, Almelo, Holland

1925
Cast **7th** G&J carillon providing 38 of 43 bells for St. Jan's Cathedral, 's Hertogenbosch, Holland

1925
Cast **8th** G&J carillon of 35 bells for St. Joseph Church, Tilburg, Holland, installed by Eijsbouts

1925
Cast and installed **9th** G&J carillon of 53 bells for Park Avenue Baptist Church, New York, NY, USA (see 38th)

1926
Cast and installed **10th** G&J carillon of 43 bells for Mercersburg Chapel, Barker Tower (The Henry Bucher Swoope Carillon), Mercersburg Academy, Mercersburg, Pennsylvania, USA

1926	Cast and installed **11th** G&J carillon of 23 bells for Jefferson Avenue Presbyterian Church, Detroit, Michigan, USA
1927	Cast and installed **12th** G&J carillon of 35 bells for Grover Cleveland Tower, Princeton University, Princeton, New Jersey, USA, gifted by the Class of 1892
1926–27	Cast and installed **13th** G&J carillon of 53 bells for the Peace Tower, Houses of Parliament, Ottawa, Ontario, Canada
1927	Cast and installed **14th** G&J carillon of 43 bells for St. Chrysostom's Church (The Crane Memorial Carillon), Chicago, Illinois, USA
1927	Cast and installed a chime of 8 bells for Grosse Pointe Memorial Church, Grosse Pointe Farms, Michigan, USA (later expanded by Petit & Fritsen to 47 bell carillon)
1927	Cast and installed **15th** G&J carillon of 23 bells for Soldiers' Tower, University of Toronto, Toronto, Canada
1927	Cast and installed **16th** G&J carillon of 24 bells for Dutch Reformed Church, Barneveld, Holland
1928–35	Cast and installed **17th** G&J carillon of 23 bells for Beaumont Tower, Michigan State University, East Lansing, USA 12 bells added 1950, 6 added in 1952, both by Petit & Fritsen; 4 bells added by G&J in 1957 using Taylor foundry (CFJ has passed away by 1950)
1928	Cast and installed **18th** G&J carillon of 50 bells for Norwood Memorial Municipal Building (The Walter F. Tilton Memorial Carillon), Norwood, Massachusetts, USA, gifted by Walter F. Tilton
1928	Cast and installed **19th** G&J carillon of 23 bells for the Ward-Belmont School, Nashville, Tennessee, USA
1928	Cast and installed **20th** G&J carillon of 23 bells for the Plummer Building, the Mayo Clinic, Rochester, Minnesota, USA
1928	Cast and installed **21st** G&J carillon of 23 bells for Bond Street, London, England
1928	Cast **22nd** G&J carillon providing 19 of 23 or 24 bells for St. Petrusbanden (St. Peter-in-Chains Church), Hilvarenbeek, Holland; installed by Eijsbouts
1927-28	Cast and installed **23rd** G&J carillon of 23 bells for St. Patrick's Church, Dumbarton, Scotland

1929	Cast **24th** G&J carillon providing 40 of 46 bells for Onze-Lieve Vrouwe Church, Breda, Holland
1929	Cast **25th** G&J carillon of 42 bells for City Hall Tower, (Dutch Reformed Church) Enschede, Holland
1928	Cast **26th** G&J carillon of 25 bells for St. Maarten's Church, Sneek, Holland
1929	Cast and installed **27th** G&J carillon of 48 bells for the Louvain University Library, Louvain, Belgium, gifted by sixteen American Engineering Societies
1929	Cast and installed a G&J chime of 8 bells for St. Paul's Episcopal Church, Cleveland Heights, Ohio (later expanded by van Bergen to 23-bell carillon; the Harry A. & Mariah H. Seabrook and Thomas Family Memorial Carillon)
1929	Cast and installed **28th** G&J carillon of 23 bells for Thomas J. Emery Memorial Tower, Mariemont, Ohio
1928	Cast and installed **29th** G&J carillon of 32 bells for The Odeon Theatre, London, England; see, #33rd below; original bells were returned to G&J and used as stock bells
1930	Cast **30th** G&J carillon of 42 bells for St. Plechelmus Basilica, Oldenzaal, Holland
1930	Cast **31st** G&J carillon of 35 bells for St. Jan-Evangelist, Liège, Belgium
1930	Cast and installed **32nd** G&J carillon of 35 bells for the YMCA, Jerusalem, Israel
1930	Replaced entire Odeon Theatre Carillon of 32 bells (29th above) 33rd G&J carillon, London, England
1931	Cast and installed **34th** G&J carillon of 30 bells for the Galen L. Stone Tower, Wellesley College, Wellesley, Massachusetts, gifted by Mrs. C. Nichols Greene of Boston
1931	Cast and installed **35th** G&J carillon of 23 bells for the Chapel of Our Lady (José M. Ferrer Memorial Carillon), Canterbury School, New Milford, Connecticut, gifted by Mrs. José Ferrer
1931	Cast and installed **36th** G&J carillon of 42 bells for the Hôtel de Ville, Seelin, France
1931	Cast **37th** G&J carillon of 25 bells for Netherlands Reformed Church, Winschoten, Holland

1931	Cast and installed **38th** G&J carillon of 72 bells for the Riverside Church (The Laura Spelman Rockefeller Memorial Carillon) New York, NY, USA; gifted by John D. Rockefeller, Jr.
1932	Cast and installed **39th** G&J carillon of 18 bells (1926) and added 5 in 1932 for the Chobham estate of H. O. Serpell, Surrey, England
1932	Cast and installed **40th** G&J carillon of 23 bells for the Church of Our Lady, Saltley, Birmingham, England
1932	Cast and installed **41st** G&J carillon of 72 bells for the Rockefeller Memorial Chapel (The Laura Spelman Rockefeller Memorial Carillon) University of Chicago, Chicago, Illinois; gifted by J. D. Rockefeller, Jr.
1932	Cast and installed **42nd** G&J carillon of 49 bells for Wellington War Memorial Tower, Wellington, New Zealand
1933	Cast and installed **43rd** G&J carillon of 23 bells for the Chapel of St. Peter and St. Paul, St. Paul's School (The Houghton Memorial Carillon), Concord, New Hampshire, USA
1934	Cast and installed **44th** G&J carillon of 23 bells for the Christ Church, Grosse Pointe Farms, Michigan, USA; G&J added 7 bells in 1938
1934	Cast and installed **45th** G&J carillon of 44 bells for the School Tower, Bourneville, England, gifted by George Cadbury of the Cadbury Company
1935	Cast and installed **46th** G&J carillon of 23 bells for the Settlers' Campanile, Port Elizabeth, South Africa
1935	Cast and installed **47th** G&J carillon of 23 bells for City Hall, Germiston, Transvaal, South Africa
1935–36	Cast and installed **48th** G&J carillon providing 34 of 35 bells for St. Johns' Kirk, Perth, Scotland
1936	Cast and installed **49th** G&J carillon of 25 bells for the Campanile Tower (Memorial Carillon), University of Wisconsin, Madison, Wisconsin, USA; 1937 G&J added 5 bells.
1939–43	Cast and installed **50th** G&J (electric-keyboard) carillon of 44 bells for Grace Cathedral, San Francisco, California, USA (most of these bells were installed in

the Tower of the Sun for the Golden Gate Exhibition
from 1939–41)

1947   Cast and installed **51st** G&J carillon of 23 bells for the
Christ Episcopal Church, Charlottesville, Virginia, USA

1947   Cast and installed **52nd** G&J carillon of 36 bells for the
First Presbyterian Church (The Walter N. Maguire Memorial
Carillon), Stamford, Connecticut, USA

1949   a travelling carillon **53rd** of unknown size was cast and
based at the G&J foundry in Croydon;
the bells were later dispersed

After CFJ retirement and death

1951   Cast and installed 54th G&J carillon of 51 bells for the
Memorial Chapel, Culver Military Academy, Culver, Indiana, USA

1952-54   Cast and installed 55th G&J carillon of 37 bells for
St. Nicholas Church, Aberdeen, Scotland; 11 bells added in 1954

*Most of the carillons by Gillett & Johnston, for Holland, were installed
by the Royal Eijsbouts Bellfoundry*

APPENDIX 3

Casting at
Gillett & Johnston Bellfoundry

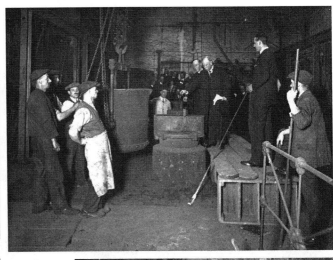

Excerpt from lecture on bell casting by Cyril F. Johnston

The design of the bell having been determined, two sweeps or strickle boards (as they are called) are then cut — one to the desired shape of the inside of the bell, one to that of the outside.

We will consider the inside first — a core is built up of bricks, having a solid cast iron plate as foundation, and having a comparatively small hollow space at the centre.

In this centre is pivoted a vertical bar with an arm fixed to the bar at right angles. To the arm is fixed the inside sweep which is revolved round the core, shaping in its circular course to the required diameter a layer of loam which has been plastered on to the body of the core. The loam is put on in a semi liquid state rather like thick mud — or perhaps porridge sounds more genteel — and it is made up of materials mixed into the right proportions — sand, cowhair, etc. The core is then put in a large specially constructed oven for a few days so as to dry gradually and set firmly.

The outer part of the mould is constructed by lining an iron case with loam and striking the mould in (foundry language) with the outside sweep [strickle]. The case is then also put in the oven to dry. It is on this, the outer mould, that inscriptions are stamped, the impressions being filled up when the metal is run, thus forming the letters in "bass relief" on a bell.

The mould, [now having set to desired conditions] is then placed over the core, taking a bearing at the bottom and clapped to the base-plate.

Now between the inner mould (the core) and the outer mould (the case) is the space corresponding in section all the way round to that of the bell that is to be cast.

The moulds being ready, the metal which has been melted in a reverbatory or air furnace, is run into a big ladle or cauldron capable of taking some tons of molten metal. The ladle is then lifted by tackle suspended from a traveling crane and the metal is poured into the moulds.

The next day, or even the day after that, according to the size of the casting, the moulds are parted and the bell extracted.

The composition of the bell is pure copper and tin, roughly speaking in the proportions of three and a half to one. May I say in passing that there is no gold, silver or precious stones in modern bell hanging, and there is no evidence of any in the old bells. . . .

Now we have arrived at the cast but not the last stage of the bell. The next process is the trimming.

After that it has to be drilled under the big machine so that bolts may pass through the top to suspend it by . . .

The next journey is to the tuning shed, and here, ultimately its career as a good or bad toned bell is decided. Of recent years what is known as the Five-Tone Simpson Principle of tuning has come into force, and I venture to say that this method has affected the greatest revolution that the bell world has ever seen. In some instances, the bells might be fairly well in tune with one another as single notes (though even this is rare).

The bell used to be treated as possessing only one tone, whereas it really has many, of which at least five are now under absolute control, . . .

Now-a-days, the bell is revolved on the table or a big boring mill weighing some tons, and different tones of the bell are carefully paired off by means of a tool-post with a cutter inserted in order to bring the harmonics into proper relationship with one another, and at the same time, to put the bell as a whole into accurate tune with the rest of the peal [or carillon].

The bell is then ready for attaching the fittings and hanging in the frame.

The first G&J tuning machine, bought by Cyril F. Johnston, in 1905, with his own money; his father A. A. Johnston having been reluctant to acquire one

Top left: Cyril F. Johnston with the small tuning machine; the bell is the tenor of the new ring of ten for St. Peter's Church, Croydon, England, cast in 1912
Top right: Cyril F. Johnston with the mid-size tuning machine, acquired in 1909. The bell is the bourdon for the United Methodist Church, Toronto, Canada
Right: The largest tuning machine G&J owned, bought from Warner & Son in the mid-1920s

SELECT BIBLIOGRAPHY

Ackerley, J.R. *My Father and Myself*. A Harvest Book, Harcourt Brace, Jovanovich, New York and London, 1968

Andreas, Wayne. *American Gothic: Its Origins, its Trials, its Triumphs*. Vintage Books, New York, 1975

Backus, John. *The Acoustical Foundations of Music*. W.W. Norton & Co., New York, 1969 and 1977

Baldwin, Rosa Lee. *The Bells Shall Ring*. James J. Gillick & Co., Inc., San Francisco, USA, 1940

Barker, Pat. *The Man Who Wasn't There*. Picador, New York, New York, 2001

Bennett, Daphne. *Queen Victoria's Children*. St. Martin's Press, New York, 1980

Bigelow, Arthur Lynds. *Carillon: An Account of the Class of 1892 Bells at Princeton with Notes on Bells and Carillons in General*. Princeton, NJ: Princeton University Press, 1948

Biswanger, Ray. *Music in the Marketplace: The Story of Philadelphia's Historic Wanamaker Organ*. The Friends of the Wanamaker Organ, Inc. Bryn Mawr, Pa., 1999

Bok, Edward. *The Americanization of Edward Bok: An Autobiography*. The American Foundation Inc. 1973

Boland, Charles Michael. *Ring in the Jubilee: The Epic of America's Liberty Bell*. Riverside, Ct: The Chatham Press, Inc. 1973

Buswell, A.A.J. *The Tuning Books of Gillett & Johnston (Bellfounders) 1877-1957: Foundry Chimes and Carillons*. (Unpublished: Original Gillett & Johnston Bell Records, 1877-1957, Donated to the Croydon Local Studies Library, Croydon Central Library, Croydon, UK), 1990.

Camp, John. *Bellringing: Chimes-Carillons-Handbells: The World of the Bell and the Ringer*. David & Charles, Newton Abbott, UK, 1974

Camp, John. *Discovering Bells and Bellringing*. Shire Publications Ltd., Princes Risborough, Buckinghamshire, UK, 1997

Chernow, Ron. *Titan: The Life of John D. Rockefeller, Sr.* Vintage Books, New York, New York, 1999

Cockett, Mary. *Bells in Our Lives*. David & Charles, Ltd., Newton Abbott, UK, 1973

Corbin, Alain. *Bells: Sound Village & Meaning in the 19th Century French Countryside*. Translated by Martin Thom. Columbia University Press, New York, New York 1998

Darwin, John. *The Triumphs of Big Ben*. Robert Hale Ltd., London, UK, 1986

Elphick, George. *The Craft of the Bellfounder*. Phillimore & Co., Ltd. Chichester, UK, 1988

Fosdick, Harry Emerson. *The Living of these Days: An Autobiography*. Harper Chapel Books. New York, Evanston and London, 1967

Gedenkboek: Jef Denyn. Published by Beiaardschool te Mechelen, Belgium, 1947

Godenne, Willy and Henry Joosen (eds.). *Jubileumboek, 1922–1972: Koninklejke Beiaardschool Jef Denyn te Mechelen*. Published by De Koninklejke Beiaardschool, Mechelen, Belgium 1973

Hatch, Eric. *The Little Book of Bells*. Hawthorn Books Inc., New York, NY, 1964

Howarth, David and Stephen Howarth. *The Story of the P&O*. Weidenfeld and Nicolson, London, UK, 1986

Howarth, David. *1066: The Year of the Conquest*. Penguin Books, New York, New York 1981

Jennings, Trevor S. *Bellfounding*. Shire Publications Ltd., Princes Risborough, Buckinghamshire, UK, 1999

Jennings, Trevor. *Master of My Art: The Taylor Bellfoundries 1784–1987*. John Taylor and Co., Ltd., Loughborough, UK, 1987

Johnston, Cyril Frederick. *Why I Started an Intensive Study of the Tuning of Bells*. Unpublished lecture by CFJ, London, UK, 1948

Johnston, Nora. *A Memoir*. Foreword by Margo Halsted, Introduction by Jill Johnston, A Remembrance by Lady Rosemary Evelyn Price. Print Means Inc., New York, NY, 2002.

Johnston, Ron, Graham Allsopp, John Baldwin, and Helen Turner. *An Atlas of Bells*. Basil Blackwell Ltd., Oxford, UK, 1990

Keldermans, Karel and Linda. *Carillon: The Evolution of a Concert Instrument in North America*. Springfield, Ill., Springfield Park District, 1996

Keldermans, Linda (ed.). *Proceedings of the 12th Annual World Carillon Congress*. Springfield, Illinois, 2001

Lapping, Brian. *End of Empire*. St. Martin's Press, New York, 1985

Lehr, André. *The Art of the Carillon in the Low Countries*. Lannoo Printers and Publishers, Tielt, Belgium, 1991

Longford, Elizabeth. *Victoria R. I.* Harper & Row, New York, London, 2001

McAuley, Robert. *The Liners: A Voyage of Discovery*. Motorbooks International Publishers, Osceola, WI, 1997

Miller, Robert Moats. *Harry Emerson Fosdick: Preacher, Pastor, Prophet*. Oxford University Press, New York, 1985

Miller, William H. *The Last Atlantic Liners*. Conway Maritime Press Ltd., London, UK, 1985

Motture, Peta. *Bells and Mortars and Related Utensils*. London, UK, V&A Publications, 2001

Muccigrosso, Robert. *American Gothic: The Mind and Art of Ralph Adams Cram*. University Press of America, Washington D.C., 1979

Nicholson, John. *Arthur Anderson: A Founder of the P&O Company*. T. & J. Manson, Lerwick, Shetland Islands, UK, 1932

Petre, Diana. *The Secret Orchard of Roger Ackerley*. George Braziller Inc., New York, New York, 1975

Pickford, Christopher J. *The Steeple, Bells, and Ringers of Coventry Cathedral*. C.J. Pickford, Bedford, England, 1987

Pound, Reginald. *Selfridge*. Heinemann, London, UK, 1960

Price, Frank Percival. *The Carillon*. London, UK, Oxford University Press, 1932

———. *Bells and Man*. Oxford University Press, New York, USA, 1983

Rayleigh, Lord John William Strutt. *The Philosophical Magazine*, 1890

Rice, William Gorham. *Carillon Music and Singing Towers of the Old World and the New*. Dodd, Mead and Co., New York, New York, 1925

Rank, Otto. *The Myth of the Birth of the Hero*. Vintage Books, New York, 1964

Rice, Harriet Langdon Pruyn. *In the Carillon Country: Journals of Belgium and the Netherlands*. The Cayuga Press, Ithaca, New York, 1933

Rockefeller, David. *Memoirs*. Random House, New York, USA, 2002

Sanderson, J. (Gen. Ed.). *Change-Ringing: The History of an English Art*. Vol. I. The Central Council of Church bell Ringers. Guildford, UK, 1987

Serber, Lee. *The Golden Age of Ocean Liners*. Todtri Productions Ltd., New York, New York, 1996

Shand-Tucci, Douglass. *Boston Bohemia 1881–1900. Ralph Adams Cram: Life and Architecture*. University of Massachusetts Press. Amherst, Massachusetts, 1995

Shaw, Antony and Ian Westwell. *World in Conflict 1941–45*. Fitzroy Dearborn Publishers, Chicago—London, 2000

Simpson, Canon Arthur Barwick. "Why Bells Sound Out of Tune." *Pall Mall Magazine*, London, UK, 1895

———. "How to Cure Them." *Pall Mall Magazine*, London UK, 1896

Sobel, Dava. *Longitude*. Penguin Books USA Inc., New York, New York, 1995

St. Aubyn, Giles. *Queen Victoria: A Portrait*. New York, New York, Atheneum, 1992

Ulrich, Kurt. *Monarchs of the Sea: The Great Ocean Liners*. Tauris Parke
    Books, London, UK, 1998
Walters, H. B. *Church Bells of England*. E.P. Publishing Ltd., Wakefield,
    West Yorkshire, UK, 1977

RESEARCH FACILITIES

Beiaardmuseum, t.a.v. Jo Haazen, Frederik de Merodestraat 63, 2800
    Mechelen, Belgium
    http://www.beiaardschool.be/marc/index_en.htm
Beverley Local Studies Library, Beverley Library, Champney Road, Beverley
    HU17 8HE, United Kingdom
    http://www.familia.org.uk/services/england/east_riding.html#RESA
    VAIL
Buffalo Public Library, Central Library, 1 Lafayette Square, Buffalo, NY
    14203-1887
    http://www.buffalolib.org/libraries/central/index.asp
Croydon Central Library, Research Division, Croydon Clocktower,
    Croydon , Surrey CR9 1ET, United Kingdom
General Register Office for Scotland, New Register House, 3 West Register
    Street, Edinburgh, Scotland EH1 3YT
    http://www.gro-scotland.gov.uk/
    http://www.scotlandspeople.gov.uk/index.php
Gillett & Johnston, Unit 9A, Twin Bridges Business Park, 232 Selsdon
    Road, South Croydon, Surrey CR2 6PL, United Kingdom
    info@gillettjohnston.co.uk
Grace Cathedral Archives, Grace Cathedral, 1100 California Street, San
    Francisco, California 94108
    http://www.gracecathedral.org/archives/
Hampstead: Heath Street Baptist Church, 84 Heath Street, Hampstead,
    London NW3 6TE, United Kingdom
Historical Library, Greenock, Scotland
Libraries and Archives of Canada, National Archives of Canada, Percival
    Price Collection. 395 Wellington Street, Ottawa, ON K1A 0N4
    CANADA. http://www.collectionscanada.ca/4/7/m15-459-e.html
Library of the Central Council of Church Bell Ringers. 10 Lugg View
    Close, Hereford HR1 1JF, United Kingdom
Mercersburg Academy, The Academy Library, Lenfest Hall Learning
    Center, 300 East Seminary Street, Mercersburg, PA 17326
    http://www.mercersburg.edu/
National Archives and Research Administration, 201 Varick Street, New
    York, New York 10014-4811
    http://www.archives.gov/facilities/ny/new_york_city.html
New York County Vital Records. New York County Clerk. 60 Centre
    Street, New York, NY 10007-1402

New York Public Library, Research Division, 5th Avenue, New York NY
Peninsular and Oriental Steam Navigation Company, P&O Nedlloyd,
        Beagle House, Braham Street, London E1 8EP, United Kingdom
        http://www.ponl.com/topic/home_page/language_en/
Mudd Library, Princeton University, One Washington Road, Princeton,
        New Jersey 08544. libweb@princeton.edu
Probate Department, Principal Registry of the Family Division, First
        Avenue House, 42-49 High Holborn, London WC1V 6NP,
        United Kingdom   http://www.courtservice.gov.uk/
Royal Exchange Archives, The Mercers' Company, Mercers' Hall,
        Ironmonger Lane, London EC2V 8HE, United Kingdom
        http://www.mercers.co.uk/mainsite/pages/default.html
Scarborough Library, Vernon Road, Scarborough, North Yorkshire, YO11
        2NN, United Kingdom
        http://www.northyorks.gov.uk/libraries/branches/
        scarborough.shtm
St. Andrews University Library, North Street, St Andrews, Fife, Scotland
        KY16 9TR. http://www-library.st-andrews.ac.uk/
The Anton Brees Carillon Library, Bok Tower, 1151 Tower Blvd. Lake
        Wales, FL 33853
        bokbells@cs.com
The British Library, St Pancras, 96 Euston Road, London, NW1 2DB,
        United Kingdom   http://www.bl.uk/
The Family Records Centre, 1 Myddelton Street, London EC1R 1UW,
        United Kingdom. http://www.familyrecords.gov.uk.htm
The Historical Society of Pennsylvania,1300 Locust Street, Philadelphia, PA
        http://www.hsp.org/
The National Archives, Kew, Richmond, Surrey, United Kingdom
        http://www.nationalarchives.gov.uk/
The National Maritime Museum, The Caird Library, Greenwich, London
        SE10 9NF, United Kingdom. http://www.nmm.ac.uk/
The New York Historical Society,170 Central Park West, New York,
        NY 10024
        http://www.nyhistory.org/
The Ringing World, Penmark House, Woodbridge Meadows, Guildford
        GU1 1BL, United Kingdom
The Riverside Archives, The Riverside Church in New York City, 490
        Riverside Drive, New York, NY 10027
        archives@theriversidechurchny.org
The Rockefeller Archive Center. 15 Daytona Avenue, Sleepy Hollow,
        NY 10591
        http://archive.rockefeller.edu/

The University of Chicago Library, 1100 East 57th St., Chicago, IL 60637
http://www.lib.uchicago.edu/e/index.html
University Library, University of Madison, WI

GLOSSARY

Reprinted in edited form from GCNA website
with kind pemission from Carl Zimmerman

Nouns
tower bell

a cup-shaped cast bronze bell, of a size suitable for hanging in a tower; normally thicker at the **sound bow** where the clapper strikes. All tower bells in listed instruments are presumed to be hung *dead* unless otherwise stated. The exception is *rings*, where the reverse is true.

carillon bell

a *tower bell* which has been tuned so that its various partial tones (*hum tone* and "overtones") are in harmony with its *strike tone* according to widely accepted principles of tuning. [Compare this brief definition with the full official definition on the GCNA Home Page.]

strike tone

the apparent initial pitch of a bell when struck. It is this pitch which is used throughout these pages to describe the notes of bells.

hum tone

the lowest audible pitch produced by a bell. The hum tone typically develops after the *strike tone* is first heard, and typically persists after other partial tones have become inaudible. In a properly tuned *carillon bell,* the hum tone will be an octave below the *strike tone;* this sometimes causes confusion in listeners as to the actual pitch of the bell.

bourdon

the heaviest bell of a *carillon,* or of the diatonic/chromatic range of a carillon. Rarely, a carillon will have a **sub-bourdon** which is separated from the next higher note by more than two semitones. It is possible (though even more rare) to have more than one sub-bourdon; this is found only in old European carillons, where these bells do double duty as swinging bells when the carillon is not in use. The corresponding word for the heaviest bell of a *ring* (and sometimes of a *chime*) is tenor.

great bell

a *tower bell* which weighs 4 tonnes or more, or which has a *strike tone* of F#(0) or lower. In the heaviest *carillons,* the *bourdon* and possibly a few other bass bells may fall into this category.

287

site

a single musical instrument made of tower bells (a **tower bell instrument**), or a collection of such bells in one place. Except in the case of *great bells* and three 6-bell rings in North America, all sites listed in these pages contain at least 8 bells.

carillon

(1)—"a musical instrument consisting of at least two octaves of *carillon bells* arranged in chromatic series and played from a *keyboard* permitting control of expression through variation of touch." This implies use of a *baton keyboard*.

(2)—a *site* having at least 23 *tower bells* in at least two octaves of mostly chromatic series, but falling short of the "traditional" carillon either in the lack of tuning of the bells or in the type of mechanism (e.g., *electric keyboard* or solely automatic operation).

(3)—an automatic mechanical tune-playing mechanism, usually found as auxiliary equipment on a *ring* in England; this distinctively British usage of the word is not employed in these *site* data pages.

(4)—a *chime* played from a mechanical *keyboard*; this distinctively French usage of the word is not employed in these *site* data pages.

A **tubular carillon** is an instrument composed of at least two octaves of **tower tubes**; these are cast from bell metal and are comparable in weight to tower bells, but are shaped rather like oversized **orchestral chimes,** or like the **chimes** of a grandfather clock or a doorbell. This instrument may have either a purely mechanical action or an electro-mechanical action.

carillonist / carillonneur

a person who plays the *carillon.*

Of French derivation, the term "carillonneur" has long been used in the English language, and obviously forms the basis for the name of The Guild of Carillonneurs of North America (GCNA).

chime

(1)—a musical instrument consisting of at least 8 *tower bells* arranged in a diatonic (or partially chromatic) series, and upon which tunes can be played by some means, but with too few bells to be called a carillon. A **tubular chime** is similarly composed of **tower tubes,** and is a smaller version of a **tubular carillon** (see above).

(2)—any collection of at least 8 *tower bells* which is not a *carillon* by either definition (1) or definition (2) above (e.g., a large *zvon*).

chimer

a person who *chimes* the bells (i.e., plays a chime.)

ring

a set of at least 3 *tower bells* hung for full-circle ringing in either British (change-ringing) or Veronese (concerto) style, normally in diatonic series starting from the tonic note of the major scale in the bass. (There are rare instances where the minor scale or the Mixolydian scale is found.) In the few instances where a ring has an added semitone, it is typically used to provide for a lighter (and smaller) diatonic range for ringing (i.e., change-ringing).

ringer

any person who *rings* one or more bells; more specifically, one who *rings* a swinging tower bell by means of rope and wheel; most specifically, a member of a team of **change-ringers**.

peal

(1)—a group of *tower bells* hung for swinging, each at its own natural pendulum frequency, and therefore at random with respect to each other; swung either by ropes or by individual electric motors. There is no standard arrangement of pitches for a peal; they may fit a fragment of a scale, or a common chord (e.g., a major or minor triad), or none of these.

(2)—the performance, by a band of **change-ringers**, of at least 5,000 changes, non-stop; on a *ring* of 7 or more bells, no two changes may be the same.

(3)—a *ring*. This definition is fiercely held by some change ringers, while being strongly deprecated by others.

glockenspiel

a set of *tower bells* (usually relatively small in size) hung *dead* and played with an automatic mechanism to accompany the operation of several moving figures which perform for viewers. Such an instrument may be either *carillon-sized* or *chime-sized*.

zvon

a set of *tower bells* hung *dead* with clapper ropes rigged for Russian-style rhythmic ringing; normally few (if any) of the bells fit into any musical scale, and there are large gaps between the pitches of some adjacent bells, particularly the heaviest. A zvon may be either *carillon-sized* or *chime-sized*.

campanile

a free-standing **bell tower,** i.e., a tower containing a single *tower bell,* a *peal* or any of the other **tower bell instruments** named above, or a free-standing tower designed and built for that purpose even though it does not currently house any bells. A bell tower which is built into (and not simply connected to) another building is not properly called a campanile.

keyboard

any of several different devices which permit one person to play all the bells in an instrument by hand, with one key per bell. The key size and arrangement vary according to the mechanism used:

baton keyboards, found in all *traditional carillons* and some *chimes,* have keys that are shaped somewhat like batons, have direct mechanical linkage to the clappers of the bells, and are arranged in two rows like the black and white notes of a piano;

"pumphandle" (American) or **"barrow-handle"** (French) keyboards are found in *chimes* with direct mechanical actions much heavier than those of carillons, and the handles are usually in a single straight line;

electric keyboards are similar to those of an organ, and typically use relays to control hammer solenoids, which may strike the bells on the inside or the outside.

baton keyboards are played by striking a key gently or briskly with the partially-closed fist; pumphandle keyboards are played by grasping a handle and pushing down with a full arm stroke; and electric keyboards are played with the fingers.

console (or clavier)

the case or framework which holds a *keyboard;* it may also contain a pedal keyboard or pedalboard by which the heaviest bells can be played with the feet as well as (or instead of) the hands. A pedalboard is always present for *traditional carillons,* sometimes for *chimes,* and never for *non-traditional carillons.*

chimestand

(1)—the *console* of a mechanical-keyboard *chime* (either *baton* or *pumphandle*);

(2)—a wall-mounted rack to which are tied ropes leading to the clappers of a *chime;* sometimes called a **taut-rope clavier.** When used as auxiliary equipment with a ring, the ropes are connected not to the clappers but to externally-mounted under-hammers. In the original design, commonly called an **Ellacombe stand** after its inventor, each hammer when at rest is out of the path of the swinging bell. To shorten the hammer stroke for better control when playing, the hammers can be partially raised by retying the ropes at a different point; but they must later be lowered out of the way to permit the bells to swing without interference. An improved design uses a movable tie bar to enable all of the hammers to be raised or lowered simultaneously without retying any of the hammer ropes.

transposition (n.)

the musical interval (or the number of semitones) between any note on the *keyboard* and the pitch of the bell connected to that key. Example: If a C key is connected to an E-flat bell, the instrument **transposes** up a minor third (3 semitones).

If note and pitch are identical, the transposition is zero and the instrument is said to be in **concert pitch.** Actually, this is true only if the heaviest C bell in the instrument weighs between 2 and 3 tons. Lighter instruments may transpose upward an octave or even more.

Most carillons and chimes are transposing instruments. But unlike other musical instruments, the transposition is not standardized—it varies considerably depending upon the weight of the instrument, which in turn was determined by the size of the tower, the funds available for construction, and other factors.

Verbs
chime

(1) (*v.t.*)—to swing a bell just enough for the clapper to strike, often on only one side of the bell rather than on alternating sides.

(2) (*v.t*)—to sound one or more bells by any method (colloquial).

(3) (*v.t.*)—to emit the sound of a bell (colloquial), as in the old clock bell inscription, "To tell the time, we chime."

peal

(1) (*v.t*)—to sound the bells of a *peal* (n.) by swinging.

(2) (*v.i./v.i.*)—to sound a bell by any method.

ring

(1) (*v.t*)—to participate in a team of change-ringers.

(2) (*v.i./v.i.*)—to sound a bell by any method.

Adjectives
carillon-sized

having 23 or more *tower bells*, regardless of any other characteristics.

chime-sized

having 8 to 22 *tower bells*, regardless of any other characteristics.

dead

refers to *tower bells* which are hung in a fixed (i.e., non-swinging) position. This is typical of *carillons, chimes* and *zvons*.

For a comprehensive explanation of terms listed in this glossary, please visit the home site of the *Guild of Carillonneurs of North America:* gcna.com

INDEX

293

Index

Index